Edward J Benfold

William J Westfold

Nicole Benfold

Alexandra Benfold

USS BENFOLD (DDG 65)

Best Regards,
Alfred W. Murray

Dorothy A Warda

COMMANDING OFFICER 3/30/99

Onward With Valor,

M. E. FERGUSON III
Commander, U.S. Navy
Commanding Officer

Fair winds,
CDR D. M. Abrashoff

i

The Green Wave And The Navy:

The History of The

USS BENFOLD (DDG - 65)

Redrosebush Press

The Green Wave and the Navy:
The History of the USS BENFOLD

© 1999 by Danny K. Edgar & Craig E. Burgess

First Printing

Printed in the United States of America by Commercial Printing, Wenatchee, Washington.

Published by:
Redrosebush Press
PO Box 2163
Wenatchee, WA 98807-2163
(509) 662-7858
ptl2163@aol.com
http://maxpages.com/guidelines

ISBN 0-9651909-5-1

Photography by the US Navy
and Craig E. Burgess
Typesetting & Design by Redrosebush Press
Printing by Commercial Printing
Binding by Lincoln and Allen Bindery

Dedication

The Green Wave And The Navy: The History Of The USS BENFOLD (DDG - 65) is dedicated to the family of Edward C. Benfold, to crew members - - - past, present and future - - - of the USS BENFOLD and to the students in the three schools in Audubon, NJ: Haviland Avenue Elementary; Mansion Avenue Elementary; Audubon Jr. - Sr. High. They are the individuals who made this book a reality.

Foreword

The Borough of Audubon, New Jersey, is a very special place. It has a population of approximately 9,000 residents and is the only town its size in the United States to have THREE Medal of Honor recipients. The citizens of Audubon are very proud of this special position of honor and have shown their pride in patriotism in ways that have attracted the attention of citizens everywhere. This PRIDE is a grass roots tradition that has reached far beyond the territorial boundaries of Audubon. It has touched the spirits of educators and military leaders across the country and has served as the inspiration for the book you are about to read.

What makes the Borough of Audubon so special? The answer is that its residents have shown in their actions what many merely express with words - - - and their actions reflect the true meaning of PATRIOTISM. They take pride in waving the American Flag; they take pride in remembering all those veterans who have fought - - - and given their lives - - - so that freedom will endure; they take pride in showing their children why growing up in Audubon is so special.

The information, the photographs, the interviews and the poetic tributes that make up this salute to Audubon will serve as a model for patriotic pride: a model that will enable YOU, the reader, to gain a deeper appreciation for the values that make our nation great - - - values reflected in the friendship that has been established between "The Green Wave" and the US Navy, an ongoing friendship that began with the Christening of the USS BENFOLD, a naval destroyer named in memory of Audubon resident and Medal of Honor recipient Edward C. Benfold, and that will continue to strengthen during the 21st century.

Join Petty Officer Danny K. Edgar and me as we take you on breathtaking journeys through the history of a town, the history of a hero, the history of a ship in the Naval Fleet and the history of a friendship between the residents of a town and the crew members of a naval destroyer . . . . . from the beginning of the 20th century to the present and beyond.

Table Of Contents

Introduction by
Petty Officer Edgar, USN

My first poem was a tribute to fellow shipmates who were advanced to Chief Petty Officer: a great honor and tribute to themselves and to their career. (Following the advancement in rank, the shipmates are known simply as the Chief.) A copy of the poem *Hail to the new Chiefs* was given to the five new Chiefs. After the ceremony, each Chief personally thanked me, saying the poem was a great tribute. Each one then asked whether I had written any other poems. I said that I had and shared them with other shipmates. As they read them, they responded, in amazement: "Petty Officer Edgar, YOU wrote these'?"

With encouragement from my shipmates - - - and in particular TM1 Shawn Ross - - - I started writing more about life on the USS BENFOLD, about my shipmates and about our maiden voyage. When the ship returned to San Diego in February, 1998, from its maiden voyage - - - a 6 - month deployment - - - I had a collection of poems written.

On the ship's 2nd birthday, March 30, 1998, I met Mr. Craig E. Burgess and showed him some of the poems I had written. (Several of my shipmates knew that he was coming on board and also knew that he was a writer and encouraged me to introduce myself.) It was a meeting that has developed into a strong friendship that I will always cherish. I can see why he is a true inspiration to other people. For me, he has become more than a friend: he has become my mentor.

Craig is the brainchild of *The Green Wave And The Navy: The History Of The USS BENFOLD* and I feel honored to have my name associated with the book. Writing this book with Craig has truly been a humbling experience. My inspirations for the book I owe to the men and women of The USS BENFOLD: the backbone of the ship. In the Navy, you're taught teamwork. We're not only a team of 300 plus sailors: we are also a family. Every sailor that has been, or currently is, on board knows what it's like to be a part of "The Best Damn Ship In The Navy"!

The community of Audubon is a big part of our family, from the care packages to the support from the residents to the letters from the students. Seeing sailors' eyes AND their smiles when reading letters from students in Audubon was a big lift while in the hostile area of the Middle East during our maiden voyage. Sailors who hadn't received mail were now writing back to the students AND receiving mail.

Audubon has become for some of us a second hometown. When the ship had its Christmas Party in December, 1998, Audubon was there, through gifts donated for door prizes - - - to the delight of crew members and their families or guests. Sailors who have gone to Audubon come back with stories of new friends. They are proud to be associated with The USS BENFOLD and with Audubon.

I hope that my contribution to this book will be a fitting tribute to the crew members, to the ship, to Edward C. Benfold, to the town of Audubon, to the world's greatest Navy and - - - last, but not least - - - to the families of the crew members who support us, take care of the family at home, pray for us and give us their love, especially during the Iraqi crisis, or any crisis that calls for the show of military presence. Without them, we could not fulfill our duties the way we do.

In addition, I hope my collection of poems in the book will give the reader some insight into a sailor's point of view of life on board, of our thoughts and of what it's like being far from home during a 6 - month deployment. May the poems add to your enjoyment of *The Green Wave And The Navy: The History Of The USS BENFOLD.*

When you opened the cover of the book, you saw the Coat of Arms for the USS BENFOLD (DDG - 65). As a member of the crew, let me explain the symbolism:

THE SHIELD

The Aegis shield denotes the capability of DDG - 65 to conduct operations in multi - threat environments. Dark blue and gold are the colors traditionally associated with the Navy. The Lion embodies the courage and strength displayed by Hospitalman Benfold in combat. The escutcheon bears a red cross, alluding to Benfold's medical service and personal sacrifice in saving the lives of others. A background of red above blue in the manner of a Taeguk underscores his service in Korea. The black pellets symbolize the heavy artillery and mortar barrages during his heroic action.

THE CREST

The reversed star, in medium blue and white, denotes the Medal of Honor, posthumously awarded to Hospitalman Benfold for his spirit of self-sacrifice and extraordinary heroism. The crossed Navy sword and Marine Mameluke signifies Benfold's service with the First Marine Division in Korea.

THE SUPPORTERS

The halberds symbolize vigilance, resolve and battle preparedness while suggesting the USS BENFOLD's Vertical Launch System capabilities.

Introduction by
Educator And Poet Craig E. Burgess LFIBA, MOIF

I am a lifelong resident of the Borough of Audubon, New Jersey, and have been influenced in a very positive way by many special individuals who helped develop the person I am today - - - teachers, coaches, neighbors, classmates and, of course, my loving parents.

After graduation from Audubon High School and from Rutgers University, I dedicated 26 years of my life to a teaching career. My goal as an educator has always been that of showing students how what they learn in the classroom applies to their daily lives. When this approach to teaching is implemented, the learning process takes on a new and dynamic dimension - - - memorization is replaced by investigation, exploration and creativity.

The educational environment in the Borough of Audubon is one which encourages young citizens to investigate, explore and create. The results have been exciting: students in the two elementary schools did research and published a history of the borough, based upon personal interviews with residents and upon materials found in historical documents. Students at the high school designed a special memorial site to keep alive the memory of those AHS graduates who fought for our nation's freedom during the 20th century. The incentive of these young citizens was not a grade, but the joy of achieving something positive in and for the community.

My incentive for doing the research for this book is two-fold: first of all, I want to celebrate the achievements of the students in the Audubon school system by honoring their efforts through a narrative and photographic history of their activities; secondly, I want to give something back to the community which I have called home for fifty-five years.

A special moment for me as I began to do research for this book was the chance meeting with Petty Officer MS1 Danny Edgar. His talents as a writer will become evident as you read his work in the pages of this tribute to the friendship between a town and the crew of a naval vessel. Petty Officer Edgar is a keen observer and has a special skill for communicating ideas - - - from factual accounts to thoughts which penetrate the emotions of the reader. His observations have made it possible for me to gain a deeper understanding of and a greater appreciation for the life of those men and women who serve our nation in the Navy.

On the inside back cover of the book you will find the Coat of Arms of Audubon High School. As a resident of the borough, let me explain the symbolism:

THE GOAT

The goat represents the agricultural history of Camden County, in which Audubon is located.

THE PLOWS

The plows represent the State of New Jersey, the "Garden State". This symbol is found on the seal of the state.

THE WAVES

The seven waves represent the original seven sections of Audubon. The symbol of a wave is used, since the mascot for the school is a GREEN WAVE.

THE OPEN BOOK

The open book represents the search for knowledge.

THE INSCRIPTIONS IN LATIN

AMICITIA = Friendship
VERITAS = Truth
AEQUITAS = Equity (Impartiality).

Special Acknowledgments
Petty Officer Edgar

Writing material for this book is like a dream . . . . and I would have had no dream without the following people who believed in me:

Tom Porter	For four straight years you were the father figure I needed in my life.
Carol Chitwood	I used to think that I spent more time in your office than I did in the classroom. Now I know why.
Dan Schmidt	For inviting me into your family.
Carol Schmidt and Marilyn Eye	For being mothers to me.
James Barnhill	You watched over me in high school . . . and you still do. Thank you.
Master Chief Scheeler	You're the Man.
MSCS Jacobs	For making me see the light.
MSC Danner	For *Hail To The New Chiefs*, which I was proud to write.
The Crew of the USS BENFOLD	What else is there to say?
All of my Commanding Officers	Thanks for being great leaders.
My Grandmother	When I went to live with you, my whole life did a 360. I will never forget that.
Laura	For being there through everything.
Kristen	You will always be "Daddy's Little Pumpkin".
Marvin & Marie Young	For treating me as one of your own.

Petty Officer Earl Davis

Whose advice has always been welcome and right on target.

Paul Jackosalem

You are an asset to the Navy and your future is bright. Keep charging!

The Community of Viburnum, Missouri and the teaching staff of Viburnum High

Who helped prepare me for the challenges I would face in today's world.

Special Acknowledgments
Craig E. Burgess

Without the support of the following individuals and groups, this book would never have become a reality.

Mr. William Westphal

Principal of Audubon High School, whose efforts in support of Project Memorial have produced many special rewards.

The students of the Project Memorial committees

For continuing a special tradition of patriotism in Audubon.

The members of the Murray - Troutt American Legion Post # 262

For ongoing support of the patriotic events planned by students and residents.

Mr. Bob Hoover

The Audubon resident who initiated the friendship between the borough and the crew of the USS BENFOLD back in 1994 and who has contributed a great deal to the success of the program in the community. He saw the value of establishing bonds of friendship between Audubon and the crew of the USS BENFOLD and turned a vision into a treasured reality.

Vincent Boris
Walter Casebeer
Ted Deusch
Joan P. Goss
Ethel Peters Gray
Ruth Hall
Dr. Harry A. Ingham
Maria Kelley
Russell Lyons
John McDermott
Stanley Mojta
Elsie Schuler

Residents of Audubon who provided written documents and photographs used in this book AND who agreed to provide information about Audubon in taped interviews with me as part of my research.

The gifted and talented students from Mansion Avenue and Haviland Avenue Elementary Schools

Published in 1995, your exciting book on the history of Audubon will forever be a cherished part of the archives in town. Your participation in the penpal program with the crew of theUSS BENFOLD has brought many a smile to the faces of the crew members.

Members of the Audubon Fire Department and Police Department

The friendship you have extended to the crew members of the USS BENFOLD, as well as your support of the special events planned by the students, is greatly appreciated.

Staff of the Free Public Library in Audubon

Your support of the project AND your willingness to take messages for the local poet without an answering machine helped make the dream a reality.

Margaret Stanton
Dawn Washington
Sandy Gandy
Kim Robinson

Four hard - working, patient and efficient employees at the Office Max location in the Lions' Head Plaza in Somerdale who handled all of my requests for copies with a smile.

Captain Mark E. Ferguson, III, 1st Captain of the USS BENFOLD

You made the friendship between the Navy and Audubon a reality. Your visit to the 3 schools in 1997 is an experience that will always be cherished by the students.

LT K. C. Marshall, Navigator / Historian, USS BENFOLD

Without your support, Chapter III would have been impossible to complete. Thanks for the input!

Commander D. Michael Abrashoff and LCDR Alan Stubblefield USS BENFOLD

Thanks for allowing me to come on board to meet with officers and crew members during 1998 and 1999 as I did my research.

Command Master Chief Robert Scheeler USS BENFOLD

Lasting friendships are made possible thanks to people like you!

Mrs. Dorothy Waida	Your contributions have been invaluable. Your willingness to share articles and photographs pertaining to Edward C. Benfold added much to Chapter II.
Mr. Edward J. Benfold	How can I ever thank you for making available some of the special documents (such as the citation signed by President Dwight D. Eisenhower following the heroic death of your father) that appear in Chapter II ?

As part of my research for this book, I sent out questionnaires to a number of individuals, asking for factual and subjective input that could add to the value of the overall work. The following deserve a special mention for their contributions . . . .

Captain Mark E. Ferguson, III
Commander Sinclair Harris
Command Master Chief Robert Scheeler
Senator John A. Adler, State Senator representing Audubon
Commissioner Donna Sadwin, Audubon
Mrs. Dorothy Waida
Mr. Edward J. Benfold

Mrs. Rosann Endt, Principal of Haviland Avenue Elementary
School in Audubon

Mrs. Linda Gringeri. Principal of Mansion Avenue
Elementary School in Audubon until 1998

Mr. Frank Keller, History II Honors Instructor at AHS

Melanie Aubrey   Derek Everman
Scott Johnson   Anthony Simeone
The four AHS students in the Class of 1994 who designed and carried out the construction and dedication of the Memorial site.

Mr. Al Murray, Mayor in Audubon at the time of the
Commissioning of the USS BENFOLD

The Venerable Robert N. Willing

Interim Rector at St. Mary's Episcopal Church in 1995 who conducted the special service at the stained - glass window for the members of the USS BENFOLD who came to Audubon in August.

The Rev. Dr. Ronny W. Dower

Rector of St. Mary's since 1997 who has supported my efforts in including the church history in this book.

Mr. James Realey

Who has done extensive research into the "Jersey Devil", a colorful part of the history and culture of the area.

**Mrs. Agnes Trione and
Mrs. Kathleen Whitaker**

Faculty advisors for the A.P.P.L.E. publication in 1995 on Audubon history. Thanks for allowing me to praise the work of the students at HAS and MAS in this book.

Kathy Jakubowski

Representative from the Audubon Grade School PTA (MAS) who gave me permission to use the design from the 95th Anniversary Tapestry Afghan as the cover page for Chapter I.

To all the citizens in Audubon who have supported the students in their patriotic activities over the years. This book is a reflection of that support.

**Janet Butler, Manager
Tracy Brickner, Lab. Technician
Jerry Pinner, Sales associate**

Employees at the Echelon Mall location of Ritz Camera Centers for excellence in quality and service, assisting with photo developing while I was working on the book.

Thanks to each and everyone of you for your enthusiastic encouragement, cooperation and support.

Co-author Petty Officer MS1 Danny
K. Edgar receives a certificate and his
Enlisted Surface Warfare pin from
Commander D. Michael Abrashoff,
2ndCaptain of the USS BENFOLD.

Co-author Craig E. Burgess takes
a tour of the USS BENFOLD
during a visit in March, 1997.

Chapter I
The History of Audubon

LOW-STOKES NICHOLSON
FARMHOUSE 1758

AUDUBON NATIONAL BANK 1923

RAILROAD STATION 1892

AUDUBON
ESTABLISHED 1905
NEW JERSEY

THE MANSION 1740 & 1853

CENTURY THEATER 1920's

COMMUNITY CENTER

FIRST SCHOOL HOUSE
CHERRY STREET 1895

AUDUBON HIGH SCHOOL 1926

FIRE COMPANY #1 1908

COMMISSIONED BY AUDUBON GRADE SCHOOL PTA

2

As we begin our historical journey, we will focus on highlights of the history of the Borough of Audubon. The borough was incorporated in 1905, but several major developments took place during the last decade of the 19th century. Town historians have traced "Audubon in the making" back to 1646 in England. In 1941, resident Ed Danielson did extensive research and put together a comprehensive history of the town. In 1988, resident Dr. Harry A. Ingham wrote a delightful booklet, describing what life was like in the first three decades of the 20th century. Most recently, the students in the gifted and talented programs at the two elementary schools in town conducted interviews with residents and put together an 85 - page history of Audubon as part of the borough's 90th anniversary. This book, published in the Spring of 1995, met with overwhelming success in the community and a second printing was required to meet the demand. As the borough approached its 95th anniversary, members of the PTA of Mansion Avenue Elementary School produced a tapestry afghan featuring well - known landmarks. The afghan design is shown on the cover page for this chapter.

The seal for the borough, shown on the previous page, contains a shield with three plowshares, symbolizing the agricultural nature of the town in its early years. The land was divided into a number of tracts or farms, the most well - known among them being the Linden, Sheets, Cedarcroft, Collins, Bettle, Nicholson and Orston. In our research we discovered that the great, great grandparents of Mr. Abel Nicholson (who purchased the Nicholson house in Audubon in 1789), Samuel and Ann Nicholson, came from Orston County of Nottinghamshire, in England in 1775. The Orston tract included land from the west side of the White Horse Pike to 4th Avenue and from Oak Street to Cherry Street.

Our journey begins in the year 1892 . . . .

The Orston Train Station in Audubon as shown on a postcard from
the early years, prior to Incorporation.

1891 - 1900

1892   The history of public education in Audubon began when a carriage house on Chestnut Street was moved to Cherry Street and converted into a one-room school building. Students attended this school from Audubon and the surrounding neighborhoods of Oaklyn, Haddon Heights and Barrington.

1893   The first church in Audubon, Logan Memorial Presbyterian, was founded. It was located on Merchant Street near the White Horse Pike.

1895   The oldest organization in the borough, Defender Fire Company, was organized. The first apparatus of the company was a hand - drawn hook and ladder which was housed in what was then Schnitzler's Hall, located at the corner of East Atlantic Avenue and Pine Street. A horse - drawn chemical wagon was purchased that year at a cost of $400.00.

(see photo below)

AUDUBON'S FIRST FIRE ENGINE

Purchased in 1895 at a cost of $400, it helped launch a proud history in the annals of volunteer firefighting in South Jersey.

1897 The first baseball team was formed in Audubon. The team played on a field between Chestnut and Pine Streets.

1900 Mr. Robert Tweed rented a piece of land from the Cedarcroft Tract and then, on July 3rd, bought a cow. It was the beginning of what was to become Suburban Dairies on Oakland Avenue.

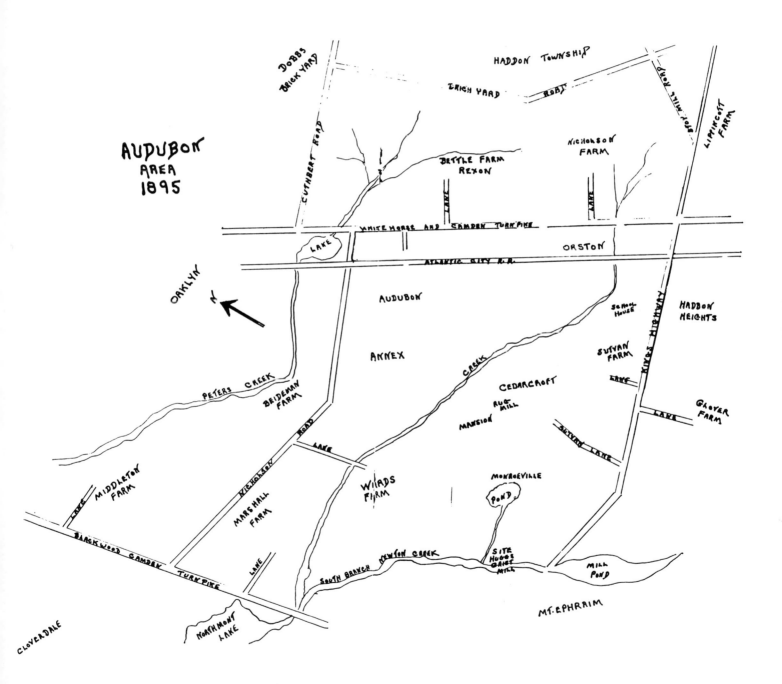

While doing research, we found a poem, written by Mrs. Julia A. Herald.
It provides a beautiful description of the early years in town . . . .

Audubon In Its Infancy

Oh, little, thrifty, Jersey town,
Along the Reading Line;
Though near enough to city marks,
Thy country sights are fine.

Thou breezy, sunny, open spot,
Whose air a tonic is;
Convenient both to train and car,
Yet full of rural bliss.

Thy little dwellings stand apart,
Just dotted here and there,
But designating happy homes,
Where life is not all care.

Thy little chapel on the hill
A welcome warm extends -
To every human being she
An invitation sends.

The stubble filled, December fields
Are brown and barren now;
Where lately stood the golden grain -
stood earlier the plough.

The roads are furrowed
And the mud shows Jersey's golden sand;
The smooth and far famed White Horse Pike
Runs through thy fruitful land.

Now stand thy tall denuded trees,
Exposed to winter's blast,
But strong and sturdy to resist
The Storm - King to the last.

Thy softly swelling, brown clad hills,
Though few, and small, and low,
A gently rolling slope describe,
O'er which the cold winds blow.

The little smithy stands beside
The Pike, unswerving, long.
Dark crimson are its painted walls -
Each day the anvils' song.

The country store, post office is,
Where people come and go,
At night and morn the mails arrive,
And deal out weal or woe.

Oh, little, thrifty, Jersey town,
Along the Reading line,
Long may the roof - trees shelter those
Who toil, but ne'er repine.

Long life and growth, young Audubon!
Long life to thee and thine!
May God with health your homesteads bless,
And cause hope's sun to shine.

Merchant Street 1908

1901 - 1910

1902   The Defender Fire Company moved from Schnitzler's Hall into its new building at West Atlantic Avenue and Oak Street.

A trolley line from Camden through Audubon to Haddon Heights was put in operation. The line later was extended as far as Clementon.

Trains of the Pennsylvania Reading Seashores Lines were already coming through Audubon on tracks located between East and West Atlantic Avenues.

1903   Construction on Audubon's first regular school house was begun at the corner of Oakland Avenue and Oak Street. It would become known as School No. 1.

1904   Population growth prompted local school authorities to close down the Cherry Street one-room school. For a while, Audubon students attended classes at the Haddon Heights Public School on Kings Highway and in the auditorium of Schnitzler's Hall.

Residents of all the settlements in the area voted to combine into one town, to be called Audubon.

1905   The town officially became known as Audubon on February 20th and, in May, became a borough. The town was named Audubon in honor of the 19th century naturalist and artist John James Audubon (1785 - 1851) The name was suggested by the wife of naturalist Samuel Nicholson Rhoads. The Rhoads lived in the Mansion House from 1898 - 1912 and Mrs. Rhoads suggested the name because there were so many birds around the area.

In June, the Audubon Police Department was established. At the time, the population was about 800.

School No. 1 at Oakland Avenue and Oak Street was completed as a four - room brick building and classes began.

1906   A second church in Audubon, The Methodist Church on the corner of Graisbury Avenue and Wyoming Avenue, was founded.

Redmen's Hall was erected on Merchant Street between West Atlantic Avenue and Oakland Avenue. The building is at the left of the photo shown below, taken along Merchant Street in 1916.

1907   Audubon Volunteer Fire Company # 1 was chartered. This second Fire Company in Audubon was first organized in 1905.

1908   The Audubon Post Office, which had been located on a site on West Atlantic Avenue south of Merchant Street, was transferred to a new location at 48 West Atlantic.

1910   The population in the borough had risen to 1,300.

1911 - 1920

1911   Robert Tweed and William Matlack became partners. The two gentlemen bought milk wholesale and processed it.

1912   Construction began on two new elementary schools in town: School # 2, located on Wyoming Avenue between Oak Street and Mansion Avenue - - - on the west side of town; School # 3, located on Haviland Avenue between Graisbury Avenue and Pine Street - - - on the east side of town. Both buildings were originally four - room structures.

1913   Holy Trinity Lutheran Church was organized by 33 members meeting in the home of Frank C. Lauer. Subsequent meetings were held in Schnitzler's Hall.

Note: At this point, we would like to say a little more about Schnitzler's Hall. In the 50th Anniversary book, published in 1955, the following entry was included: "It would be impossible to compile a history of Audubon, however brief, without directing attention to Schnitzler's Hall. Within the walls of this still - standing building began much of the civic, religious, patriotic, fraternal, educational and recreational life of the community. Built shortly before the turn of the century, and enlarged from time to time , it housed a store, fire department, church groups, public school classrooms, borough government and was Audubon's first movie theater. The first movie shown there was *"The Smugglers"*, sponsored by the Defender Fire Company, and followed by a doughnut social. Both the Masonic Lodge and the Eastern Star Chapter had their origins in the building. The availability of other meeting quarters and the erection of the Highland and Century theaters gradually reduced the importance of Schnitzler's Hall, and today it contains only a store and several dwelling units. The auditorium is still intact, although never used as such."

In his book, *"Audubon and the surrounding areas as I remember them"*, published in 1988, Dr. Harry A. Ingham recalls that the Hall was known as the Audubon Opera House and that Saturday was a big day at the location, with admission to the movies ten cents. (The photograph below of the former Schnitzler's Hall was taken by this book's co-author, Craig E. Burgess, on Saturday, February 13, 1999. On the left is a photo taken about 1920.)

Schnitzler's Hall—early home of community activities

10

Note: Throughout the history of the borough, several sets of postcard scenes were produced, showing various locations around town. Two of these postcard scenes are presented on the following page. They come from a collection of photos in the possession of Audubon resident and former Mayor Stanley Mojta. We know that the photos were taken during the first decade of the century because both postcards were mailed: the card at the top was postmarked November 13, 1909; the card at the bottom postmarked August 18, 1910. Both cards were sent for one penny!

Another photograph of the town that we found interesting is the one shown on this page. It shows the fire house on Merchant Street. Notice the spelling of the name of the town . . . . and the name of the street.

DAVIS AVE BUNGALOWS
AUDUBON N.J.
'S '10

Carries branched the X

ATLANTIC AVE AUDUBON N J '10

Wyoming 50 g graysberry audubon

An Early Fourth-Of-July Parade

This picture was taken during the days prior to our entry into World War I. Wyoming Avenue
looked quite different from today. Note Methodist Church in background.

1916   The Century Theater was built on the White Horse Pike near the intersection with the King's Highway..

The Weekly Visitor, a newspaper that began publishing in 1914, moved from Haddon Heights to a new location, next to the Audubon Fire Company in Audubon. It later relocated to the corner of Chestnut Street and West Atlantic Avenue.

1918   The Audubon Sewage Disposal Plant was built.

1919   One of the borough's leading institutions, the Audubon National Bank, was founded and started operations in Redmen's Hall on Merchant Street.

The photos below show the bank, then and now.

Audubon National Bank's first home

1920   The Murray-Troutt American Legion Post # 262, which was started in 1919, was granted its permanent charter on September 9th. (A temporary charter had been granted earlier in the year, on May 18th.) Meetings were held in various homes of veterans, as well as in Brights Hall and in the Defender Fire Hall.

School No. 2 was enlarged and additional rooms were added to School No. 3.

Note: As we complete our summary of the history of Audubon from 1911-1920, we would be remiss if we did not include a comment made by longtime resident Ted Deusch. Mr. Deusch wrote about his childhood in an essay called *"Growing up in Audubon in the early 1900s"*. The essay was published in two segments in the Spring and Summer issues of *South Jersey Magazine* in 1997. The photo and caption shown here clearly reflect life during the decade and one person's initial reaction to the paving of the dirt roads.

Growing Up In Audubon
In the early 1900's
by Ted Deusch

Merchant Avenue, Audubon, looking west from Atlantic Avenue. As a 5 year old I had been used to seeing Merchant Street like this. After being away for most of the summer of 1917, I came home on the train with my mother. She had trouble making me get off the train. I looked at a newly paved street and insisted we were not at Audubon.

Already mentioned were the tracks of the Pennsylvania Reading Seashore Line that pass through Audubon. The Reading Line was also planning to build tracks that would take passengers from Gloucester to Haddonfield. A gully was dug in the early years of the 20th century, but the tracks were never laid because construction became too costly. Where the gully crossed Haviland Avenue - - - dividing the northern end from the southern end of the avenue - - - a suspension bridge, held by large cables that were fastened at each side by two steel towers, was built. It was known as the "Swinging Bridge" and provided a shortcut for those students attending School # 3 who lived on the north side of the gully.

"SWINGING BRIDGE"

In our interviews with lifelong residents, we heard many stories about the bridge and about the swimming hole in the gully that was used as a recreation site.

The "Swinging Bridge" was removed in 1941 so that the steel could be used in the war effort.

Shown is an old photo of the "Swinging Bridge", an early landmark in the Borough of Audubon.

Note: Many longtime Audubon residents refer to the plan for building the Railroad tracks in this area as "Thompson's Folly."

One of the principal means of transportation in the area in the second decade of the 20th century was the trolley line. Owned by the Camden and Trenton Railway Company, the system was purchased in 1910 by Public Service Corporation. One of the routes of the trolley line connected Federal Street in Camden with Clementon and made stops in Woodlynne, West Collingswood, Oaklyn, Audubon, Orston (Audubon), Haddon Heights, Magnolia, Stratford, Laurel Springs and Garden Lake (Lindenwold). There are several locations in Audubon and Haddon Heights, along West Atlantic Avenue, where tracks from the trolley line can still be seen by residents.

Longtime Audubon resident Mr. James Realey, who has done much research into the legend of the "Jersey Devil", tells of several 'sightings' of the creature by residents who were riding the trolley line back in the early days of the town.

16

1921 - 1930

1921   The Defender Fire Company purchased its first piece of motorized equipment: a 1917 Model-T Ford Truck to carry buckets, hose and other items used in fire fighting efforts.

On April 26th the form of government changed from councilmanic to commission form.

Audubon passed an ordinance forcing bathing women to wear longer stockings and raincoats on their way to local swimming pools.

1922   In August, Sunday baseball was abolished in the borough. In the words of historian Ed Danielson: "a baseball fiasco was had during the ballgame" - - - a game that took place on the borough field the first Sunday in August. Then Mayor Mr. Conway Bennett issued a statement that was published in the local papers:

"There will not be any disturbance in Audubon Sunday afternoon. The borough commissioners will not tolerate anything that will give our fair town a bad name in the outside world. We are ready to preserve the peace, whatever may occur."

The Mayor had made his comment at a local commissioners' meeting on Tuesday evening and, although a game between the Audubonites and the Girard Field Club of Philadelphia was scheduled for the following Sunday afternoon, it was canceled and Sunday baseball in Audubon came to an end. (History of Audubon, Danielson, 1941: p. 54.)

The Audubon Library became part of the Camden Library system.

1923   The Audubon National Bank moved from Redmen's Hall to its own building on the corner of West Atlantic Avenue and Merchant Street.

In August, there was a trolley strike. Freeholder Charles T. Wise of Audubon expressed countywide disillusionment regarding this action.

Note: This same year, busses replaced the electric streetcars in parts of East and South Camden. The streetcar system continued to operate throughout Camden County until 1935.

On October 1st, Audubon became an independent branch of the Camden Post Office.

1924   In January, Casper Piez, chairman of the building committee of the American Legion Post # 262, purchased a lot on West Graisbury Avenue and Lake Drive, on which the Post erected its Post Home. The new building was dedicated on July 4th and the first meeting was held at the new location on July 15th.

On October 21st, the Borough of Audubon took over the financial aspect of the purchase of equipment for the Defender Fire Company.

Longtime Audubon resident John McDermott told us about a local figure who reached international prominence this year. Bishop John Boccela, who attended Camden Catholic in his sophomore year in high school, became the head of the 3rd Order of St. Francis and, in 1924, the Bishop of the Franciscan Order, with headquarters in Ismer, Turkey.

1925   Mr. S.F. Dietrich, who had purchased *The Weekly Visitor* in 1919 from its owner, William E. Evans, erected a new building to house the paper at the corner of Chestnut Street and West Atlantic Avenue.

1926   Additional classrooms were added to School # 3 on Haviland Avenue.

The practice of sending the borough's children to Collingswood for their high school education ended when the high school building was erected on Edgewood Avenue.

Below is a photo of Audubon High School, from the late 1920s

Note: Under the leadership of Dr. William L. Fidler, supervising princi-pal. this high school rapidly attained stature as one of the best in the state.

John McDermott remembers well the last week in September, when Heavyweight Boxing Challenger Gene Tunney, while preparing for his fight with then Champion Jack Dempsey, stayed in the home of Mr. Campbell at 340 West Graisbury Avenue. Tunney stayed at the Audubon residence from Thursday until Sunday and won the championship against Dempsey that weekend.

Note: Gene Tunney retired from his boxing career undefeated in 1928 after holding the title of World Champion for two years. Dempsey had held the title from 1919 - 1926. Some controversy surrounded one of the fights between Dempsey and Tunney, centering around what has been called "The Long Count". Tunney survived and went on to defeat Demp-sey in this famous bout.

See the photos of Dempsey and Tunney below.

Gene Tunney

Jack Dempsey

1927:   The Police Department in Audubon was officially formed.

Audubon Fire Company # 1 dedicated its present headquarters on Merchant Street at Virginia Avenue.

See photo below.

IT WAS A GREAT DAY

Audubon Fire Co. No. 1 really put on the dogwhen in 1927 it dedicated its present headquarters as can be seen by the gala trappings and natty attire of building and personnel. The dude on the left was not a fireman.

Audubon
National Bank

"The Bank Public Confidence Built"

Suburban
Motor Co.

Authorized
Ford
THE UNIVERSAL CAR
Dealer

Clinton Avenue and
Kendall Blvd.
OAKLYN, N. J.

—o—

*"The Place That Gives
Good Service"*

Keystone 74 *Bell 1034*

2240 lbs.
TO THE TON

Audubon
Ice & Coal
Co.

201 Oakland Ave.

YARD
Opposite Station at Audu

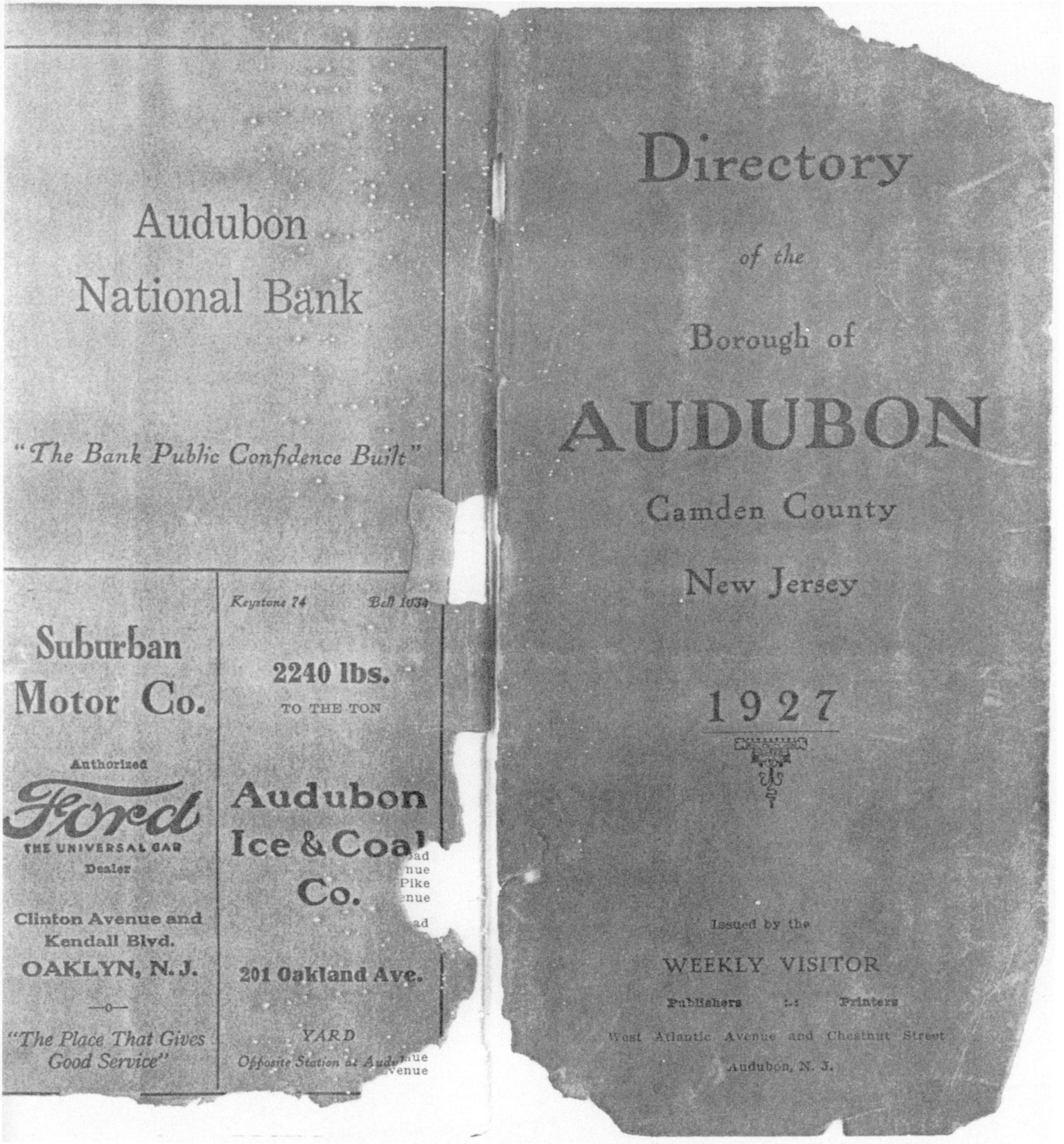

Directory

of the

Borough of

AUDUBON

Camden County

New Jersey

1927

Issued by the

WEEKLY VISITOR

Publishers :: Printers

West Atlantic Avenue and Chestnut Street

Audubon, N. J.

22

The Weekly Visitor published a Business Directory for the borough. It listed the Commissioners, the churches, the lodges and organizations, schools, fire companies and an alphabetical listing of the businesses in the borough.

Note: The ads in the Directory often contained special slogans. These slogans included:

"The Bank Public Confidence Built" for the Audubon National Bank;

"The little theatre with the big shows" for the Highland Theater at East Atlantic Avenue and West Pine Street;

"We are always ready to Clean and Dye for you" for the Morris Jacobs Fashionable Tailor Shop at 121 West Merchant Street;

"2240 pounds to the ton" for Audubon Ice and Coal Company at 201 Oakland Avenue.

(See ads from the Directory on preceding pages.)

1928: Defender Fire Company got its third piece of apparatus: a Hale City service ladder truck.

1929: The Audubon Sewage Disposal Plant was remodeled and expanded for greater capacity.

American Legion Post # 262 purchased an ambulance, which was presented to the borough for use whenever there should be need of such a conveyance. With this purchase, ambulance service was inaugurated in the borough.

As mentioned earlier, Audubon High School opened its doors for the first time in September of 1926. Prior to that date, students from Audubon went to Haddon Heights High and Collingswood High. Some of the students began their high school career in February and, as a result, in 1929, there were TWO graduating classes at AHS: one in February; one in June. There were also TWO graduating classes in 1930, with the class of 1930 being the first class to have spent the entire four years at AHS.

Le Souvenir, the AHS Yearbook, was published for the first time in February of 1929. A special dedication to Dr. Fidler and Miss Kramer was included in the first issue. (See next page)

Note: It is interesting that in both 1929 and 1930, class poems were written and placed in the yearbook. The June class of 1930 even had its own song. Theses items are presented for their historical value on the following pages. What a surprise to learn that the CLASS COLORS in 1929 were not GREEN AND GOLD but RED AND BLUE!

—————— . ● ⚜ [LE SOUVENIR] ⚜ ● . ——————

Dedication

To our Principal and Supervising Principal, who at all times have given us their unending support and cooperation, we, the class of February, 1929, affectionately dedicate this, the first edition of Le Souvenir.

Class Poem

Oh, Alma Mater, great and grand,
We're leaving you behind
To venture forth in unknown land,
Seeking Fortune's shrine.

We've trained ourselves to stand the fight
And never shall we die,
But struggle onward to the light
As we've been taught and by

Your guidance tried and true
We'll battle on, each one
Playing squarely all, the time,
Not stopping till we've won.

We've learned to play the game of Life;
We've learned the rules, each one;
And we'll return you two-fold gain
When we our task have done.

Oh Audubon, our Mother school,
Your '29 has gone.
We've given you the best we've had,
And when our curtains drawn.

We hope that we our task have done
The best that it could be;
And with the setting of our sun
Our memory stays with thee.

Goodbye! Our time has ended.
Success has called us on.
You've made us men and women and
We're grateful though we've gone.

We hope that Future's times may bring
Glory, Honor and that thy
Coming classes your praises sing
This our prayer, Audubon, Goodbye!

"HERB" OWENS '29

Farewell

Class Poem of the February Class of 1930

Our school days are ended
And now we must part,
As down a new pathway
In life's lane we start.
With courage and bravery
We'll fight our way through;
And always dear High School
Our thoughts are of you.

And now at commencement
We let fall a tear,
As farewell we say to
Our class-mates so dear;
In the years of the future,
We often shall sigh
For the good times together
At Audubon High.

-Dorothy Carter

Class Song of June Class of '30

(Words and music by Herbert A. Poole)

Goodbye Audubon, we are through,
Goodbye, we are leaving you.
The time to part has come to us too;
With sad aching heart, we must bid you adieu.
The crossroads of life we have met,
A new goal of strife we have set.
For you, Audubon, we would do---we would die!
Goodbye, Alma Mater, goodbye.

Goodbye Audubon, we are through,
Oh, school, ever faithful and true.
Your protecting arms must now lose their hold;
You've saved us from harms and from worries untold.
But now we must bear our own weight;
And now each must find his own fate.
For you, Audubon, we would do---we would die!
Goodbye, Alma Mater, goodbye.

Goodbye, Audubon, we are through;
We'll soon be a mem'ry to you.
The world calls us on, and we must abide;
And when we are gone, we'll have you as our guide.
A parting farewell, one and all;
We go now to answer the call.
For you, Audubon, we would do---we would die!
Goodbye, Alma Mater, goodbye.

Class Poem of the June Class of 1930

The time has come, dear classmates,
When we must bid "adieu"
To all the school day pleasures
Our happy hearts once knew.
It scarce seems possible that all
The joys that we have known
Are only fondest memories
Of days that now are gone.
They are the dearest souvenirs
We hold within our hearts,
But seem to us the dearer,
Now the time has come for us to part.
The fun we've had together,
The joys and sorrows, too----
The sharing of our fortunes,
If the skies were gray or blue----
The times we've argued "hot and hard"
With laughter or with tears----
Are all but tend'rest mem'ries
To follow through the years.
Like the fragrance of a rosebud
Wafted on the evening air,
Those mem'ries of our days together
Touch us, greet us everywhere.
And now the parting hour has come;
Farewell, Alma Mater, farewell

Our hearts are overbrimming
With words we cannot tell.
How we've loved thee, Alma Mater,
Guardian of our youthful dreams!
May thy spirit ever lead us
With its radiant beams
Of the light that never darkens;
May we hold thy standards high,
Fare thee well, dear Alma Mater----
It is hard to say good-bye!
As we go upon our journey,
All along the paths of life,
As we join the thronging masses
In the world of toil and strife,
May we see beyond the common,
May we see alone the best.
Let us make our lives so steadfast
That our hearts may stand the test.
There isn't a word in all the world
As sad as the one, "Farewell."
There isn't a word that's half so hard
For human lips to tell.
And so our hearts are heavy
As we bid Audubon "Adieu!"
The mem'ries that are sweetest
Are the days we've spent with you.

- Betty V. Price

1930: The record shows that the population in Audubon was 8,903 in an area of 1.6 square miles. The population breakdown was: 4,394 white males, 4,510 white females and 15 black persons. Of the total, 6,069 were of native parentage, 2,158 were of foreign or mixed parentage and 661 were foreign born whites. (Danielson, p. 66)

One final note on the decade of the 20s: one of the big events at school # 2 was the annual May Day Festival. Girls competed for best - looking Maypole and the boys drilled to a stirring rendition of *Stars and Stripes Forever*, which emanated from a Victor Talking Machine called a Victrola.

The Faculty

The Parrot

Editor In Chief	Betty Price
Associate Editor	George Rippel
Literary Editor	Jean Eaton
News Editor	Louise Maier
Jokes Editor	Gilbert Jones
Business Manager	Hedrick Ravenell
Asst. Business Manager	Robert Francis

Scribes

Girls' Athletics	Jeanne Weber
Boys' Athletics	Jonas Morris
Club	Elizabeth Miller
Compositor	Theodore Deusch
Faculty Advisor	Paul M. Dare

1931 - 1940

In the decade of the 1930s, the public library in Audubon was located in the basement of School # 2 (now the Mansion Avenue School) and was open three afternoons and three evenings each week.

One of the local newspapers in Audubon during the decade was the *Bi-Town Orator*, serving the communities of Audubon and Oaklyn. The offices of the paper were located at 58 West Atlantic Avenue in Audubon.

By the end of the decade, the Post Office moved to its new location on Merchant Street. The cost of sending first class mail from Audubon to Camden and nearby towns was 2¢.

In the area of development, the decade was highlighted by improvements in roadways and lighting. By the end of the decade there were 34 miles of concrete or hard - surfaced streets, sidewalks, curbs and gutters. Audubon had become a 100‰ "paved" town and a model for other municipalities to follow in highway construction. Gone was the nickname of "MUDABON", given to the borough during the decade of 1911 - 1920. (Welcome to Audubon, pp. 7 - 8) In addition, by the end of the 1930s, Audubon had the distinction of being one of the best lighted municipalities in New Jersey.

With this as a general background, let's now take a closer look at some of the events of note during the decade . . . .

1931   On January 31st, Audubon Post # 262 of the American Legion was changed to Murray-Troutt Post # 262 to honor the memory of two veterans of World War I.

1932   Defender Fire Company obtained a 1000 - gallon Maxim Pumper.

The new ambulance service in Audubon, under the auspices of Murray - Troutt Post # 262, purchased a new vehicle. Purchases were also made in 1935, 1938 and 1940 as the service continued to increase in the community.

1934   Activated traffic control lights were installed on the White Horse Pike at Merchant Street and at Pine Street. When a car on Merchant or Pine approaches the pike, the traffic light automatically turns to green for the driver to "go". In addition, two automatic lights were installed, at the White Horse Pike and Kings Highway and at West Atlantic Avenue and Kings Highway, to help regulate traffic in Audubon.

1935   A First Aid Squad was organized within the ranks of Audubon Fire Company No. 1.

On the next several pages, several photos are shown, indicating life in the mid - 30s:

Recreation: going to the movies at the Century Theatre (known then as the HUNT'S CENTURY)

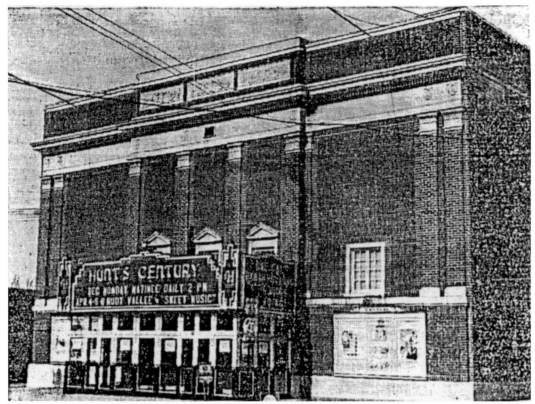

CENTURY THEATER IN 1935 — Rudy Vallee was starring in "Sweet Music" at the Century Theater as the Class of 1935 was preparing for its Washington Trip. Right of the theater (not shown) was Tegge's Drugstore. In addition to movies, the Century Theater for many years in the '20s and early '30s had "Eight Acts of Vaudeville," starring some of the biggest names on the circuit.

and swimming along the shores of Haddon Lake.

HADDON LAKE AUDUBON, N.J. #1947

33

Police: a photo of the force in 1935

AUDUBON'S FINEST — Audubon's Police Department in 1935 included the above stalwarts, all of whom are deceased with the exception of Rudy Creyaufmiller (later police chief). Front row, left to right: Sgt. Dewey Parker, Chief Frank Kelly and Sgt. Jack Parker. Second row, same order: Vic Dorwart (who passed away in May, 1985), Frank Holroyd, Bill Roarke, Rudy Creyaufmiller, "Pete" Mehrer (who married Miss Crozier, a fifth grade teacher at No. 1 School), Thorkild (Andy) Anderson and Fred Mollenkopf. Back row: Ray Marriner (who died earlier this year), John Gribley and Lyman Fuller.

and one of the vehicles at Pine Street. (This photo also shows the Traffic Signal box and an ad for the movies.)

PINE STREET AND THE PIKE — This mid-1930s photo shows police car and unidentified officer with pedestrians at the corner of Pine Street and White Horse Pike. Note traffic signal box with theater posters announcing coming shows at the Century Theater. "Doc" Schuler the chiropractor had his house and office at far right. Entire block is now a bank and a WAWA convenience store.

Transportation: the trolley system

Haddon Heights Line Franchise Car At Clementon, March 1937
Last Car Operated at Camden

and the Audubon Railroad Station.

AUDUBON RAILROAD STATION — This 1930s photo shows commuter train with its coal-fired steam engine pulling into Audubon railroad station at Merchant Street and Atlantic Avenue. Gatetender's house can be seen in background. Gatetender was John Markel.

This is a photo, taken in 1935, of one of the steam locomotives of the Pennsylvania Reading Seashore Lines. The photo was taken between Merchant Street and Pine Street from the West Atlantic Avenue side of the tracks. Dr. Harry A. Ingham recalls that one of the engineers with PRSS, Bill Wardoff - - - an Audubon resident - - - would play the tune *"Home Sweet Home"* on the locomotive whistle as the train passed through the borough at about 10:30 pm. The tune was heard almost every weekday night and residents looked forward to this special 'event'.

1936 The borough deeded part of its western boundary - - - Haddon Lake, with 10 acres of land adjoining - - - to the Camden County Park Commission, to be incorporated in the $10,000,000 County Park System. An additional 5 ½ acres of ground were purchased by the Park Commission to provide ample parking for cars, swimming pool and bathhouse. The section of land was part of the Hampshire plot at the corner of Kings Highway and Lake Drive.

  During the next two years, the Park Commission built a swimming pool (1937) and a playground (1938) on the site.

1937 A concrete stadium seating 3,500 persons was erected along the Walnut Street side of the High School at a cost of $36,000. This structure increased total seating capacity (in the bleachers and in the new stadium) to 8,000 persons. Workers from the WPA (Works Progress Administration) built the stadium as one of many projects in the county. The County WPA pulled thousands of men and women off relief and put them to work in every corner of the county. (See the photo of the new concrete stadium on the next page.)

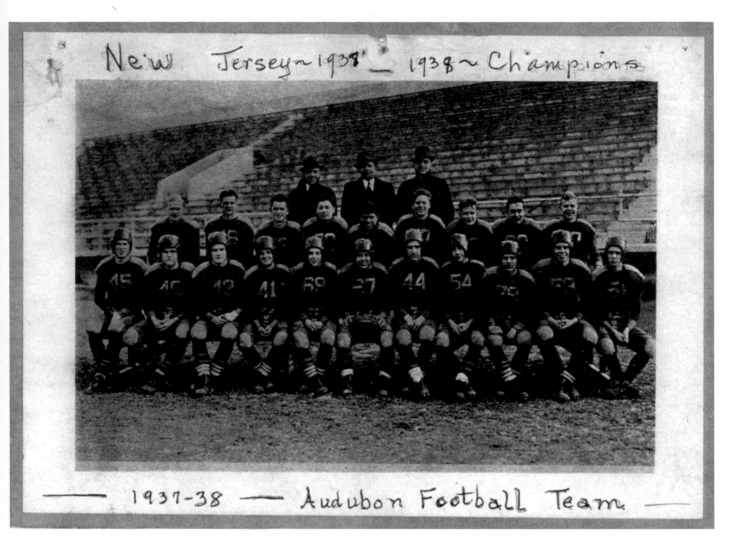

New Jersey~1937 – 1938~Champions

1937-38 — Audubon Football Team

Former resident of Audubon and AHS grad Ruth Hall brought this photo to the Free Public Library to add to the collection in the facility's Archives. It shows the New Jersey State Championship Football Squad of AHS. In the background can be seen the new concrete stadium at AHS which was constructed in 1937 - - - in time for the 1937 fall season. The photo also shows the 'uniforms' used by team members in the 1930s.

1939   Medal of Honor recipient NELSON V. BRITTIN graduated from AHS.

The Audubon Board of Education and the Commissioners published a 36 - page booklet entitled *WELCOME TO AUDUBON*, containing photos and important activities in the borough.

On February 1st, SUBURBAN DAIRIES merged with ABBOTTS DAIRY. (See ad next page.)

Washington Terrace, Audubon, N. J.

New Quarters For Postoffice

Audubon Branch Moves to Merchant Street Next November

PART OF MORRIS STORE

New quarters for the Audubon branch of the Camden Post Office have been secured at 107-109 West Merchant street, according to an announcement made today by postal authorities.

It is understood that the present location at the rear of the Audubon National Bank, West Atlantic avenue, has been found of inadequate size and and it is mainly because of this the decision to change was effected. Future post office quarters are to be located in the Frank Morris building store and upon completion of extensive alterations, will provide nearly three times the space available in the present building.

While the post office department is scheduled to take possession of the new quarters on October 1, it is understood occupation will not be made until a month later. The rental agreement runs for 10 years.

Plans call for extension of the Merchant street building as far back as the alley and the erection of a new and modern front. The Morris store will operate on the east side.

The announcement of the new post office location comes as welcome news to Audubon business men who feared transfer might be made to Oaklyn. Much credit for keeping it in the borough goes to the efforts of Wilbert Davis, president of the Audubon National Bank, and to a committee representing the Audubon Chamber of Commerce.

———o———

1939

(cont.)   On Thursday, June 22nd, the *Weekly Visitor* carried an article on plans to relocate the Post Office to Merchant Street, following extensive alterations to the Morris Department Store. Morris leased part of the property at 107 Merchant Street to the U.S Government for the new Audubon Post Office.(See article on previous page). The Frank Morris Store held a huge rebuilding sale in July, featuring spectacular savings, such as . . . .

> 55 ¢ men's ties on sale for 39 ¢.
> 25 ¢ kiddies' Play Suits on sale for 10 ¢.
> Ladies' Fine Muslin slips on sale for 25 ¢.
> $1.00 Men's Van Heusen Sportshirts for 69 ¢.

The new combined Post Office and Department Store was opened in November.

On July 4th, the Murray-Troutt Drum and Bugle Corps performed for the first time. This group, known nationwide as the "BON - BONS" remained in existence for nearly 40 years and gained a reputation as the best marching corps in the State of New Jersey. (See the photo of the group, taken in July. at the Legion Post Home on Graisbury Avenue and Lake Drive, below; and the photo of some of the members of Post # 262, taken earlier in the decade at right).

LEGION POST 262 — The Murray-Trout American Legion Post 262 in Audubon was once one of the most active organizations in the community. This 1930s photo shows legion home the post members built at the corner of Graisbury Avenue and Lake Drive in the 1920s. Building now is a church.

Pride of Audubon Legionnaires

—Photo by Alfred Dotts.

Members of Murray-Troutt Post No. 262, American Legion, are justly proud of the above Girls' Drum and Bugle Corps sponsored by their organization. The first all-girl Legion unit in the State of New Jersey, these lassies, resplendent in blue and gold uniforms, made their initial appearance in the local Fourth of July parade. They will also represent the Post in competitive drills at the State Legion convention being held September 7, 8 and 9, at Cape May.

In August, ground was broken for a 279 - room apartment house on the West side of the White Horse Pike, near Merchant Street. Units extended for 375 feet along White Horse Pike and back to East Atlantic Avenue and the complex was predicted to be the finest and most modern apartment house in South Jersey.

After months of expansion work at the corner of Merchant Street and the White Horse Pike, the veterinary hospital of F. Herbert Owens was converted from what "had been an adequate dog and cat hospital into one providing all the necessities and conveniences known to science". (See illustration and article on the next page)

Note: The veterinary hospital was in existence for more than forty years. When it closed in the 1980s, the property remained for sale for almost a decade. It is now the site of a new Equity Bank location.

At the National Education Association Convention in San Francisco, Dr. Fidler, the supervising principal of the Audubon Schools, was elected chairman of the New Jersey Delegation. (See the article and photo on the next page.)

Mr. Frank Oldham, teacher at AHS, returned safely from his annual bycicle tour of Europe on board the Holland America Lines Veendam. With him on this year's tour was another AHS teacher, Miss Florence Tyson. Considerable fear for their safety was manifested by their friends when the German armies began their push into Poland. The two, along with others participating in the annual tour directed by Oldham, had left on the line's Rotterdam on June 27th and arrived in Amsterdam at the end of the month. They returned on September 6th and were particularly fortunate in returning home unharmed.

Note: On the next page, we have included a cartoon from September 7 that appeared in the *Weekly Visitor*. It is a reflection of the changing times!

Having completed his history of Audubon after years of intensive research, Ed Danielson of 511 Third Avenue in Audubon put an article in the *BI - TOWN ORATOR* (on September 7th) requesting pictures of past borough officials so that he could complete his work on a pictorial history.

Wins New Honor

DR. WILLIAM L. FIDLER

At the annual convention of the National Education Association now being held in San Francisco, Dr. William L. Fidler, supervising principal of Audubon schools, was elected chairman of the New Jersey delegation. He is attending the convention. In addition to the position he occupies in Audubon, Dr. Fidler is president of the New Jersey Education Association.

To Better Care for Pets

AUDUBON ANIMAL HOSPITAL

As the result of an extensive program of expansion, Audubon has now become the home of one of the most modern and complete animal hospitals in New Jersey.

For months workmen have been busy on the premises of F. Herbert Owens, Jr., V. M. D.,, 36 White Horse pike, transferring what had already been an adequate dog and cat hospital into one providing all the necessities and conveniences known to science.

A trip through the new hospital reveals and abundance of light together with equipment that even to the inexperienced lends an atmosphere of respect and confidence. The entire building is steam heated, and air-conditioned by the latest and most efficient system known. Temperature is controlled thermostatically from the ward room.

In addition to a tastefully furnished and decorated waiting room, the hospital has a complete laboratory, operating room, ward accommodating as many as 25 pets in spotless and vermin-proof cages, six concrete runways, and a fully equipped pharmacy.

Many intricate instruments are to be found in an abundance, including an X-Ray machine, Dia-Thermy and Physio-Therapy equipment and other essential details in the armamentarium necessary to combat the diseases of small animals.

1939

(continued)   Mrs. Dorothy Lillagore, proprietor of the "Dorothy Sweet Shop" at 273 West Kings Highway, announced that she would open her new "The Dipper" on September 15th at the site of the former A&P store on the White Horse Pike between Vassar and Princeton Roads. "The Dipper" will have a dance floor, as well as a soda fountain. Music will be supplied by a recording machine with all the latest numbers.

On Sunday, September 24th, the Audubon Chamber of Commerce chartered an Express Train from Audubon to the New York World's Fair. Admission to the Fair was 50¢ and the roundtrip train fare was $2.70. The train left Audubon at 7:55 am, arrived at the World's Fair at 10:45 am, left the Fair at 10:45 pm and returned to Audubon at 1:45 am on Monday, the 25th.

The Audubon High School Concert Choir gave a special performance at Convention Hall in Atlantic City on November 9th. The Concert was a highlight of the 1939 New Jersey Education Association Convention.

In November, new traffic lights were installed at the White Horse Pike and Kings Highway.

On November 3rd, the Audubon Women's Club observed its 25th anniversary with a dinner at the Walt Whitman hotel in Camden.

On November 30th, the Audubon Women's Club purchased a lot on East Atlantic Avenue and Chestnut Street, on which the organization planned to build a club house in the Spring of 1940. It had a frontage of 59 feet and a depth of 197 feet, facing Atlantic Avenue. The purchase price of the lot was $100.

Several other major events took place in the year 1939: The Audubon National Bank celebrated its 20th Anniversary on September 20th; A grand opening was held for the Audubon Skating Rink on Friday, September 7th, after extensive renovations (Admission was 25¢ for ladies and 35¢ for gentlemen); the opening of the Audubon schools was delayed from September 6th until September 20th, because of a second case of infantile paralysis in the borough (for the two week period, Sunday schools and theaters were also closed to all children under the age of 18); Volunteer Fire Company No. 1 held a successful Firemen's Carnival on the grounds of the fire house on Merchant Street opposite Virginia Avenue. Articles about these events, along with some of the interesting ads for local shops that appeared in the September 7th issue of the *BI - TOWN ORATOR,* are presented on the following five pages. The store ads are placed by geographic location within the borough.

Bi-Town Orator

58 W. Atlantic Avenue, Audubon, N. J.
Telephone Audubon 681

Co-Publishers and Editors

HOWARD J. HEINZ   JOHN J. RYAN, JR.

JOSEPH MAYERS   GEORGE MURPHY
Managing Editor   *Circulation Manager*

SUBSCRIPTION—$1.00 A YEAR; THREE CENTS A COPY

Advertising Rates Upon Application

All communications should be addressed to the Bi-Town Orator, Audubon, N. J. *Unsigned communications not acknowledged.*

Thursday September 7, 1939

"The Bank Public Confidence Built"

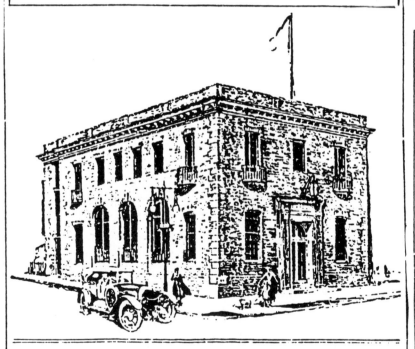

Audubon National Bank To Celebrate Twentieth Anniversary

The Audubon National Bank is this month, celebrating it's twentieth anniversary. Twenty years of achievement! Twenty years of faithful service! Twenty years of striving to become a social benefit! This is the record of the Audubon National Bank.

Since 1919, Audubon National Bank has thwarted every economic upheaval and presents now as it did then, a bank of confidence. During the two decades of the bank's existence, layman of all types, professional men of every vocation have passed through its doors recognizing it as a sound

and successful organization. There are approximately 6,000 depositors who now enjoy the services this bank renders. The law firm of Riggens & Davis of Camden, are still the active bank solicitation representatives as they were since the bank was organized.

Due ot the diligent efforts of the former Charles F. Wise, Dr. I. G. Seiber, William Lamont, William Hanselman, Cooper L. MacMillan, John J. Dempsey, Harvey E. Ulrich, and Wilbert Davis, the bank's governing body and officials was formed. Of the former

Continued On Page 8

PRICE THREE CENTS

School Opening Deferred In Audubon Following Second Paralysis Case

Announcement Made After Joint Meeting Of Commissioners, Health Officials And School Board

To Open September 18, Dr. W. L. Fidler States

Health authorities in Audubon have taken the first step in infantile paralysis prevention by deferring the opening of schools from September 6 to September 18. Sunday schools and theatres will be closed to children under 18 years of age for the same period.

The announcement came as a distinct surprise to teachers and students as it had previousy been stated by health officials that there was no apparent danger of changing the regular routine. Dr. W. F. Burns, President of the Board of Health, issued the following official statement Friday evening:

"It has been decided that in view of the cases of infantile paralysis in the county schools of the Borough of Audubon, the moving pictures, and Sunday Schools be closed to children up to 18 years of age, until September 18, 1939, or at the discretion of the Board. This resolution was adopted at a special meeting of the Borough Commissioners and the Board of Education."

Dr. W. F. Burns

It is believed that the action was taken after it was discovered that a second case of paralysis had broken out in the borough. The stricken boy is Edward Tulane, Jr., of 15 N. Logan avenue. His case is reported to be only slight and physicians claim he is recovering rapidly.

At the present time these are only precautionary measures being taken by borough officials. However, Dr. Burns stated that if any further developments arise, added measures will be taken.

The Audubon school system had been scheduled to open on September 6. Health authorities have stated that if there are no indications of further spreading of the disease the schools will open according to the new schedule.

Mr. Arja Hopkins, president of the board of education in Audubon, stated that the action concerning closing Sunday schools and movies had been taken after long consideration at special joint meeting held Friday. It was believed that such a precautionary measure would aid in keeping down any possibility of spreading.

Dr. Burns said that although there was no fear of a growing paralysis epidemic in Audubon, the members of the three borough bodies had taken the action because they believed that parents throughout the borough would be in constant worry if the school were open and rumors continued to circulate through the county.

"It is possible," Dr. Burns said, "that the cases may have resulted from exposure in some other locality and it would take about ten days after return of the individual to tell if there were any traces of the disease."

In announcing that the schools had been closed for the temporary period, Dr. William L. Fidler, supervising principal of Audubon schools, said that the teachers meeting scheduled for last Tuesday had been indefinitely postponed.

Late Wednesday night it was not known whether or not the new ruling would effect the start of high school football practice. Coach Jim Picken returned from Canada late Tuesday and con-

(Continued on Page 8)

43

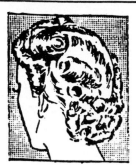

1940   As we come to the end of the decade of the 1930s, we want to add one more ad that will help you visualize the changes in movie entertainment that have occurred during the 20th century. We found an ad for the Highland Theatre, complete with photos of the stars, prices for various showings of the film and, of course, the special gifts for ladies in attendance. (see the ad for "Destry Rides Again" on this page.)

NOTE: The owner of the Highland Cleaners, located at the corner of West Atlantic Avenue and Chestnut Street, provided this flyer. She explained that the store's name was derived from the name of the famous Theatre, located one block away.

Note: One final note of interest about the decade of the 1930s: Telephone Numbers in Audubon began with the three letters AUD, followed by four numbers. The system was later changed to LI 6 and LI 7 and then to 546 and 547, still in use in the 1990s.

1941 - 1950

This decade began with the outbreak of World War II. Many of the events and activities in Audubon were related to the war effort. As part of the research for this book, interviews were conducted with seversl longtime residents, who shared their experiences in taped discussions that are now part of the archives of the Free Public Library.

1941   A housing project for war workers appeared in Audubon. It was built as a result of the thousands of laborers who moved into Camden County during the first years of the decade. This sudden growth in population stimulated real estate development and housing construction in Camden City and the suburban towns. Camden County received $1.5 Billion worth of war contracts, as the U.S. Government recognized the area's growing military importance: New York Shipbuilding, Mathis Shipbuilding, Quaker Shipyard, RTC Shipbuilding Corporation.

Ed Danielson, the historian for the county American Legion, completed his extensive history of the borough of Audubon. As part of this work, he included a poem which he had composed to describe some of the changes that occurred in town since Mrs. Herald had described the area in her poem. His selection was based on the poem of Mrs. Herald and reflected his impressions of Audubon. (See next page).

The American Legion Post Monument, formerly located on the White Horse Pike at Pine Street, was relocated to the High School grounds, facing Edgewood Avenue.

1942   The Audubon Auxiliary Police Association was incorporated.

The Defender Fire Company received a new Maxim 75 - foot aerial ladder.

Note: It was about this time in the early part of the decade that the famous "Swinging Bridge" - - - the old Haviland Avenue foot bridge - - - was taken down so that the steel could be used in the war effort.

Many of Audubon's citizens enlisted in the service during these years. Three of these citizens will be mentioned at this point in our travels through the borough's history.

AUDUBON - FIFTY YEARS LATER

Edgar N. Danielson (1941)

Oh, little, thrifty, Jersey town
Along the Reading Line.
Where once stood little dwellings,
Has expanded with the time.

Today the stubble filled, December fields,
That were brown and barren then,
Have been replaced with Homes and Stores
That make our memories slim.

The sunny, breezy, open spots,
Where air a tonic is;
Convenient both to train and car,
Still yet is full of rural bliss.

The roads that used to be furrowed,
With the mud of Jersey's yellow sand;
Have all been paved
And now, are the finest in the land.

The smooth and far - famed White Horse Pike
Runs through our prosperous land,
Taking cars from every nation
To the Playground of the world.

The softly swelling, brown clad hills
That were few and small and low
Are now replaced with landscapes
That really make a show.

The country store, where the Postoffice stood,
Where people came and went,
Has been replaced with the modern kind,
And our mail and parcels sent.

Oh, little town of Audubon,
While in your infancy,
Dreamed of great things for the future
Which today is a reality.

May long life and growth continue,
As we proceed along,
To every living citizen
In good ole Audubon.

Vincent Boris   1923 - - - - -

Vincent was in the service for 2 ½ years, from 1942 - 1945. He served on the European front in WW II in A Company, 34th Division. While stationed in Italy, his division was preparing for an attack against the Germans. Because of his height, he was recruited to help in the crossing of a river. Being tall, he and several comrades took a rope across the river and held it while the others crossed. The banks of the river were filled with landmines. He was blinded in one eye when one of the mines exploded. He received the Purple Heart and, on October 10, 1998, the Distinguished Service Medal. (see photo to the right)

Russell Lyons   1925 - - - - -

Russell has lived his entire life in Audubon. In 1942, at the age of 17, he enlisted in the Navy. He was stationed in the Pacific, having volunteered for duty on board a PT Boat, and spent 1 ½ years in the area between the Philippines and Borneo. In an interview, he explained how the torpedo tubes were replaced by racks because of the danger that existed with the buildup of salt in the tubes.

Ethel Peters Gray

Ethel moved to Audubon in 1939 and enlisted in the Army in 1944. She was in the Transportation Corps and was stationed at Camp Kilmer in New Brunswick, New Jersey. She is one of only two women in Audubon whose name is listed on the WW II Monument at the American Legion Post site on Chestnut Street. One of the PFCs who was also stationed at Camp Kilmer was Red Skelton.

50

After the war, Ethel worked in several hospitals, including the Audubon Hospital on Vassar Road (which was later moved to Stratford and became part of the Kennedy system).

In the interview, she mentioned that she has one of the railroad ties that were to be part of the line running through the Gully on its way from Gloucester to Haddonfield.

The photos to the left show Mrs. Gray in her uniform with the insignia of the Transportation Corps and sitting on the cab of one of the trucks (upper right). On the following page is a photo she took of PFC Red Skelton in 1945.

Note: The American Legion Post Monument serves as a symbol of the patriotism of the borough of Audubon. It honors ALL the citizens in the community who served in World War II, fighting for our freedom. A special service is held at the Post site at East Atlantic Avenue and Chestnut Street each year on Memorial Day. (See photo page 53)

1947 The housing project that was built in Audubon in 1941 for war workers was officially incorporated as Audubon Park. Prior to this year, the project had been known as Audubon Village.

1949 Medal of Honor recipient Edward C. Benfold graduated from Audubon High School. He did not attend the graduation ceremony in June because he had enlisted in the Navy in May. (See Chapter II for the entire life story of Edward C. Benfold.)

Little League baseball became a reality in Audubon.

1951 - 1960

1951   Nelson V. Brittin was killed in action in Korea on March 7th. He later was the recipient of the Medal of Honor. In addition, a street in Audubon was named in his memory and an elementary school in Fort Stewart, Georgia was named in his memory.

1952   Edward C. Benfold was killed in action in Korea on September 5th. He later was the recipient of the Medal of Honor. In addition, a naval destroyer, the USS BENFOLD (DDG-65), was named in his memory.

1953   The wife of Edward C. Benfold was presented the Medal of Honor at a special ceremony at the Philadelphia Naval Yard on July 16th.

The "Bon Bons" Drum and Bugle Corps took 2nd place honors at the VFW National Competition.

Note: We thought that readers would would enjoy seeing several of the comic strips popular in 1953. (see the comic section on the next page.)

Photos of one of the PRSS trains coming through Audubon and the Orston Depot are presented on the page following the comic page. Notice the gatetender and the gate house at the crossing in the photo of the train.

1954   St. Mary's Episcopal Church, White Horse Pike and Green Street in Haddon Heights, dedicated a stained-glass window in memory of parishioner and Medal of Honor recipient Edward C. Benfold in November. The window is the Baptismal Scene and is quite special in that there appears in the lower right corner a stained-glass image of the Medal of Honor.

On November 19th the Masonic Lodge in Audubon opened its new Temple at 305 East Atlantic Avenue, on the site of the old Highland Theatre.

Note: Since 1931 Lodge meetings had been held on the 2nd floor of the Audubon National Bank Building, 100 West Merchant Street.

HILADELPHIA INQUIRER. THURSDAY MORNING. AUGUST 20, 1953
BIG BEN BOLT
HI, CHAMP...HEY, WHAT'S THE SCOOP ON TODAY'S SHOOTING?
NOTHING SPECIAL THAT I KNOW, BOYS... JUST SOME ROUTINE FIGHTING SHOTS.
THE CHIEF SAID SOMETHING MIGHT EXPLODE AROUND HERE TODAY....WELL, WHATEVER IT IS THAT'S COOKING, BOLT'S NOT IN ON THE MENU.
I GOT THE SAME FEELING I HAD ONE NIGHT A COUPLA MINUTES BEFORE I WAS HIJACKED IN SINGAPORE IN '32!
IT'S JUST A MOVIE WE'RE MAKING, SPIDER... RELAX AND GET A SUNBURN!
DICK TRACY
BACK ON HIS ICE CREAM CYCLE, 3-D MAGEE PREPARES FOR HIS MASTER STROKE.
I'D BETTER CHECK TO BE SURE THAT THE LITTLE DARLINGS ARE ALL IN THE BOX. AH, YES.
FIRST, LOSS OF SPEECH; THEN, COMA AND PARALYSIS. YES, THE PERUVIAN BLUE-BACK ANT IS A MIGHTY MITE.
MEANWHILE—
UNCLE CANHEAD, WE'RE GOING TO GET ANOTHER ICE CREAM BAR. ARE YOU WAITING FOR ICE CREAM MAN, TOO?
SORT O
STEVE CANYON
PRINCESS, OUR RESERVES HAVE CLOSED THE LINE WHERE THE SNOWSLIDE SWEPT THE ENEMY DOWN THE MOUNTAIN!
BUT THE RED GUNS CONTINUE TO FIRE! THE TIME FOR TEA AND CAKES IS NOT AT HAND!
MEANWHILE - FAR TO THE EAST A CAMEL TRAIN MOVES TOWARD THE MOUNTAINS...
A BOMBARDMENT OCCURS AT OUR DESTINATION!
AWAKEN THE HEAD HOOLIGAN!
ZZZZZZ
MARK TRAIL
HAVE YOU SEEN TOMMY AMOTOKTUK?
THIS OLD ONE DOES NOT UNDERSTAND A WORD THE KRABLOONAK SAYS!
HOLY SMOKE, JOHNNY, WHAT'S WRONG WITH THESE PEOPLE?
DEY DON'T WANT YOU TO KNOW WHERE DIS TOMMEE IS, MA FREN!
HEY, I HAVE AN IDEA...THAT BOY MIGHT TALK!
HENRY
ESCALATORS
BEETLE BAILEY
I HOPE YOUR COMPANY AREA LOOKS BETTER TODAY, CAPTAIN!
IT WILL, SIR! I MADE THE MEN CLEAN AND SCRUB EVERYTHING!
WHERE'S THE TEN BUCKS YOU SAID YOU'D PAY BACK TODAY?
I PUT IT IN YOUR JACKET POCKET ON YOUR BED THIS MORNING!

ORESTON DEPOT H CRES
AUDUBON N.J.

1955: The old pumper of the Defender Fire Company, purchased in 1932, was replaced by a new Maxim 1000-gallon pumper.

OLDEST NATIVE

MISS MARY MARSHALL

Born in 1887 on one of Audubon's last remaining farms, she has continued to remain a resident of the community to this day. Her home is on a portion of the farm where she was born.

Audubon celebrated its 50th Anniversary with a week-long celebration. A special honoree at the Anniversary was Miss Mary Marshall, born in 1887 and the oldest living native of the community. (See photo and caption at the left.

On the following three pages are photos of the two Fire Departments in town, a listing of professionals and organizations that sponsored activities during the week-long celebration and some of the businesses in town in 1955. (Compare these with the businesses listed in 1939 to see the changes.)

DEFENDER FIRE COMPANY

OFFICERS AND MEN OF DEFENDER FIRE COMPANY — 2 WEST ATLANTIC AVE.

AUDUBON VOLUNTEER FIRE CO. #1

OFFICERS AND MEN OF THE AUDUBON VOLUNTEER FIRE CO. NO. 1 — MERCHANT STREET

Professional Men of Audubon Cooperating

I. Grafton Sieber, M.D.
Russell Stuart Magee, M.D., F.A.C.S., F.I.C.S.
C. E. Filkins, M.D.
Henry Tatem, M.D.
Wilmer F. Burns, M.D.
John Horner, M.D.
Edward Stuart Magee, M.D.
Ernest F. Doherty, M.D.
William R. Stevenson, M.D.
Raymond A. Baker, M.D.
Walter Schuler, D.C.
John H. Hayes, D.O.
Russell Howell Hunt, O.D.
F. Herbert Owens, V.M.D.
Ellis Bulk, B.S.Phar.

S. W. White, D.D.S.
Harry A. Ingham, D.D.S.
Julius L. Pearl, D.D.S.
Henry A. Belasco, D.D.S.
M. Bradin, D.D.S.
Wilbert Davis, D.S.C.
Jonas Morris, D.S.C.
Charles Wise, D.S.C.
Elwood Bigler, C.P.A.
Marshall Hammon, C.E.
George L. J. Neutze, R.A.
J. Claud Simon, Atty.
Warren Douglas, Atty.
Charles H. Stevens, Atty.
Edward W. Eichman, Atty.
Harold P. Gleaner, Atty.

Direct Organization Donations

Audubon Fathers Association
Scout Mothers, Boy Scout Troop 57 of Audubon
Boy Scout Troop # 88 of Audubon
Cub Pack # 131 of Audubon
Boy Scout Troop # 57 of Audubon
Grade School Parent-Teacher
    Association
Audubon High School P.T.A.
Audubon Wildlife Society
Audubon Citizens Republican Club
Audubon Women Citizens
    Republican Club
Wyandotte Council #83, D. of P.
Sunshine Club of Audubon
Murray-Troutt Unit 262, American Legion
    Auxiliary

Audubon Lions Club
Audubon All-Girls Corps
United Spanish War Veterans
Women's Club of Audubon
Women's Democratic Club of
    Audubon
Murray-Troutt Post 262
    American Legion
Audubon Auxiliary Police Assn.
Star of Audubon Lodge #106
Camp 54, P.O. of Ar.
Ladies Auxiliary Defender
    Fire Co. #1
Ladies Auxiliary Fire Co. #1
Audubon Volunteer Fire Co. #1
Defender Fire Co. #1

AUDUBON, NEW JERSEY

This color photo, taken in 1955 at the corner of the White Horse Pike and Kings Highway, shows the Century movie theater. Notice that the traffic signals are mounted on poles fastened in the cement along the curb. In the 19902, these signals are on poles that are extended out over the intersection and, due to ever - increasing amounts of traffic, have a special green arrow for left hand turns which were installed in 1998.

1956   Following a serious injury to a school child early in the year, a meeting was held and volunteer crossing guards were recruited to work with the Safety Patrol to help control vehicular traffic.

1957   The Audubon Safety Patrol, founded in 1941, was awarded a trophy for best appearing and best marching group in the nation in a competition in Washington, DC.

The "Bon Bons" Drum and Bugle Corps from Audubon captured 2nd Place in the American Legion National Competition in Atlantic City. They missed winning the title by less than 1/10 of a point in the scoring.

1957

(cont.)   During the summer, a building was erected at the back of the Holy Trinity Evangelical Lutheran Church for a heating plant and the entire heating system of the church was changed.

The present Audubon Public Library was constructed next to the old School # 1 on Oakland Avenue and opened its doors in November. (see photo below)

Work began on the construction of the Black Horse Pike Shopping Center.

1958   On November 14th and 15th, the Audubon Fathers' Association put on the Western Musical Satire *"Jazze Get Your Gun"* on the stage of the High School.

Note: The Fathers' Association in Audubon was founded in the early 1920s and was one of the most active organizations in town. In the Playbill for their 1958 show (which included Mr. Vince Boris in the role of barkeeper) listed the following ongoing activities sponsored by the group: Youth Week, The Job Poppa Program, a Scholarship Fund, Boys' State, the Grade School Christmas Party, Girls' Hockey Camp, Boys' Football Camp, a Little League Team, the Cub Pack and the Brownie Troop in town and support of the Korner Canteen.

On October 4th, the annual Drum and Bugle Corps Competition was held at the High School. The program featured 4 Junior Corps plus a special exhibition by the "Bon-Bons" and the "Musketeers" from Upper Darby, PA on the theme: "The King And I".

1959   On September 6th, ground was broken for a new Educational Building for the Holy Trinity Lutheran Church.

1060   On May 8th, the cornerstone for the Educational Building of the Holy Trinity Lutheran Church was laid.

On September 11th, the new Educational Building was formally dedicated.

A special holiday postcard, featuring the "Bon-Bons" All Girl Drum and Bugle Corps was issued. The organization had become one of the most recognized and accomplished Corps in the nation. (See the postcard below)

1961   -   1970

The decade of the 1960s brought some major changes to the face of Audubon. Some new organizations were beginning to function within the borough, a business that had existed since the turn of the century closed its doors, four apartment buildings came into existence and the population continued to grow. A major celebration took place in the middle of the decade when Audubon helped the state of New Jersey review the first three hundred years of its existence. Here are just some of the highlights.

1961   The Women's Club in town made one room in the Community Center - - - previously the site of School # 1 on Oakland Avenue near the corner of Oak Street - - - available to all adult organizations in town. This room, on the first floor of the building, had been remodeled (combining two small rooms into one large meeting area) at a cost of $8,500.00.

Work began on construction of two apartments houses on he property owned by Abbotts Dairies at 211 and 230 Oakland Avenue. This building project marked the end of a dairy business that was begun back in 1900 by Robert Tweed.

This year marked the first full year of operation for the Audubon Business Association, founded in order to promote a better business atmosphere in Audubon and to improve the present facilities for the public.

A dream come true was realized for Audubon Police Sergeant William P. Ulrich, who had established a Policewomen's Association, a group of volunteers, to serve as school crossing guards back in 1956. This group of women was an asset to Ulrich's Safety Patrol program in town. On May 12th permission was granted to have the Policewomen's Association march with the Safety Patrol in the parade in Washington, DC. The event was a fitting tribute to Ulrich and all his efforts over 15 years working with the young students of the Safety Patrol.

A girls' Softball League was organized in town and a second boys' baseball team was entered in the Interborough Youth League. Both teams were organized under the auspices of Audubon Sports, Inc., an organization formed in 1960.

On May 6th, the Audubon Chapter of the S.P.E.B.S.Q.S.A., Inc. presented a Barber Shop Singing Festival at Audubon High School. Six barbershop groups performed in this concert. The Audubon Chapter had its beginning in Woodbury in 1949 and moved to

Audubon in 1955, meeting every Tuesday evening in School #
2 at Oak Street and Wyoming Avenue. (See photo of the group below)

AUDUBON CHAPTER, S.P.E.B.S.Q.S.A.

1962   Audubon Sports, Inc. entered teams in softball, baseball
and football. The football team, the Audubon Eagles, traveled to
Harrisburg, PA and to Athens, GA for post-season bowl contests.

At Audubon High School, an electronics course was added
to the Science Department curriculum and was offered to 11th and
12th grade students. By 1964, the new program had been expanded
into a two-year offering.

1963   The Audubon Business Association sponsored the first
"Miss Audubon Business Association" contest. The event was a
huge success.

As support for the Audubon Sports, Inc. program continued
to increase, with the backing of many local businesses, the softball
program was expanded to five teams and permission from the Audubon Park Board of Education was received to play games on the
Audubon Park field. In addition, a baseball team for boys ages 16-18
was entered in the Garden State Baseball League.

In May, work began on another apartment building, the Imperial Arms, located at the White Horse Pike and Merchant Street
(across the street from the veterinary hospital).

1963

(cont.)   As of September, the total enrollment in the three schools in Audubon was as follows:

School # 2, 599; School # 3, 365; AHS, 1,272.

The Audubon Manor Apartments, located at 624 White Horse Pike, opened for rental in October.

1964   The Audubon Rotary Club, first organized in 1945 with a charter membership of 20 local business and professional men, began its 19th year of work in the community. The president of the organization this year was Dr. Ernest Schreiber and meetings were held every Tuesday at Compton's Log Cabin.

The Audubon Lions' Club celebrated its 10th Anniversary. This organization sponsored an annual Halloween Parade in town, a tradition that continues through the 1990s.

The Audubon Women's Club celebrated its 50th Anniversary.

Audubon published a special Tercentenary Book which provided many facts about the 300 year history of the State of New Jersey, as well as information about the first 59 years of the borough. A summary paragraph in this book reads as follows: "Our town includes two elementary schools, in use, one former school used as a Community Hall and our oldest and smallest school on Cherry Street, now a private dwelling. (See the photo of this Cherry Street landmark, taken in 1999, on following page.)

There are also six growing churches, two fire companies and a library. We have a bank, a Post Office, a railroad station, and the essential stores, divided between Merchant Street and Orston. We have two War Monuments, listing the 125 men serving in World War I (5 killed), and the 1,021 men and women (27 killed) who followed the colors in World War II. Our only lack is a cemetery and there was one of these on the Graisbury Tract near Pine Street and the Railroad, in which many of that family, the Breechs, Spragues, Glovers, etc., were laid to rest. The records state that the railroad "ran through the grounds and so has been lost sight of." "

1965   The Audubon Public Library had a circulation of 27,910 items and had come a long way since its opening in November of 1957.

1966   The Murray-Troutt American Legion Post # 262 sold its Post Home on the corner of Graisbury Avenue and Lake Drive and began holding meetings at the Audubon Community Center, next to the Public Library.

1967   Audubon Little League, founded in 1949, had its most successful season ever. The All-Star team won the District 14 Championship and then went on to be Section 4 Champs and State Runner-up in tournament competition.

At the end of the decade of the 1960s, one tradition came to an end. At Audubon High School, for almost 40 years, only Seniors were allowed to enter the building through the Main Entrance at Chestnut Street. Even underclassmen walking with members of the Senior Class had to enter the building through other entrances. For many AHS grads, the end of this tradition was greeted with sadness. (See the photo of AHS and its Main Entrance, taken in November, 1998, on following page.)

1971   A major change took place at School # 2 on Wyoming Avenue between Oak Street and Mansion Avenue: a new building was constructed (beginning in 1970) on the former playground of the school. The old building was then torn down and became the palyground. Because the Main Entrance of the school was located on Mansion Avenue, the school was renamed the Mansion Avenue School (MAS). (See the then and now photos below: Then was 1939; now is 1999)

School No. 2, Wyoming Avenue and Oak Street. Audubon's Public Library and the Meeting Room of Borough Commissioners are in This Building.

1971

(cont)   The Audubon All-Girl Drum and Bugle Corps, the "Bon Bons", won THREE National Championships: The World Open; the U.S. Open and the VFW Nationals.

On February 8th, a self-service photocopy machine was installed in the Public Library.

1972   Due to high costs of maintaining membership, the Library withdrew from the County Library system. The Library was officially incorporated.

At Audubon High School, two additions were made to the existing structure: C Building and a Library. AHS was now a complex that extended from Walnut Street to between Pine and Oak Streets on Edgewood Avenue.

The Audubon Pool, a center of recreation for borough residents since 1940, was closed to the public. The building, containing locker and rest rooms became a storage site for the Camden County Park system and remained in that state until the early 1990s.

1974   The Public Library on Oakland Avenue became known as the Free Public Library of Audubon.

1975   Defender Fire Company celebrated its 80th Anniversary. It housed an Imperial 100' Aerial ladder truck. (See the cover for the Celebration Book on the next page. Note the image of a yacht in the center. It represents the "Defender", the American yacht that defeated the British yacht, "Challenger" in the 1895 yachting competition. The company was named in tribute to that victory.)

What was thought to be the oldest tree in Audubon, an oak tree at 712 Bringhurst Avenue, over 17 feet in circumference, was severely damaged in a freak storm and had to be cut down. Some residents say that the "Old Pin Oak" dated back to the 1680s and, thus, was nearly 300 years old.

80th ANNIVERSARY
1975

DEFENDER

1895

AUDUBON, N. J.

HOUSING

IMPERIAL 100' AERIAL

1976   Plans were being made to demolish the abandoned train station at East Atlantic Avenue and Merchant Street. Audubon resident and AHS graduate William J. Judd rescued the building and converted it into a dental office. (See the photos, then (1976) and Now (1999) on this page and the following page.)

Train stops find a new station in life

Courier-Post photography by Ron Karafin

Dentist William J. Judd rescued this station in Audubon from the wreckers, and it now serves as his offices. The eyesore was restored by the doctor in 1976 with landscaping help from the Audubon Women's Club.

72

Former PRSS Train Station, now the dental offices of William J. Judd
(Photo, February, 1999)

Track repair cars from Amtrak pass by the former PRSS Train Station at Merchant Street in Audubon in February, 1999.

1976
(cont)   July 4th was a very special day in the borough as the residents help the nation celebrate its Bicentennial.

1977   In August, another community landmark announced that it was closing its doors to the public. The historic Century Theatre, known in the 1970s as the Coronet, gave notice that it would close on September 3rd. The town, that at one point in its history had three theatres, now would have none! (See photo below and article on next page)

Courier-Post photography by Evangelos Dousmanis

Three-year-old Man of Steel Gary Greener strikes a familiar pose outside the Coronet Theatre, due to close next month.

Curtain coming down on Coronet

By JULIE BUSBY and ROBERT BAXTER
Of the Courier-Post

AUDUBON — Vaudeville acts, rock groups, and Superman have danced, blared or soared across the Coronet Theatre stage for half a century.

But the Coronet, following the trend of so many of South Jersey's old-time movie palaces, is about to take its last bow.

William Milgrim, president of Milgrim Theatres, confirmed yesterday that the 1,300-seat theater will screen its last film on Sept. 3. He refused to comment on the circumstances behind the closing or the future of the building.

WHILE 150 patrons marvelled at the celluloid feats of Superman last night, Coronet manager Chester Delikate, 62, said he had not been informed about the theater's demise.

"I don't know anything about it," he said. "But sometimes the manager is the last to know about these things."

Delikate, who has worked at the Coronet for nine years, said the chain has charged between $1.50 to $4 per customer for films shown over the past decade.

The theater was recently packed for a month when "Deer Hunter" was booked and "Bloodline" also proved to be a financial success when it previewed earlier this month.

The final film to flicker across the screen next month will be "Beyond the Poseidon Adventure."

"WE HAVE good days and we have bad days. It depends on what's playing and sometimes the films are real dogs," Delikate said. "This is a good theater and we do a lot of business so you can't really blame the management."

The vast structure, which boasts a stage, organ loft and dressing rooms, may be the victim of competition from newer theaters housed in the malls and the burden of operating costs.

"Sometimes the large theaters just can't compete with the malls or big cinemas that have first-run movies," said relief projectionist Robert Semler, one of 15 Coronet employees. "We're facing the end of an era and the next five years might prove to be the last for large movie houses."

The theater's most popular film was "The Sting," buttered popcorn always rates as the audience's favorite snack, and moviegoer's antics have never changed from the silent era to the "blood and guts" cinematic genre.

"Some things never change," said cashier Beth Gallagher of Haddon Heights. "People are always trying to get in on a child's rate."

THE DEATH knell for the theater was almost sounded in July when the Exxon Corp. appeared before the zoning board for permission to build a gas station on the site.

But the zoning board rejected the proposal, saying the facilities were in violation of the borough's master plan.

Audubon's only movie theater to survive the whims of filmgoers and the economy, the Coronet was built in the early 1920s as a vaudeville house.

According to film buff Allen Hauss of Marlton, finances ran thin and the Coronet — then known as the Century Theatre — reopened as a silent movie house.

FIVE YEARS later, the building was expanded and entertainers such as Abbott and Costello and Charles Laughton appeared on stage. The last act to play there was the pop group "The Association" in 1966.

The borough's two other movie houses met their economic death years ago. The Highland Theatre is now a Masonic lodge and the Opera House at Atlantic and Pine streets has been converted into a shoe store.

Hauss said the Coronet was built during the heydey of theaters. An orchestra pit, chandeliers, a balcony and a lobby — all the drawing cards that made a visit to the theater a magical experience — were a part of the Coronet, he said.

The Westmont Theatre, the Harwan Theatre in Mount Ephraim, and the Broadway Theatre in Pitman are among the few remaining old-time entertainment showplaces.

Hauss lamented that Audubon is not the only town to lose a big movie house or theater.

THERE ARE no theaters in Camden since the Midway was recently demolished for a federal project. The Princess is now a union hall, and the Grand, Savar, and Roxie are only memories.

The Ritz in Oaklyn and the Crescent on the Black Horse Pike have become porno theaters, a theater in Haddon Heights has become a restaurant, and theaters in Maple Shade and Haddonfield have been demolished.

But the trend of theater closings did not ease the loss of the Coronet for movie fans last night.

"It's a shame because the kids really enjoyed it," said Pat Greener of Haddon Heights, who brought her Superman costumed son, Gary, and two other children to the theater.

1977   The "Bon Bons", the All Girl Drum and Bugle Corps
in Audubon, disbanded after nearly 40 years as a community
organization.

Note: From 1969 until 1977, the "Bon Bons" NEVER lost
a National Drum and Bugle Corps Competition!

On November 17th, the ground breaking took place for
an addition to the Free Public Library of Audubon. The addition
added a children's room, a storage area and an office to the existing facility.

1978   The new addition to the Free Public Library was dedica-
ed in July.

1979   The Audubon Lions' Club celebrated its 25th Anniversary. A special recognition was given to the service organization
in the 4th of July book.

Renovations began on School # 3, now known as the
Haviland Avenue School (HAS). (See photos of the school,
Then and Now, on the next page: Then, 1939, Now 1999)

As we close the summary of the 1970s, we present an aerial photo of the
former Swim Club, (page 78) taken in 1977. On page 79 we present some of the
businesses in town in the mid 1970s. (Compare them with those in the 1930s and
the 1950s.)

Another important addition to the borough in the 1970s was the Audubon
Arms Senior Citizen Apartment Complex. It was constructed on Nicholson Road
near the Black Horse Pike Shopping Center. It later became known as the Audubon
Towers. (See photos of the AUDUBON TOWERS, completed in 1980, on page 80)

School No. 3, Haviland Avenue South of Graisbury. Grade School
Pupils From the Eastern Section of Audubon Attend Here.

PETE'S HAIRSTYLING

B.H.P. SHOPPING CENTER

AUDUBON, N. J. 08106

FATHER & SON SHOES

AUDUBON SHOPPING CENTER

BELINS' ARCO SERVICE

WHITE HORSE PIKE & TAYLOR AVE.

AUDUBON, N. J. 08106

GARDEN STATE BINDERY

11 EAST TAYLOR AVENUE
AUDUBON, N. J. 08106
547-8993
RAY C. ADAMS

ALBO T. V. & APPLIANCE

AUDUBON, N. J. 08106

For Appointment Call 547-1471
VALENTI'S HAIRSTYLING
27 WEST MERCHANT STREET
AUDUBON, N. J. 08106
"A Full Service Salon"
Mary Valenti, Prop.

(609) 546-4881
ROBERT P. JORDAN
Dental Laboratories
ROBERT P. JORDAN, C.D.T.
101 WEST MERCHANT STREET
AUDUBON, N. J. 08106

SALLY SHOP
111 W. MERCHANT ST.
AUDUBON, N. J. 08106
Women's Wearing Apparel
Sewing & Knitting Supplies
Phone 547-6106

AUDUBON NEWS AGENCY

116 W. MERCHANT STREET
AUDUBON, N. J. 08106

Under New Management

GRIFFITHS' EXXON STATION

200 WHITE HORSE PIKE
AUDUBON, N. J. 08106

547-9393

BENTLEY'S
HOUSE OF SHOES

301 E. ATLANTIC AVE.
AUDUBON, N. J. 08106

SCOLA'S BARBER SHOP

317 E. ATLANTIC AVENUE

AUDUBON, N. J. 08106

FRANK'S FOOD MARKET

300 WYOMING AVENUE

AUDUBON, N. J. 08106

JULIANNA STEFAN
Interiors
Draperies — Interior Appointments
37 E. KINGSHIGHWAY
AUDUBON, 6, N. J.
547-9484

SMITH'S FLOWERS

557 W. KINGS HIGHWAY

AUDUBON, N. J. 08106

STARRETT' GULF SERVICE

KINGS HWY. & EDGEWOOD AVE.

AUDUBON, N. J. 08106

A treasured photo was taken in 1980 at Audubon High School: a photograph of five generations of teachers at AHS. The 1980 edition of the school's yearbook was dedicated to these five individuals, all of whom graduated from AHS and then returned to the school as teachers. We are presenting the photo and the yearbook dedication in this history of Audubon because they provide some insight into the special nature of the community.

Note: Miss Housel lived on Washington Terrace in Audubon and, after retiring, moved to Camden, Maine, where she still resides. Mr. Westphal is now the Principal of Audubon High School.

Pictured, l. to r.: Miss Louise Housel, Mr. George Kinkler, Mr. William Westphal, Mr. Jake Messenger, Mr. Joseph Brown. (Photo taken in 1980)

Thanks to Beth Connatser(Bunny Messenger), AHS Class of 1965, for the photo and article!

Audubon's Five Generations

We, the class of 1980, proudly dedicate this yearbook to the five generations of A.H.S. teachers. The yearbook staff feels that it is a unique quality of Audubon High School that those individuals who have gone through the educational system here have gone on to be educators and then returned to their own school to teach.

This teaching chain started with Mr. Jake Messenger who began teaching at Audubon in 1926 when the school first opened. Mr. Messenger taught a variety of subjects, such as chemistry, physics, and math. Mr. Messenger was loved by some but always respected by all. He was known for his cigars and his frequent use of the phrase, "hit the wall".

Mr. Messenger taught Miss Louise Housel, who began teaching social studies and foreign language in 1937. As the advisor of our yearbook, Miss Housel named it "Le Souviner." She taught language at A.H.S. and took upon herself the position of department chairman. In her spare time, Miss Housel enjoys the theater, ballet, and opera and is especially known for her gourmet cooking.

Mr. Messenger and Miss Housel both taught Mr. George Kinkler who began teaching in 1952. Mr. Kinkler presently teaches math and serves as advisor of Audubon's golf club.

Mr. Messenger, Miss Housel and Mr. Kinkler all taught Mr. William Westphal. Mr. Westphal began teaching math at his alma mater in 1965. He is now chairman of the math department as well as serving as assistant to the athletic director.

All four of these dedicated professionals taught Mr. Joseph Brown. Mr. Brown began teaching at Audubon in 1976 in the social studies department. He is also the advisor to the Senior Class.

For greatly contributing to the education of the Audubon youth, we, the class of 1980, would like to dedicate our yearbook to you Mr. Messenger, Miss Housel, Mr. Kinkler, Mr. Westphal, and Mr. Brown.

1981 - 1990

1981   In November, and Audubon legend, John "Jake" J. Messenger passed away. He began teaching at AHS in 1926, the year the school opened, and after retiring "officially" in 1972, continued on the staff as a tutor until 1978. The AHS Class of 1935 included an article about his life in their 50th Reunion booklet. (See article below)

"Jake" Messenger — A Legend In His Time

OBITUARIES   NOVEMBER 14, 1981

John J. Messenger, 'Mr. Audubon High'

By MARGARET SCOTT
Of the Courier-Post

AUDUBON — Services for John "Jake" J. Messenger, who taught mathematics and science at Audubon High School for more than 50 years, will be at 1 p.m. tommorrow at Foster's Funeral Home, 250 White Horse Pike here.

Mr. Messenger died Thursday at West Jersey Hospital, Southern Division, Berlin, after a long illness. He was 79.

"Jake was Mister Audubon High School; he was the cornerstone, a legend," Audubon principal Henry R. Gilbert said yesterday. "There will never be another teacher like him. He was a master."

After attending the University of Pennsylvania and Rutgers University, New Brunswick, Mr. Messenger began teaching at Audubon in 1926, the year the school opened.

"There are so many stories and so many things to say about him. He was an unbelievable person. He was zany, he was different and the kids loved him," Gilbert said.

"His ability to reach and motivate kids was phenomenal. He was unorthodox but effective.

The story is told that it was easy to tell when Jake Messenger's chemistry class was in session by the number of explosions or common to find him in the faculty lounge, legs crossed and a cigar in his mouth, meditating.

In his younger days on the staff, Jake Messenger was an assistant football coach and would spin on his heels when his team made a pleasing play.

He also initiated an annual dinner for Audubon male faculty members that he called "Jake's Gents."

"It was chauvinistic, but we loved it. It was a big jamboree to honor some male on the faculty. But when he went, the group went, too. We just couldn't do it without him," Gilbert said.

Mr. Messenger officially retired in 1972 but stayed on the school's staff as a tutor until 1978.

"He really didn't want to stop teaching and I'm sure he was older than the retirement age anyway when he did retire," Gilbert said.

"No one ever did find out how old he was, but there's a great story that he took some years off his age because he didn't have a birth certif-

icate and no one could prove he was older."

While he was growing up in upstate Pennsylvania, his house burned down and his birth certificate burned with it.

After living here since 1926, Mr. Messenger moved to Tabernacle earlier this year to live with his daughter.

During World War II, Mr. Messenger was in the Army Specialist Corp and taught mathematics and science to soldiers at Amherst College, Amherst, Mass.

Mr. Messenger was a honorary fireman in Audubon with the volunteer Fire Company No. 1.

He is survived by his wife, Estella, of Tabernacle; two daughters, Jacklyn Sileika of Tabernacle and Beth Connatser of Tennesse; four grandchildren; two brothers, and one sister.

Friends may call at the funeral home between noon and 1 p.m. on Sunday. Internment will be at the Crescent Burial Park, Pennsauken.

Memorial contributions can be made to the Audubon High School scholarship fund.

83

1982   The foot bridge at Graisbury Avenue over the Pennsylvania Reading Seashore Lines tracks was demolished after being declared unsafe. (See photo and caption below)

LANDMARKED REMOVED — The Old Graisbury Avenue Bridge across the Pennsylvania-Reading Seashore Railroad tracks falls victim to the sledgeball in August, 1982, after being declared unsafe for foot traffic.

1983   At Audubon High School, some additional improvements were made to classrooms, hallways and science labs.

1984   During the first week in May, a new Girls' Softball field, (See photo below) built across the street from the Audubon Shopping Center at the end of Hampshire Avenue, was dedicated. The field was built in tribute to Mr. Lee Jones, the individual who organized the Girls' Softball League in Audubon in 1961.

At a Memorial Day service at the home of Post # 262 of the American Legion, a Monument honoring Audubon residents who were killed in the Korean and Vietnam conflicts was dedicated. The monument includes six Audubon heroes, among them Medal of Honor recipients Nelson V. Brittin and Edward C. Benfold. (See photo of monument below, taken in 1999)

IN HONOR OF
THOSE WHO SERVED
OUR NATION

KOREA
JUNE 1950 — JAN. 1955
KILLED IN ACTION
NELSON V. BRITTIN   EDWARD A. HELMES
WILLIAM J. CONNELLY, JR.   JAMES E. OPIE, JR.
EDWARD BENFOLD
CONGRESSIONAL MEDAL OF HONOR

VIETNAM
DEC. 1961 — MAY 1975
KILLED IN ACTION
GUY P. GUADAGNO

HEROES LIVE BEYOND THE TOMB
DEDICATED MAY 28, 1984

1985   The Junior Women's Club celebrated its 50th Anniversary.

The AHS Class of 1935 celebrated its 50th Reunion on June 15th at Tavistock Country Club. One very special member of this class is Walter Casebeer, who was honored by the community in 1998 as the Grand Marshall of the 4th of July Parade. Walter is active in many organizations in town, including the Fathers' Association and the Historical Society. He has helped plan semi-annual luncheon reunions for the Class of 1935 for more than a decade.

Prior to the Class Reunion, the Class of 1935 received a letter from President Ronald Reagan (shown below).

THE WHITE HOUSE

WASHINGTON

April 5, 1985

To the Class of 1935,
    Audubon High School:

On the occasion of your 50th reunion, I am pleased to extend my warm greetings.

I know that this occasion brings fond memories and renewed friendships. Coming together in this way, you honor your community, your school and your fellow graduates. You also reaffirm the American tradition of fellowship and goodwill.

Nancy joins me in offering our best wishes for a happy celebration. God bless you.

Ronald Reagan

Note: Walter Casebeer served in the army in World War II as a medic aboard hospital ship Acadia. He was stationed in Africa, Italy and France during the war. Another Audubon resident, Jonas Morris (son of Audubon Businessman Frank Morris), was stationed at Oran, Africa, where he worked as a foot doctor. After the war, Morris opened an office on Merchant Street. Casebeer and Morris met several times during the war. The photos below show both men at Morris' quarters in Oran (photo at left: Morris, right; Casebeer, left) and on board the hospital ship Acadia (Morris at left; Casebeer at right). On the following page is a letter written to Casebeer by Morris from Oran on January 3, 1944. (The athletic stadium at Cherry Hill High School West is named The Jonas Morris Stadium in honor of Morris.)

No. 79180

PASSED BY

To
Pfc. Miller Cashier
350 N. Duichberry ave
Audubon N.J. 21-59

from J.C. Morris 33271506
Med. Det. 2° Conv. Hosp.
G. A0371 %O.P.M. N.Y.C. N.Y.

Dear Will.   1/3/44 Africa.

You fellows sure pulled out fast from here, worried that maybe you had to take the boreal on the boat across for you. There is some more mail for you at the Red Cross (xmas cards) Tell Bernie the bottle boy he was looking for, came down to the boat about an hour after you left. You missed all the bad weather, it's rained every day since you left. The pictures I took of you on deck came out fine, the rest not so good. The girl working with me (the Pt.) was transferred to the 43rd General and I have charge of the whole "works" now, it's been a headache but Jack & Joe are good men, so all will be O.K. I hope you had a pleasant trip. Take it easy while you are home and don't eat out of any mess kit!! "Thanks a million" for your dishes.

Sincerely
Jerr

All is Well

V -MAIL

88

1986   Mr. Nelson V. Brittin, one of Audubon's three Medal of Honor Recipients, was honored again when an elementary school in Georgia was named in his memory. In Audubon, a street, Brittin Avenue, is named in his memory.

1987   Audubon Little League was the District 14 Runner-up in tournament play.

1988   On September 3rd, the Murray-Troutt American Legion Post # 262 held a dedication ceremony for its new headquarters, located at 20 Chestnut Street (between White Horse Pike and East Atlantic Avenue).

Audubon resident Dr. Harry Ingham published a book entitled "Audubon and the Surrounding Areas as I Remember Them".

1990   Audubon Little League inducted its first citizen into the League's Hall of Fame, Mr. Al Powell.

On October 19th, the new Audubon Municipal Complex, located along Nicholson Road next to The Audubon Towers Senior Citizens' Apartments, was dedicated. The Police Station and Tax Office were moved from their former location on Oak Street, between West Atlantic Avenue and Oakland Avenue, into the Municipal Complex. The Police Station is on the first floor; the tax office is on the second floor, along with the offices of the three commissioners. (See the photo and caption on the next page)

AUDUBON MUNICIPAL COMPLEX
DEDICATED ON OCTOBER 19, 1990
The former Graduate Hospital Medical Center was completely renovated to encompass
the needs of the Municipal government operations including the Tax Office, Public Works
Administration, Construction Code Office, Police and Court facilities.

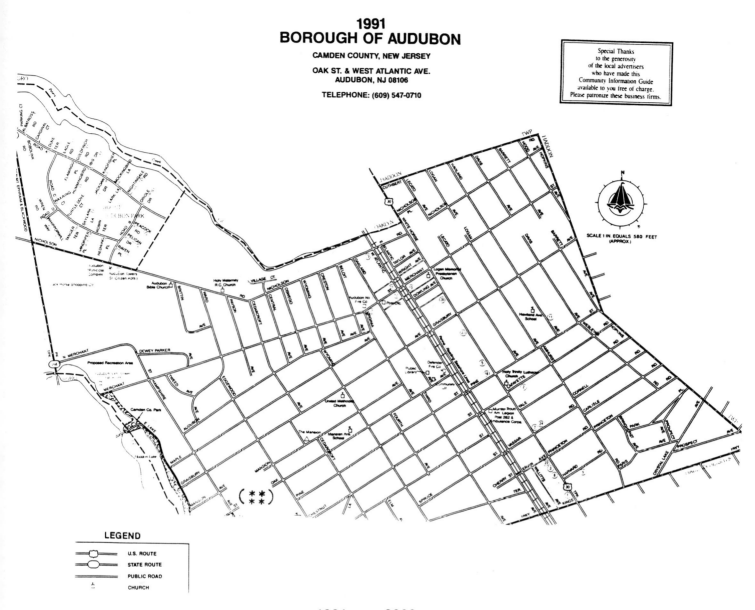

1991

BOROUGH OF AUDUBON

CAMDEN COUNTY, NEW JERSEY

OAK ST. & WEST ATLANTIC AVE.
AUDUBON, NJ 08106

TELEPHONE: (609) 547-0710

SCALE 1 IN. EQUALS 580 FEET
(APPROX.)

LEGEND

U.S. ROUTE
STATE ROUTE
PUBLIC ROAD
CHURCH

1991 - 2000

As we enter the last decade of the 20th century, we begin with a map of the borough that was published in 1991. At the time of the printing, the borough offices were still listed as Oak Street and West Atlantic Avenue, right next to the Defender Fire Company Headquarters. The new building for the borough was constructed in 1990 at a site along Nicholson Road, as shown on the previous page. On the map, the borough of Audubon Park, incorporated in 1947, is at the upper left corner. Route 30 (The White Horse Pike) divides the East side of town (to the right) from the West side. One block west of Route 30 are the tracks for the railroad, which is still in use today for freight. The (**) shows the location of the high school campus, which runs from Walnut Street to Oak Street along Edgewood Avenue.

1992   On May 2nd, the baseball field at Walnut Street and Hampshire Avenue was officially dedicated. Greenberg Field was named in honor of longtime AHS baseball coach and faculty member Hank Greenberg. (See photo of the field below)

On August 30th, the Philadelphia Inquirer published an article about Audubon entitled: "A Tight Fit makes a tight-knit town". The caption for one of the photos in the article reads: "Audubon residents don't mind displaying old-fashioned, small-town pride, as shown by the patriotic display in a barbershop window". (Refer to the article and photos on pages 93 and 94)

The Audubon High School Alumni Association was reborn, after being inactive for almost 40 years.

Mrs. Dorothy Waida, widow of Medal of Honor Recipient Edward C. Benfold, was notified that the U.S. NAVY would shortly begin construction of a new destroyer that would be named the USS BENFOLD (DDG-65)

A tight fit makes for a tight-knit town

By William H. Sokolic
SPECIAL TO THE INQUIRER

For a town named after the most famous bird-watcher of all, Audubon has few places to watch birds.

The borough doesn't have its own park, per se. There are a few ball-fields, though. And there's a county park — Haddon Lake Park — which straddles Haddon Heights and Mount Ephraim.

Audubon is a quiet spot where old-er homes line rows of shady streets. But it has a dearth of open space. The town is quite compact. People are close, and so are their homes.

The problem is one the city is at work on. Officials are looking for ways to create open, tranquil set-tings, and there now is a plan to convert the old sewage-treatment plant to a 13-acre municipal park with baseball and soccer fields, pic-nic areas and jogging tracks.

This is a proud town, and one of the things that folks take pride in is the town's petite size. The public schools are small. Lots of the houses are small. Even development in this tiny borough on the New Jersey side of the Walt Whitman Bridge has been, well, rather small-scale.

The last major project was 36 town-

For The Inquirer / TOM MIHALEK

Audubon residents don't mind displaying old-fashioned small-town pride, as shown by the patriotic display in a barbershop window.

houses off Nicholson Road more than two years ago. Fewer than 30 vacant lots are left in the 1½-square-mile borough. Only a handful of new homes will be built this year, accord-ing to the borough's Planning Board office.

More people left Audubon — a once-fertile farming community — than moved in over the last two decades, said Audubon Mayor Alfred Murray, who, at 31, is one of the youngest mayors in New Jersey. The population decreased from 10,700 in 1970 to 9,200 in the 1990 census.

Recently, however, Audubon has

Living In: Audubon

POPULATION: 9,205 in 1990.
MEDIAN HOME PRICE: $100,000 ('91).
INCOME: $12,392 per capita in 1987, 15% below 7-county suburban avg.

Audubon Borough

CAMDEN COUNTY

seen young couples stake a claim to their town.

"Three years ago, the town was much grayer," Mayor Murray said.

Little Audubon is indeed having a small boom.

Seventy-one houses were sold in Audubon since the year began, with an average sales price of $101,561.

See AUDUBON on M8

93

For The Inquirer / TOM MIHALEK

Many of the small homes on Audubon's tree-lined streets are several decades old. Although the borough has lost more people than it has gained during the last 20 years, more younger families are arriving.

In Audubon, small-town verities are revered by its loyal residents

AUDUBON from M1
according to the Camden County Board of Realtors.

Jacqueline and Barry Dembowski are among those flocking here. Earlier this year, they paid $120,000 for a spacious, 78-year-old four-bedroom house, their first home. "Audubon is reality-centered. It's definitely middle America," said Jacqueline, who grew up in the wealthy enclave of Bryn Mawr.

The small-town feeling that's woven into the borough's fabric is a draw, city officials said.

"It's also the kind of town where people stay," said Murray, whose family goes back four generations.

Affordable housing is another selling point. "You get more for the money than in, say, Philadelphia," said Jacqueline Dembowski, 28, who moved here with her husband and children from an apartment in nearby Collingswood.

The borough affords convenience to Philadelphia via the Ben Franklin or Walt Whitman Bridges and via public transportation. Barry Dembowski, 27, can get to the Hospital of the University of Pennsylvania, where he works as a researcher, in 45 minutes.

Center City Philadelphia is only 15 minutes away on either bridge, and the Cherry Hill Mall is a mere 10 minutes away.

However, Jacqueline Dembowski, whose three children all are under 6, said she was impressed with the city's close-knit school system.

While city schools in some other towns have been gulped up by larger

A circular fire bell is mounted on a display pillar near the Defender Fire Company in Audubon.

systems, Audubon steadfastly retains its own school district, which consists of two grade schools and a high school.

People here think they've got something really big in their small schools.

"A small school is better able to meet the needs of students," said Audubon School Superintendent John Polomano.

The student population has increased 15 percent over the last four years, Polomano said. The bulk of the increase has been at the grade school level, but high school enrollment has risen from a low of 600 students to nearly 750.

The rising school population is one indication that young couples have moved in, Murray said. So, too, is participation in activities such as Little League baseball.

"It's a parochial town," said Murray. "There's a strong sense of community pride."

Still, Audubon gets it share of older newcomers. Barbara Heck, 46, and her parents, Marian and Harold Hecht, moved to Audubon in March from the Fairview section of Camden. It wasn't much of a move in distance — they still attend the same church and shop at the same stores.

"But we have more room and more privacy now," Barbara Heck said.

In a way, they found their own open space.

Vital statistics

Estimated taxes: About $2,300 on a median-price home.

School district: Audubon.

Transportation: Buses: New Jersey Transit No. 450 to Cherry Hill Mall and Camden; No. 403 along White Horse Pike and into Philadelphia. No. 457 to Philadelphia.
Trains: PATCO High-Speed Line. Collingswood or Ferry Avenue station.

Shopping: Black Horse Pike Shopping Center on the Black Horse Pike.

1993   Four students from Audubon High School requested a meeting with Principal, William Westphal. They presented a proposal: the construction of a special Memorial Site on the campus to honor the school's THREE Medal of Honor recipients.

1994   On February 20th the Audubon All Girl Drum and Bugle Corps (The "Bon-Bons") Alumni Association came into existence, sponsoring a reunion banquet at the Cherry Hill Hyatt. This organization, in existence from 1938 until 1977 was among the top activities ever in Southern Jersey and the most notable successful organization from Audubon. In 1982 the "Bon-Bons" were named by the World Drum Corps Hall of Fame as the "ALL TIME GREATEST ALL GIRLS CORPS".

The Audubon Savings Bank on the White Horse Pike opened for business.

Pep Boys relocated its Black Horse Pike store in the Audubon Shopping Center, building a new store on what had been the parking lot area for Korvette's and later Bradley's department stores.

On Monday, July 4th, the new Medal of Honor Memorial Site was dedicated in a special ceremony attended by representatives from all of the Armed Forces. (See the pre-dedication flyer and the photographs of the Memorial on the next two pages.)

Note: The photo of the Memorial Site was taken on November 11, 1998. Since the dedication, citizens in town have placed flowers at the base of the Memorial every year, along with notes thanking the students for helping maintain the site.

Samuel M. Sampler
U.S. Army

Edward C. Benfold
U.S. Navy

Nelson V. Brittin
U.S. Army

Audubon High School Project Memorial Committee, announces the dedication of its Memorial to the Audubon Medal of Honor Recipients.
Monday, July 4, 1994, 4:45 - 6:30 pm.
Audubon High School

 Scott Johnson

 Melanie Aubrey

 **Anthony Simeone**

 Derek Everman

SAMUEL M. SAMPLER

IN MEMORY OF HIS BOLD CHARGE THROUGH
HOSTILE FIRE RESULTING IN THE SURRENDER
OF TWENTY-EIGHT ENEMY SOLDIERS NEAR ST.
ETIENNE, FRANCE 8 OCTOBER 1918. HE
DIED ON 19 NOVEMBER 1979

EDWARD C. BENFOLD

IN MEMORY OF THE SELFLESS SACRIFICING
OF HIS OWN LIFE FOR THE LIVES OF TWO
COUNTRYMEN HE WAS KILLED WHILE
DEFENDING THE WOUNDED IN KOREA
ON 5 SEPTEMBER 1952

NELSON V. BRITTIN

IN MEMORY OF HIS COURAGEOUS,
LEADERSHIP UNDER FIRE WHILE WOUNDED
WHICH INSPIRED HIS COMPANY AND
HELPED DEFEAT THE ENEMY HE WAS
KILLED IN BATTLE AT YONGCONG-NI.
KOREA 7 MARCH 1951

1994

(cont)   Longtime resident and educator Earnest B. Mayo composed the following poem about the Memorial site in 1997 . . . . . .

THE MEDAL OF HONOR SITE !

Way back in nineteen hundred ninety four
A team of high school students wore
A search for the reason why this school should show
The Nation's Medal of Honor on three bestowed.

No other high school in this nation has shown
A record like this for valor and heroism beyond the call.
They must have learned more of duty than walking a hall.
So what did Audubon High School teach her young?

Their Nation's honor above their own held sway;
For some it was a job well done, for others, holding a gun.
In going that extra measure, you're giving aid to others.
Your buddies need you in every spate and time.

To carry this honor and their Nation's pride,
To some it meant that they would die.
Following the footsteps of those who have gone before
Were the students of the Class of '94.

They sought to know why the duty clear
Was a job for some for their whole career.
For them there came a time and place
That they would go that extra measure, face to face.

For this extra measure to give a friend,
They would face that cost to the very end.
They gave their all and their Nation showed,
The Medal of Honor on them bestowed!

In the 4th of July celebration book, Mayor Alfred W. Murray wrote the following tribute: "We celebrate 'Project Memorial' this year. This was realized through the hard work, research and endless labor of a few of whom we are so proud. These young people from Audubon High School stand as examples of young adulthood we wish to foster. Their work will be a legacy for generations to come".

1994

(cont)   The co-author of this book, Craig E. Burgess, is a career educator and believed that the accomplishments of the students at his Alma Mater should be recognized. In July of 1995, he composed the following poem . . . . .

AUDUBON HIGH SCHOOL STUDENTS HONOR WAR HEROES

The students of Audubon High School
Have paid tribute to men from the past:
Three men who fought well for America
So that freedom forever would last.
The Nation's Medal of Honor
Was awarded to each of these men:
SAMUEL SAMPLER, EDWARD BENFOLD, NELSON BRITTIN . . .
One for bravery at St. Etienne;
The other two died in Korea
Defending our right to be free.
Three men from the same little borough:
AUDUBON is as proud as can be!

All three lived and studied in Audubon
And of that present students are proud,
So they set up a fund raising program - - -
Plus a dinner, which drew a large crowd - - -
And established a Memorial Foundation
To honor these three valiant men . . .
So their actions would long be remembered
In the future, as well as back then.

A special Memorial was constructed,
Then placed on the high school's front lawn.
A scholarship fund was created
So their sacrifice will forever live on.
A new club at the school was established
To maintain the Memorial site.
A system of lighting was connected
So that all could observe it at night.

Special services are held three times yearly
To help keep their mem'ries alive.
It's a tribute created by students:
May·THEIR efforts forever survive!

The AHS Alumni Association funded the renovation of the Rotunda of the High School.

On November 12th, the USS BENFOLD (DDG-65), was christened in Pascagoula, Mississippi.

1995   In February, a new writers' group, THE AUDUBON POETS, was organized and held its first meeting in the Free Public Library. Three writers attended the first session.

On May 31st, students in the A.P.P.L.E. program at the two elementary schools (Audubon Pupils' Program for Learning Enrichment), held an autograph session to introduce their new book. With the guidance and support of faculty members Mrs. Kathleen (Cass) Whitaker and Mrs. Agnes Trione, as well as the support of the entire community, the students published an 85 - page history of Audubon (1905-1995) and Audubon Park (1941-1995).

Note: The publication sold out within three weeks of its release. A second edition was published, which also sold out!

On August 19, the Captain of the USS BENFOLD and 30 members of the crew came to Audubon. They went to the high school, visited with residents and even played a softball game with members of the Audubon Fire Company.

1996   At the municipal meeting in April, an ordinance was introduced to merge Audubon's two existing fire departments. The proposed merger itself was not the greatest source of contention at the meeting. The contention centered on the decision to relocate both companies at the Merchant Street site, especially since major renovations to the Oak Street site had begun in 1993. (See the April 26th article from the Retrospect on the following two pages).

At a Commissioners' meeting on August 6th, a vote was taken and approval given to merge the two fire companies into one: THE AUDUBON FIRE DEPARTMENT.

Note: The merger closed the Defender Fire Company on West Atlantic Avenue and Oak Street . . . after 101 years of service to the community. (See August 7th article from the Philadelphia Inquirer on page 103)

100

Fire Company Merger Hot Audubon Topic

by Eun Sook Kang

An ordinance to merge Audubon's two existing fire departments was introduced at last week's municipal meeting.

It prompted such a controversy that some 300 residents turned out and the meeting had to be moved from the Municipal Building to the Audubon High School auditorium. And the meeting lasted almost five hours, not ending until 12:45 a.m.

According to the proposed ordinance, the existing Audubon Fire Co. No. 1 and Defender Fire Co. and Heavy Rescue Squad will be consolidated as simply the "Audubon Fire Co."

The proposed merger itself was not the greatest source of contention at last week's meeting. Rather, it was the fact that the merged company would be located at 221 W. Merchant St., the current headquarters of Audubon Fire Co. No. 1.

Members and supporters of the Defender Fire Co. are up in arms over the fact that the commissioners have selected the Audubon No. 1 headquarters as the location for the merged company. They have asked for an impartial third party to recommend the best site.

Defender backers are also decrying the fact that they undertook a major renovation of their building just three years ago. They have also charged publicly that Mayor Al Murray cannot be impartial on this issue because he is a member of Audubon No. 1.

Mayor Murray, on the advice of acting solicitor Paul Kelly, did not participate in any portion of last week's meeting concerning the fire company merger ordinance.

Due to the large audience, the meeting was moved from the Municipal Building to Audubon High School. The decision to move was made with reluctance by Commmissioners John Hanson and Anthony Pugliese, who maintained that the court room was the designated location for the public meeting as advertised in the newspaper.

One Audubon resident inquired, "Do we mean anything out here?" He explained that those forced to stand in the lobby could not participate in the meeting because no speaker system was set up in the lobby to facilitate it. The crowd agreed with loud applause, urging the commissioners to change the meeting to a different location.

Chief Tim Downing of Defender Co. made a public statement requesting that an unbiased third party consultant be utilized to advise the commissioners on the best location for the new fire department.

(continued on page 10)

101

Audubon Fire Co. Merger

(continued from page 1)

Downing explained that he supported the merger of the two fire companies, but expressed his concern regarding the zoning of the Defender property at Oak St. and Atlantic Ave. if the company were shut down. The possibility of a commercial zone at the site was a concern to residents who did not wish to have Defender Fire Co. dissolved.

It was pointed out that Defender Co. was created as the fire department for the community of Orston before Orston was incorporated into Audubon in the early years of this century. Audubon Fire Co. No. 1 also has a proud tradition and the fact that the two companies are just three blocks apart has generated a rivalry over the years.

"There has been an old rivalry between the two fire companies since I was a kid," said resident Sandy Stafford. She also agreed with Chief Downing's proposal for a third-party consultation on the merger.

Public statements were made by those who were partial to Audubon Fire Co. No. 1 and those who were partial to Defender Fire Co. as the better location for the new fire department. Traffic, safety and accessibility to equipment were major issues that residents addressed. Statements were strongly in favor of an unbiased third-party consultation.

Both Commissioners Hanson and Pugliese stated that the meeting was merely to introduce the ordinance and that no final decisions were made. During the first adjournment of the meeting, Pugliese stated, "If they (the two companies) are really interested in providing services to the town, then they should work together."

Regarding the suggestion of a third-party recommendation, Pugliese said "Do we in fact need a third party to make a decision? That is something that we (Hanson and Pugliese) will have to consider."

Commissioner Hanson added that Monday night's meeting was merely to introduce the ordinance and that no firm decisions have been made. He pointed out that the ultimate decision is up to the commissioners after the public hearing on the ordinance, which is scheduled for Tuesday, May 21.

Chief Downing questioned Mayor Murray's decision to withdraw from discussions after the ordinance had been written. He said the mayor's bias may have influenced the location of the new fire department at Audubon No. 1 during the drafting process.

After the meeting, Downing was also critical of the commissioners. "They looked down upon their own constituents," he insisted. "They were disrespectful and (the commission) seemed like a dictatorship. I feel like I'm on trial here."

Downing reiterated what was expressed by many who spoke last Monday night. "I want it (the merger) done properly and with fairness," he remarked.

The Defender chief noted that neighboring Oaklyn had effected a merger between two fire companies several years ago. In that case, the merged company moved into a new building. Oaklyn's merger, Downing said, took about six months of work from both fire companies.

A less controversial matter on the agenda of the Audubon meeting was passage of an amended municipal budget which holds the line on local purpose taxes for 1996.

"For three years the Board of Commissioners has been doing more with less to keep taxes in check," said Pugliese. "We have done that and we continue to do that."

The commissioners also passed a resolution to apply for state relief on recycling tonnage. Funds resulting would be used to employ young people for a summer job program.

Wednesday, August 7, 1996

Audubon merges fire companies

The borough has had two for 90 years. The mayor, a member of one company, did not vote.

By Lisa Kozleski
INQUIRER CORRESPONDENT

AUDUBON — A 90-year-old tradition of two fire companies serving the borough will come to an end because of last night's approval of an ordinance that merges them into a single company.

Before a crowd of about 100 that appeared fairly evenly split between supporters and opponents of the move, the borough commission voted 2-0 to make the change. The third commission member, Mayor Alfred W. Murray, did not vote because he is a member of Audubon Fire Company No. 1, one of the two companies.

As a result of the vote, beginning this fall the borough will be served by a single new company, known as the Audubon Fire Department.

It will be located on West Merchant Avenue, the site of Fire Company No. 1. The 70 volunteers there, as well as at the Defender Fire Company on West Atlantic Avenue, will be under that one roof.

Tim Downing, chief of Defender, said he was going to end his career as a volunteer fireman because "I don't want to be a member of a political department."

The commissioners postponed voting on the controversial issue in May, June and July while they awaited the return of a ladder truck that was being repaired. Once they confirmed that the truck would fit in the Merchant Avenue building, they acted on the ordinance to merge the two companies.

The merger is is expected to save Aububon's fire district more than $600,000 over the next 10 years.

Murray said in April that about $60,000 would be realized through the the sale of a rescue truck, a rescue hose wagon and a 1979 pumper scheduled for replacement in 2000. The rest of the savings will come from forgoing the future replacement of the trucks being sold, commissioners said.

Members of the Defender Fire Company had argued their station should be used because it was larger and was recently renovated.

Much of the earlier debate centered on Murray's involvement with Fire Company No. 1. The mayor, who abstained from commenting or voting on the ordinance, said he did so to avoid the appearance of a conflict of interest.

1996

(cont)   Ingalls Shipbuilding Company presented a scale-model version of the USS BENFOLD (DDG-65), carved in wood, to Audubon High School. The model was placed in the school's Rotunda.

On March 30th the USS BENFOLD (DDG-65) was commissioned in San Diego, California.

1997 In January, a branch of Equity Bank opened on the corner of White Horse Pike and West Merchant Street, across the street from the Logan Memorial Presbyterian Church. The bank was built on the site of the former Veterinary Hospital of Dr. Owens. (See photo below of the bank, taken in February, 1999)

On April 12th a new electronic scoreboard was dedicated at the Greenberg baseball field. The scoreboard was donated by the AHS Alumni Association in honor of the school's three consecutive New Jersey State Championship teams: in 1994, 1995 and 1996. (See article and photos on the following two pages.

In May, the New Jersey Department of Education sent a film crew to Audubon to record the Memorial Day service at the Medal of Honor Memorial site on the AHS campus. Highlights of the service were telecast statewide on CLASSROOM CLOSE-UP, NJ, a series that salutes activities in schools around the state.

THROWING OUT FIRST BALL: Craig Burgess, president of the Audubon High School Alumni Association, had the honor of throwing out the first ball at ceremonies last Saturday which opened the Ralph Shaw Tournament and celebrated the dedication of the new electronic scoreboard that was donated by the Alumni Association.

Audubon High Scoreboard Dedicated in Ceremony

The excitement of South Jersey high school baseball was at it's peak on Saturday and Sunday, April 12 and 13, on the Greenberg Field at Audubon High School, the site of the second annual Ralph Shaw Tournament.

On Saturday, Gloucester Catholic defeated Gloucester, 4-0, in a rain-shortened game. On Sunday afternoon, Paul VI defeated host Audubon, 3-1.

In the title game, Gloucester Catholic, a team listed in the top 20 high school teams in the nation in a USA TODAY poll, pounded out a 10-7 victory over Paul VI.

Adding to the excitement of this year's tournament was the dedication ceremony for the new electronic scoreboard at AHS, donated by the AHS Alumni Association in honor of the Green Wave teams that won the New Jersey State Championship in 1994, 1995 and 1996.

Sunday's activities began

with the playing of the National Anthem by the Jersey Surf Drum and Bugle Corps, while Audubon athlete Brian Jeres held the American flag. AHS Athletic Director Don Bordon then introduced members of the AHS Alumni Association and conducted the dedication for the scoreboard.

Alumni President Craig E. Burgess was given the honor of throwing the ceremonial first pitch following the ceremony. Burgess stated that the acquisition of the scoreboard was a true community effort.

Contributions were received from many AHS grads, from the Audubon Women's Club and from the Retrospect (which donated $5 to the fundraising effort for each new subscription during the first three months of 1997).

"Everyone in town is proud of the accomplishment of our Green Wave baseball team!" said Burgess. "The Scoreboard is a reflection of that pride."

105

1997
(cont)   On Veterans' Day, November 11th, AHS Principal and member of the AHS Class of 1960, and lifetime resident Craig E. Burgess, member of the AHS Class of 1963, initiated a new activity at the school. All incoming 7th graders were brought to the Rotunda of the high school for a 40 minute presentation on the items displayed in honor of all AHS graduates who served our nation during wartime - - - from World War I to Desert Storm. Details of the lives of the borough's three Medal of Honor recipients are included in the program and the students place flowers at the base of the Memorial site.

In December, the AUDUBON POETS released a publication entitled THE BEST OF THE AUDUBON POETS, containing poems and short stories written by 18 members of the writers' group and more than 40 full color photos taken around town. Member Earnest B. Mayo (pen name E. Bartlett M.), composed a special selection about Audubon that appeared in this publication. This piece is presented on the following page.

1998   The Audubon National Bank, which first opened in Redmen's Hall in 1919 before moving to its current location on the corner of West Merchant Street and West Atlantic Avenue, closed its doors. In recent years, it had been known as a branch of the Midlantic Bank.

A new community publication, THE AUDUBON QUILL, is mailed to all residents. This bi-monthly newsletter keeps residents up-to-date on events and activities in the borough.

The Free Public Library publishes the first issue of its quarterly newsletter.

With funds from a Mini-Grant from the County Parks' System, elementary students and parents conduct a clean-up project at the Recreation Center (on the site of the former swimming pool). Resident Craig E. Burgess was asked to write a poem for a special tree-planting ceremony. This poem is found on page 108.

MY LITTLE TOWN OF AUDUBON

E. Bartlett M.

Between the pikes of Black and White
The town of Audubon grows, its history makes.
It's no mistake, it's red and white and blue . . .
With the very young, and old folks, too.
They raise our flag up high, so all can see,
The pride we know reflected in the sky.

I walk the streets of Audubon, both narrow and wide,
Since days of Revolution War folks lived here with pride.
The tree-lined streets and paths to the place we call home,
The roads and to the driveways for shelter, not to roam.
The town of Audubon was built with cottages small and low,
No pretense here, the craftsmen built the tiny bungalow.

Along every street and drive as cedar shakes did age,
With time and weather, too, the homes look upon the sage.
None of us has ever known a house that was back when,
So we see in the houses of today the building that was then.
They've changed the now to former, and many rooms to spare,
With new, developed houses, it's known as Bungalow Town Today.

The lovely town of Audubon is home to birds of every kind;
They too live in custom-built houses not big or too refined.
Put up by owners and no two are quite the same.
You see the birds know Audubon, the town of birds of fame.
We watch and look and list the birds so varied, not the same.
They live and raise their families in Audubon's claim to fame.

The friends of birds of every kind come to sit and stare.
They take photographs that show birds were happy to be there.
The wild ducks and geese are given handsful of grain, too.
Thus the seasons come and go as seasons are known to do
And to be sure our birds come to flit and then fly away, too,
For Audubon is an open sky and not a closed up zoo.

THE PLANTING OF A SPECIAL TREE IN AUDUBON

Craig E. Burgess

Today our town will plant a tree
For all its citizens to see.
The event is part of history
Being made by you and me.

The site we chose to plant this tree
Has witnessed much activity:
A swimming pool here used to be
Where Audubon residents swam with glee.

The future growth of this new tree
Depends a lot on you and me
And on how dedicated we shall be
To making this site pollution free.

We take great pride this April day
In taking steps to pave the way
For guaranteeing, come what may,
A site on which our kids can play,

Enjoying what began today - - -
With cleanup efforts under way - - -
To put our borough on display.
"AUDUBON CARES!", reports will say.

"Its citizens have spent the day
Working hard to clean away
The weeds and trash that cause decay
To this special site on which to play."

What happens now, we all agree,
Depends on how we treat this tree.
"Take pride in our community!
Work hard to help to guarantee

That, in the 21st century,
Our children's children, filled with glee,
Will enjoy this site, AND will agree:
IT WAS WORTH WHILE TO PLANT THIS TREE!"

1998

(cont)   The photos on these two pages show the "work crew" that participated in the special ceremony. Also shown is a photo of the recreational area, taken in February, 1999.

1998

(cont)   On May 20th, AHS received two special items from the Nelson V. Brittin Elementary School in Fort Stewart, Georgia: Brittin's diploma from AHS and a portrait painted by his brother. Both items are now on display in the Rotunda of the school.

In September, efforts began to revitalize the Merchant Street businesses in town. The Merchant Street Businesspersons' Association held its first annual Sidewalk Sale.

On October 31st a new Memorial Grove, located at the rear of the Recreation Center, facing Lake Drive, was dedicated to all the youth in the community who pass away before reaching the age of 21. Two poems about the Grove and six photos of the area are presented here . . . . .

The poem on the following page was composed by Craig E. Burgess after he had attended the dedication ceremony. The poem shown in the photo to the right was written prior to the ceremony and placed on a plaque which is on display at the entrance to the Grove. It was written by Audubon resident Philip C. DiMartino.

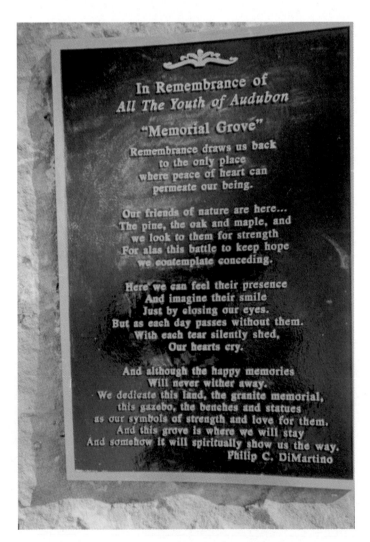

In Remembrance of
All The Youth of Audubon

"Memorial Grove"

Remembrance draws us back
to the only place
where peace of heart can
permeate our being.

Our friends of nature are here...
The pine, the oak and maple, and
we look to them for strength
For alas this battle to keep hope
we contemplate conceding.

Here we can feel their presence
And imagine their smile
Just by closing our eyes.
But as each day passes without them,
With each tear silently shed,
Our hearts cry.

And although the happy memories
Will never wither away.
We dedicate this land, the granite memorial,
this gazebo, the benches and statues
as our symbols of strength and love for them.
And this grove is where we will stay
And somehow it will spiritually show us the way.
Philip C. DiMartino

A Special Day In Audubon History

The MEMORIAL GROVE in Audubon
Is a site of which ALL can be proud,
Reflecting a caring community
In which showcasing love is allowed.
There's a garden in front of a Gazebo
And another near the top of a hill,
With a pathway of stones that connects them:
'Twas a labor of love to fulfill!

It was built in a picturesque setting,
Looking West, in plain view of the lake
Whose surface reflects all the beauty
Of those spirits whom we'll never forsake.

The Gazebo was built by the students - - -
To which all may come and reflect.
Donations were made by the residents
So that no one will ever neglect
The love that exists in Audubon
And the caring that's really sincere:
A caring that unites all the residents,
And will be strengthened, year after year.

The sun was shining in brilliance
Through the autumn-colored leaves
On the day of the GROVE'S dedication,
And each one in attendance believes
That the Lord prepared this special day
For Audubon's MEMORIAL GROVE.
So that community love and caring
Would radiate throughout the GROVE.

The dedication took place on a Saturday,
On a day known as All Hallow's Eve;
Thus the Saints of the church were all present:
An inspiring Grace they did weave
As the families of the precious departed
Were presented a commemorative gift.
Then the community was thanked for its efforts
In giving everyone's spirits a lift.

Mayor Coyle addressed all who had gathered
To remember the youth of our town
Who had passed away much too quickly - - -
Precious buds, like jewels in a crown,
Who never would blossom nor flower
And experience what life has to give,
Yet have left a lasting impression
On the town in which they did live.

The song, "*If We Hold On Together*"
Was part of the program that day.
Colene Reilly and **Renata Gordon**
The meaning of the words did convey
As they sang to those in attendance
And the tune lifted spirits quite high,
Uniting residents of all ages
Who had gathered 'neath the brilliant blue sky.

Haviland Avenue Elementary School's Principal
Read a special prayer to us all.
"*We Remember Them*" was the title;
Mrs. Endt helped each one to recall
The reason the MEMORIAL GROVE was constructed - - -
For all to reflect and take pride
In a special community's caring
For its young citizens who too early had died.

DEDICATED TO THE YOUTH OF AUDUBON

BRYAN DYLAN NISENFELD
JACQUELYN "JACKIE" HIRSCHLEIN
MERWON R. CHEW, JR.
CAROL MICHELLE FORZIATI
ALAN MENGERT
PAUL WEISE
BARRY McFADDEN, JR.

TROY C. BOEHM
RANDOLPH S. REED
RAYMOND W. BALLANTINE
THOMASINE C. BENDORF
LOUIS TETI, III
JAMES SCOTT BATTEN
SUZANNE BERNERT

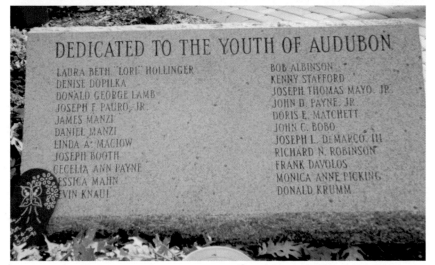

DEDICATED TO THE YOUTH OF AUDUBON

LAURA BETH "LORI" HOLLINGER
DENISE DOPILKA
DONALD GEORGE LAMB
JOSEPH F. PAURO, JR.
JAMES MANZI
DANIEL MANZI
LINDA A. MACIOW
JOSEPH BOOTH
CECELIA ANN PAYNE
JESSICA MAHN
KEVIN KNAUL

BOB ALBINSON
KENNY STAFFORD
JOSEPH THOMAS MAYO, JR.
JOHN D. PAYNE, JR.
DORIS E. MATCHETT
JOHN C. BOBO
JOSEPH L. DeMARCO, III
RICHARD N. ROBINSON
FRANK DAVOLOS
MONICA ANNE PICKING
DONALD KRUMM

116

1998

(cont)   In November, the AHS Alumni Association placed an
Alumni Garden on the high school campus, at the corner of
Walnut Street and Edgewood Avenue as a first step in a beau-
tification project for the campus.

The Texaco Gas Station on the corner of White Horse
Pike and West Kings Highway, across the street from the former Century Theatre (now a Capas Costume store and dance
studio), closed for major renovations.

On November 17, a letter was sent from the Department of the Navy to Mrs. Dorothy Moffa, sister of Medal
of Honor Recipient Nelson V. Brittin, notifying her that a
new naval vessel, a Strategic Sealift ship would be named
the USNS BRITTIN in honor of her brother. (See the letter
on the next page)

On December 6th, the first annual Holiday House
Tour was held in the borough. The event was sponsored by
the Free Public Library and was a great success. (see the
map showing the homes on the first tour, on page 119.)

The borough published an official Business Directory, listing all the stores and shops, as well as services
available, in alphabetical order by category. The opening
paragraph of the directory states, "Wherever you live in
Audubon, you're near a business district, whether the
Black Horse Shopping Center, East Atlantic Avenue,
Kings Highway, Merchant Street or the White Horse Pike.
And whatever professional services you may need, you're
bound to find them right here in Audubon. The borough
has nearly 300 businesses, easily accessible on the main
roads, tucked away along side streets, or operating quietly
as home based businesses."

1999   On January 5th, the Classic Cake Bakery at 103
West Merchant Street (across the street from the now
vacant National Bank), closed its doors forever . . . after
serving Audubon for 26 years.

DEPARTMENT OF THE NAVY
PROGRAM EXECUTIVE OFFICE
EXPEDITIONARY WARFARE
2531 JEFFERSON DAVIS HWY
ARLINGTON VA 22242-5171

IN REPLY REFER TO
4760
Ser 385/817
17 Nov 98

Mrs. Dorothy Moffa
RR2 Box 2305
Dushore, PA 18614

Dear Mrs. Moffa:

It is with great pleasure that we inform you of the Secretary of the Navy's decision to name a Strategic Sealift ship, USNS BRITTIN, in honor of your brother, SFC Nelson V. Brittin, United States Army. The Strategic Sealift Program has been commissioned by the Congress of the United States to provide ships capable of the rapid transportation of military equipment to anywhere in the world. These ships will become the centerpiece of our nation's Sealift power projection into the next century. They will help provide our nation with the ability to thwart aggression and promote stability in times of emergency.

The USNS BRITTIN, also referred to as "T-AKR 305" will be built by Avondale Industries, Inc. (AII) in New Orleans, Louisiana. The USNS BRITTIN will be the 16th of 19 Strategic Sealift ships to be delivered to the U.S. Navy. Avondale has tentatively scheduled the USNS BRITTIN christening for April 2000. As the Deputy Program Manager for the Strategic Sealift Program, I am privileged at this time to invite you and your family to attend this ceremony.

A representative of my office will be in contact with you soon to coordinate the upcoming ceremony events with you. Please feel free to contact me at (703) 602-7881, if you have any further questions regarding this matter.

Sincerely,

J. R. EXELL
Captain, U.S. NAVY
Deputy
Strategic Sealift Program

Copy to:
COMSC (PM4)
SUPSHIP NEW ORLEANS LA (Code 153)

118

AUDUBON
Holiday House Tours

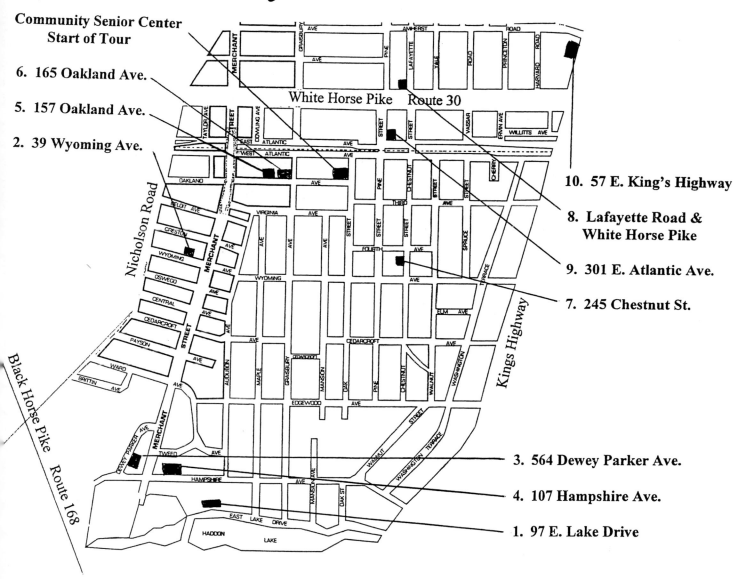

Community Senior Center
Start of Tour

6. 165 Oakland Ave.

5. 157 Oakland Ave.

2. 39 Wyoming Ave.

White Horse Pike   Route 30

10. 57 E. King's Highway

8. Lafayette Road &
   White Horse Pike

9. 301 E. Atlantic Ave.

7. 245 Chestnut St.

3. 564 Dewey Parker Ave.

4. 107 Hampshire Ave.

1. 97 E. Lake Drive

Begin your tour at any number on your map, and continue the tour as you wish. The numbers on the stops have no significance except for ticket takers. Look for the wooden Holiday House Tour markers in front of each of the homes for easy locating. There is a special invitation from the folks at Treasures in the Attic to join them at 3 p.m. and again at 4 p.m. for an impromptu sing-a-long outside the shop. Wassail will be served during the day at Treasures in the Attic. Refreshments will also be served at the Holy Trinity Lutheran Church, Community Senior Center, and Linda's Doll House. Those who are planning to attend the concerts at the Church should make special note of the times. (See brochure.)

1999

(cont)   In January, the Audubon Cold Cuts and Deli on the south corner of West Merchant Street and East Atlantic Avenue closed its doors after several decades of service to the community. (See the photo taken in February, 1999, below)

On January 18th, a film crew from the NJEA CLASSROOM CLOSE-UP, NJ came to Audubon for the 2nd time in two years. On this visit, the crew visited Mansion Avenue School and prepared a story on the tutoring program at the school: a program in which students in grades 5 and 6 offer academic assistance to students at the lower levels of instruction.

The Audubon Grade School PTA began selling a special tapestry afghan as part of the celebration of the borough's 95th Anniversary. The design of this afghan is shown as the cover page for this chapter on the history of Audubon.

Note: The Audubon Grade School PTA was first established on December 7, 1909 and is the oldest active PTA organization in the state of New Jersey.

The Free Public Library of Audubon put into effect a program which will salute the many talents of residents in the local community. The focus of the spotlight this year is poetry: the focus for the year 2000 will be painting and sketching. A poetry competition was sponsored with the support of the Audubon Poets, the local writers' group. One of the categories in the competition was "The History of Audubon". We present here the winning entry in this category, a selection written by longtime resident William H. Adam, Jr. . . . .

Yesteryears On Merchant Street

The Audubon business district, established in 1905
　　　was a nice place to shop, once very much alive.
Merchant Street, on Audubon's west side of town,
　　　was where places of business once could be found.
The Audubon Post Office, moved once again in town:
　　　what once was Rosen's Market is where it can be found.
Bass's Hardware store stood across the street
　　　from Murray's market which sold canned goods and meat.
Jacob's Tailor was a few doors away:
　　　like the other stores, they did not stay.
In Carolyn's Bakery one could buy a cookie or cake:
　　　her customers were pleased with the way she did bake.
Joe's Barber Shop is no longer there:
　　　When I was little, it's where Joe cut my hair.
At Lusch's Deli, the townspeople stopped to eat.
　　　There was also a foot doctor, up the street, for your feet.
Morris's was a children's clothing store,
　　　the Sally Shop sold women's dresses next door.
Next to the Sweet Shop, there was a drug store:
　　　prescriptions were filled there; they're filled there no more.
The Audubon Bank, the first bank in town,
　　　after 75 years, it too did close down.
The old railroad station can still be seen by the tracks:
　　　it's now used by a dentist, not for trains, like years back.
The news agency was once Bob and Ann's store:
　　　it sold soda and candy, magazines, papers and more.
The Audubon Cold Cuts, it recently closed down.
　　　Mary Jo Hair Fashions celebrates 30 years in town.
Merchant Street, on Audubon's west side of town
　　　was where places of business once could be found.

William's poem summarizes many of the changes that have taken place in the last 94 years.

Early in the year, a rebuilding project began on the lot next to Weber's Diner on the White Horse Pike between Merchant Street and Graisbury Avenue. One of the borough's oldest buildings is on the lot and the new owners renovated the old building, rather than tearing it down and rebuilding. (See photos taken in November, 1998 and February, 1999 below)

1999

(cont)   The Texaco station at the corner of White Horse Pike and West Kings Highway reopened for business. (See photo below)

As part of the celebration of its 4th "Birthday", THE AUDUBON POETS produced a 90-minute audio cassette, with selections read by 10 members of the group.

On February 26th, co-author Burgess took a walk down Merchant Street, from the railroad tracks west to Virginia Avenue. This is what he saw . . . .

101	Store for rent (formerly Connelly Ins.)
103	Connelly Insurance (formerly Classic Cake)
107	Sara's Clothing Outlet
109	Sara's Ceramics
113	Flowers by Renee
115	Store for Sale
117	Store for Rent
119	Almost Anything Collectables
121	Priscon Enterprises / Sutton Engineering
123	Big Daddy's Pizza
127 - 131	Penny Press
203	South Jersey Graphics
211	Mary Jo Hair Fashions

Having reached the Audubon Fire Company, Burgess
crossed the street and made his way back to the railroad tracks . . .

___	The Commons at Audubon, an apartment building that spans the entire block, from Virginia Avenue to Oakland Avenue.
126	The Audubon Post Office

Note: In 1998, mail was no longer picked up by the
carriers for delivery to homes in Audubon at
this location. Now, the office serves only to
sell stamps and collect mail for transfer to
Camden or Runnemede. The future of the
Post Office is uncertain.

120	Store for Sale (formerly Merchant Street Booksellers)
118	Store for Sale (formerly Dianetics and Scientology)
116	Law Offices of Frances R. Ward and David H. James
114	Vacant building
112	Vacant building
110	J & H Tax Service
	Kathryn Hewitt-Jones, Attorney-At-Law (formerly a Cable TV company)
108 B	Pregnancy Care Center
108 A	Apartment on 2nd floor
102 - 106	Building for Lease (formerly the home of the Audubon National Bank)

On March 1st, a new director was welcomed to
The Free Public Library.

In April, the Friends of the Free Public Library,
a volunteer organization founded in 1995, celebrated its
4th birthday. In late 1998, the members received a donation of $5,000.00 from the AUDUBON POETS for use
in establishing new programs for young readers in the
community.

As we come to the end of the 20th century, many changes are taking place in the borough
of Audubon: changes which will have a positive impact on the residents as we enter the 21st
century. Each year, more and more activities have been sponsored that bring together students
and residents. Some of these activities include an annual Senior Citizen Social in April and a
Christmas Luncheon in December; monthly meetings of an Intergenerational group, bringing
together students from AHS and members of the community; programs to introduce students to
professional businessmen in the community.

In the year 2000, Audubon will celebrate her 95th Anniversary as a borough. Residents of all ages will participate in a series of special events marking this special moment in history. The Free Public Library has established a special archives and is asking residents to contribute items that spotlight the borough's past. Taped interviews with longtime residents are being conducted as one means for strengthening the holdings in the archival collection.

Yet, with all of the changes that Audubon will undergo, she will still remain *"that little, thrifty, Jersey town, along the Reading Line"*.

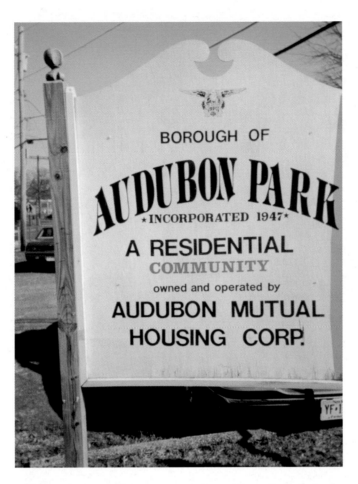

127

Chapter I: Section II
The History of
St. Mary's Episcopal Church
In Haddon Heights
The Spiritual home of Edward C. Benfold
Medal of Honor Recipient

St. Mary's Episcopal Church, located on the corner of White Horse Pike and Green Street in Haddon Heights, New Jersey, played a role in the growth of Edward C. Benfold. He was a parishioner of the church while a student in the Audubon schools, and was a member of the church choir.

Following his death in the Korean War, members of the Youth Fellowship at St. Mary's honored the memory of their friend by dedicating half of the Baptismal stained-glass window in his name. They even arranged to have a stained-glass image of the Medal of Honor placed in the lower right hand corner of the window. (See the enlarged section of the lower portion of the window on this page.) A brief history, in facts and photos, will be presented on the next several pages.

1907   Groundbreaking ceremonies took place for St. Mary's. (See photo on this page that was taken soon after work began on the church.)

1909   In June, St. Mary's was officially incorporated as a church.

1910   In January, the cedar-shingled frame church building was completed.

        In September, the Reverend Thomas Theodore Butler took charge as St. Mary's first rector.

1932   The church purchased an organ from the Laurel Springs Moving Picture Theatre, complete with steamboat whistles, bells and other sound effects.

1936   In March, the new brick addition to the original church building was dedicated. The cost of the addition was $17,000.00.

Note: A feature of the addition was a "rose" window, depicting the Resurrection of our Lord, placed in the East Wall over the altar. The cost of the window was $16,000.00 . . . only $1,000.00 less than the cost of the entire addition. (See the photos of the church before and after the addition and a picture of the "rose" window on the next two pages.)

St. Mary's in the late 1930s, following construction of the new brick addition.

St. Mary's in the late 1920s.

ST. MARY'S EPISCOPAL CHURCH, HADDON HEIGHTS, NJ
DESCRIPTION OF CHANCEL WINDOW OVER ALTAR

The subject of the window is the Resurrection. In the cross section of the window -- Our Lord is shown rising from the tomb, with attending angels removing the sepulchral shroud. At either side are the soldiers who became as dead men. Below the tomb is a symbolic treatment of Jonah and the Whale, the Old Testament prototype of the Resurrection, linking the Old Dispensation with the New. The four small scale subjects in the corners depict scenes related to the Resurrection. The bottom left hand -- the Entombment: bottom right -- the visit of the three Marys at the Sepulcher when the angel announced, "He is not here. He is risen." Top right hand corner -- Mary Magdalene meeting Christ in the garden, and mistaking Him for the gardener: top left -- The Supper at Emmaus. The window exemplifies the finest principles of stained glass as found in the windows of the 11th and 12th centuries. The above is copied from a letter from The Willet Stained Glass Company, 3900 Girard Avenue, Philadelphia 4, PA, October 29, 1951

134

1939   In mid-June an announcement was published, notifying parishioners of the change in times for the regular services for the summer months. (See the schedules for May and for June on this page) In the 1990s, services are held at 6:00 pm on Saturday and at 8:00 am and 10:00 am on Sunday.

On October 19th, Audubon High School history instructor Frank Oldham spoke about his trip to Europe at a meeting of the Service Club. (See the article about the presentation on the next page.)

AUDUBON and HADDON HEIGHTS WEEKLY VISITOR

Thursday, May 25, 1939.

————o————

St. Mary's Episcopal

White Horse Pike and Green St., Had. Hts.
REV. WALTER P. PLUMLEY, Rector

8 a. m.—Holy Communion.
9.45 a. m.—Church School.
11 a. m.—Morning prayer.
7.30 p. m.—Young People's Fellowship.

————o————

St. Mary's Episcopal

White Horse Pike and Green St., Had. Hts.
REV. WALTER P. PLUMLEY, Rector

7.30 a. m.—Holy Communion.
10 a. m.—Church school.
10 a. m.—Morning prayer.
7.30 p. m.—Young People's fellowship.

The services at St. Mary's Episcopal Church will be held earlier begining Sunday. The early celebration of the Holy Communion will at 7.30 a. m.; church school at 10 a. m., and morning prayer and sermon at 10 a. m. This schedule will be maintained until early in September.

Sunday a special service will be held at 10 o'clock, recognizing Father's Day. Betty Baird and Frank Rippel, two young people of St. Mary's, will deliver five minute addreses on "What Father Means to Me." The rector will conclude with a five minute sermon on "The Fatherhood of God."

The church school will join the congregation in this service and a number of awards will be presented to the children.

The young people's fellowship will hold its last meeting until Fall in the Haddon Heights park. Members will meet at the church at 7.30 and proced in a body to the park. The regular devotional meeting and discussion will be held, after which refreshments will be served.

St. Mary's Sunday School will continue all summer, starting at 10 o'clock. The older children will meet with the regular congregation and the younger children will meet separately. Special awards will be given for perfect attendance during the summer. Those attending Sunday schol in other churches while on vacation will be given credit for attendance upon presentation of certificate from school attended.

Plans are almost complete for the opening of the Vacation Bible School on June 26. The school will continue for three weeks. There will be Bible study, stories, handicraft, sewing, cooking, games, and carpentry. All are welcome.

————o————

Inside St. Mary's looking toward the altar and the "rose" window, in the late 1930s, following the construction of the new brick addition.

—————o—————

Audubon Teacher is Guest Speaker at Service Club

Frank Oldham, history instructor at Audubon High School and extensive European traveler, has been announced as guest speaker at a meeting of the Service Club of St. Mary's Episcopal Church, Thursday evening, October 19.

Having only recently returned from a trip abroad that took him to England, France, Germany and Switzerland, Mr. Oldham's address is said to be eagerly awaited by club members and a full attendance is expected.

Service Club members are reminded of the rummage sale to be held in Camden on October 28. Mrs. Walter Staib, chairman, will be glad to accept any articles for this affair.

—————o—————

1954   In November, the stained-glass window, designed in honor of Medal of Honor Recipient Edward C. Benfold, was dedicated. (See the photo below)

1957   The 2nd addition to the church, including a new meeting room (The West Room), an entrance wing and the expansion of the basement, was completed.

1959   At its 50th Anniversary, ground was broken for a new addition to house a Christian Day School. The Parish had 891 communicants at the time.

1961   The Christian Day School at St. Mary's was opened.

1971   Through a generous donation from parishioner Miss Linda Bunting (in 1968), the new custom-built Schantz organ was installed.

Note: The old theatre organ was sold and installed in Christ Church, Magnolia.

1976   Due to economic difficulties, the Vestry made the decision to close the Christian Day School.

1984   In June, a special service and reception were held to commemorate the 75th Anniversary of the Incorporation of St. Mary's as a church.

1995   On August 19th, a special service was held for the Captain and 30 members of the crew of the USS BENFOLD. The service was conducted by interim rector, the Right Reverend Robert R. Willing.

1999   Repairs to the large stained-glass window at the entrance to the West Room were completed. The repairs were made possible through a donation from a parishioner in memory of Medal of Honor Recipient Edward C. Benfold. (See photo on following page)

Many exciting events took place as part of the 90th Anniversary celebration, including a choir festival in which church choirs from around the area joined together for a special concert in May.

On Ash Wednesday, February 17th, the Courier-Post newspaper came to St. Mary's and captured part of the 10:00 am service. (See the photo of the Reverend Dr. Ronny W. Dower placing ashes on the forehead of parishioner Mrs. Ralph Barnwell on page 140)

COURIER~POST

Thursday, February 18, 1999

Wednesday ushers in Lent

142

1999

(cont)   On Sunday, October 10th, the Bishop of the Episcopal
Diocese of New Jersey, will visit St. Mary's to participate in
the celebration of the Parish's 90th Anniversary.

Into The 21st Century - - - - -

What lies ahead for St. Mary's? Many exciting programs and events have been initiated and planned for the future. During the decade of the 1990s, many renovations were completed, among them a new roof, a paved parking lot and the painting and refurbishing of the Crib Nursery (See photos below). In addition, the Sunday School curriculum was updated and several new programs of Christian Education for parishioners of all ages have been put into place. The Music Committee has planned a series of special choral concerts and organ recitals, with guest choirs and musicians joining with the St. Mary's singers for seasonal programs that are open to the general public. Groups such as Outreach contribute time and talent in support of special projects in the community.

St. Mary's invites residents to visit and to discover the joys of joining in worship and in social gatherings with the members of the Parish - - - an invitation expressed in verse by co-author Burgess, a lifelong member of St. Mary's. (See poem on following page)

The Bell Of St. Mary's

Have you heard the Bell of St. Mary's
On a recent Sunday morn,
Ringing out a greeting
As its sound through the air is borne?

It's sending out a greeting
From a very special place
Where friends are always welcome
From every creed and race.

It invites all those who hear it
To join our family;
To share both time and talent;
To rejoice in harmony.

Yet its message is much more than
Just a greeting to come in,
For it calls us all to dinner
Which will free us all from sin:

It announces a Communion
And a chance to share with Christ,
Partaking of the Body and Blood
Of HIM who was for us sacrificed.

Don't ignore the Bell of St. Mary's,
For it rings for ALL to hear:
A melody for the mind and spirit
Of friends both far and near.

Craig E. Burgess

Edward C. Benfold
Chapter II
The History Of A Hero:
Edward C. Benfold, USN
1931 - 1952

Ed
the age of
Edward S.
Adams Be
War II and
Atlantic),
troops to t
Merchant
Kr
Haddon H
was a colc
of both the
ter Eileen
served in 1
Ed
Station, he
Camp Pen
Ed
began that
on June 9,
In
A-Bomb '
Th
Pendleton
return to (
Edward le
he had bee
Or
action wh
was tendii
and charg
He was 21

The Audubon High School

Music Department

PRESENTS

𝓡hythm

𝓃'

𝓜usic

(A MUSICAL REVUE)

PRODUCED AND DIRECTED
By Gabriel Chiodo

pit
me
Hi
19
his

of

THE A.H.S. MIXED CHOIR

(Sopranos and Altos of the Mixed ▮▮▮ appear in Rhythm N' Music as
the G▮▮▮▮ ▮▮▮ Club)

Sopranos

Marjory Alwine	Jackie Mainor
Rosemarie Beier	Betty Martz
Dolores Braun	Jean Mattson
Shirley Burkhardt	Virginia Menk
Sally Cadmus	Marion Neel
Anna Connolly	Jane Neutze
Ilena D'Illio	Mary Nobel
Dorothy Fadio	Betty Paul
Barbara Fox	Dorothy Rowand
Vanova Gest	Marian Sherman
Esther Higgins	Gloria Waddell
Virginia Jordan	Rose Fanelli
Louise Kampf	Florence Oakley
Janet Lomax	Jeanne Mackin

Accompanists

Alberta Giffins
Helen Gebhardt

Altos

Dorothy Anderson
Janice Ayers
Doris Dietrich
Laurel Dirkes
Betty Granzow
Janice Groff
Betty Hazard
Anna Holt
Nancy Hooper
Avis Jacobs
Marion Jacoby
Alice McAllister
Angeline Minnitti
Jean Moos
Joan Radue
Gloria Rulon
Rosalie Runkle
Claire Stringfellow
Mary Jane Taylor

Tenors

William Hemsley
William Jenkins
Stuart Miller
Henry Sanderson
Richard Skidmore
Randall Terry
Mickey Vernamonti
Allan Wolff

Bass

Jimmie Harkey
Edward Benfold
Richard Peterman
William McLean
Joe Brooks
Harold Collins
Edward Davis
Edward Snelgrove

[handwritten: Edward is the only one who can hit the low bass Do. the rest are really baritones]

(The A.H.S. Symphonic-Jazz Orchestra made up of the String Ensemble under
Miss Beryl Doherty) (The A.H.S. Swing Band under Mr. Benjamin Weil)

First Violin

Miss Beryl Doherty
Carol Bartollette
Mary Jane Taylor
Albert Ruoff
Robert Ruoff

Second Violin

Laurel Dirkes
Betty Granzow
John Land

Cello

Jane Dirkes
Hope McAllister

Flute

Raymond Hartzag

Clarinet

William Buell
Norman Lore

Saxophone

Charles Epting
Albert Anderson
Samuel Raymond
James Krusch

Trumpet

Lynn White
David DiGiambardino
William Levine

Trombone

John White
John Tessman
Robert Whittaker

Bass

Mr. Benjamin Weil

Tympani

James Christopher

Drums

Harold Collins

Piano

Alberta Giffins
Helen Gebhardt

[handwritten: He had no solo part — but was in all the mixed group singing]

CREDITS

The Director of the production wishes to take this opportunity to thank
each and every individual who in any way contributed to the success of the
Revue: Dr. Charles Pierce, Miss Grace N. Kramer, Mrs. Elizabeth Schuler, Miss
Clare Aranow, Miss Lillian Eaton, Mrs. Reba Rosander, Mrs. Ruth Mervine,
Miss Gladys Lawson, Mr. Paul Dare, Mr. George Jaggard, Mrs. Mildred Lance,
all members of the Stage Crew, and any persons who may have aided us
in any way.

The A.H.S. Band Conc▮▮▮ ▮▮▮rday, February 28, 8:15

WEEKLY VISITOR, AUDUBON, N. J.

Junior Class of Audubon High School

PRESENTS

OUR TOWN

A Play in Three Acts by Thornton Wilder

DIRECTED BY

LOUISE P. HOUSEL

HIGH SCHOOL AUDITORIUM — 8:15 P. M.

FRIDAY AND SATURDAY, APRIL 9 and 10, 1948

(Produced by special arrangement with Samuel French, Inc.)

Picture Number 1: Row 1: J. Hoyt, R. Mitchell, T. Berger, J. Roland, A. Wolff, J. Mackin, B. Marriner, F. Thatcher, W. Jelonek, B. Ferguson, E. Adamson, F. Gibson. Row 2: B. Troehler, A. Rode, R. Peterman, H. Nebel, F. Mullin, R. Przybylski, P. Pflugfelder, E. Benfold, R. Cunningham. Number 2: J. Mackin, J. Hoyt, A. Wolff. Number 3: T. Berger, E. Benfold. Number 4: J. Hoyt, W. Jelonek, J. Roland.

JUNIOR PLAY

OUR TOWN
by Thornton Wilder
directed by Louise P. Housel

Cast

Stage Manager......................John Hoyt
Dr. Gibbs.....................Richard Mitchell
Joe Crowell...................Philip Pflugfelder
Howie Newsome.................Edward Benfold
Mrs. Gibbs....................Thelma Berger
Mrs. Webb.....................Barbara Marriner
George Gibbs..................Allan Wolff
Rebecca Gibbs.................Joyce Roland
Wally Webb....................Walter Jelonek
Emily Webb....................Jeanne Mackin
Professor Willard.............Ernie Adamson
Mr. Webb......................Frank Thatcher

Woman in the Balcony..........Barbara Ferguson
Man in the Balcony.................Frank Mullin
Another Woman in the Balcony.......Herta Nebel
Simon Stimson.................Richard Peterman
Mrs. Soames.......................Amabel Rode
Constable Warren............Roland Cunningham
Si Crowell........................Frank Gibson
Sam Craig....................William Troehler
Joe Stoddard..................Roman Przybylski
Assistant Stage Managers.........Anthony Vecchio
David DiGiamberardino

Edward joined the Civil Air Patrol as a cadet and served for two years, prior to enlisting in the Navy in May of 1949. The photo on this page shows Edward talking on the phone while learning the operation of a mobile phone unit with other cadets at the Camden training site.

CAP Cadets Study Mobile Radio

Operation of a mobile radio unit is being studied by the youths shown above in training with the Camden Cadet Squadron, Civil Air Patrol. Boys and girls from 15 to 18 years old can enlist in the squadron any Tuesday between 8 and 8.30 p. m. at the 114th Infantry Armory, Haddon and Wright avenues. Training includes air photography, navigation, judo and allied subjects. In the picture, left to right, are Sgt. Henry Sanderson, Pvt. Edward Benfold, W/O Paul Wine and Pvt. Lois Graham.

Picture Number 1: B. Granzow, E. McKay, F. Mullin, W. Wolf, F. Gibson, B. Steltz, E. Power, D. Fleming, J. Hoyt, J. Marsik, M. Green, H. Kling, T. Berger, J. Marston, B. Hawlk, J. Benedict, F. Craig, A. Wolff, R. Guedon, T. Gaffney, G. Dieser, E. Albertson, J. Kent, J. Markovitz, R. Peterman, R. Wilson, P. Harris. Number 2: M. Green, T. Berger, J. Hoyt. Number 3: B. Hawlk, J. Benedict, T. Berger, M. Green. Number 4: D. Fleming, J. Marsik, H. Kling, J. Marston, F. Craig, R. Guedon.

SENIOR PLAY

MY SISTER EILEEN
by Ruth McKenney
directed by George H. Jaggard

Cast

Mr. Oppopolous.....................John Hoyt	Frank Lippencott....................Frank Mullin
Ruth Sherwood.................Thelma Berger	Chick Clark........................Frank Gibson
Eileen Sherwood..................Muriel Green	Violet Shelton......................Elsie Power
Jensen ....James Kent	Mrs. Wade.......................Betty Granzow
A Street Arab...................Walter Jelonek	Robert Baker......................Allan Wolff
A Pair of Drunks............Roland Cunningham	Future Admirals..................James Marsik,
Edward Benfold	Donald Fleming, Ray Guedon, Frank Craig,
Lonigan ....Richard Peterman	Joseph Markovitz, James Marston.
The Wreck......................Robert Hawlk	Walter Sherwood................Thomas Gaffney
Another Street Arab.............Elmer Albertson	A Prospective Tenant...............Edna McKay
Mr. Fletcher....................William Wolf	The Consul......................William Steltz
Helen Wade.....................Joan Benedict	

1949: Edward was a Senior at AHS and once again participated in the Class Play, taking on the role of a drunk in the presentation of "*My Sister Eileen*". (The cast of the play, along with several photos, appears on the previous page. It is interesting to note that Edward is not in the cast photo.)

In May, Edward enlisted in the Navy. As a result, he was not at the graduation ceremony for his class at AHS. The yearbook does not even have his photo in the "Seniors" section for 1949.

On October 10th, a photo of the enlisted men in Company 279 at the U.S. Naval Training Center, Great Lakes, Illinois shows Edward (see the photo below: Edward is the 3rd from the left in the next to the back row)

CO. 279 – P. M. MAKEPEACE, E.N.C. – A. G. MEULEMAN, M.M.C. – CO. CMDRS. U.S. NAVAL TRAINING CENTER, GREAT LAKES, ILL. 10 OCT. 1949.

1950:   Edward graduated from the U.S. Naval Hospital Corps School, as part of class 31, on April 26th. His classes included Anatomy, Nursing, First Aid and minor surgery, Pharmacy, Chemistry, Materia Media and Therapeutics, Bacteriology, Hygiene and Sanitation and Radiological Safety. (The photo below shows Edward at the far left of the back row.

The next five pages show parts of the Graduation Program. Included is a summary of Edward's grades, the Mission of the U.S. Naval Hospital School, the items on the graduation program and Edward's name in the list of graduates (left column, top name).

HOSPITAL CORPS SCHOOL, CLASS-31
21 APR. 1950, GREAT LAKES, ILL.

GRADUATION
PROGRAM

U. S. NAVAL HOSPITAL CORPS SCHOOL
U. S. NAVAL HOSPITAL
Great Lakes, Illinois

²²
A - 88   anatomy
ND - 93   Nursing
MS FA - 86 First aid and minor surgery
PHAR - 92 Pharmacy
CHEM - 95 Chemistry
MMT - 89 Materia Medica & Therapeutics
BACT 89   Bacteriology
HS - 95   ~~Hygiene~~ Hygiene & Sanitation
RAD 84   Radiological safety

70.11   Final average

GRADUATION PROGRAM

WEDNESDAY, 26 APRIL 1950

INVOCATION .... C. A. HEROLD
Lt. Commander, Chaplain Corps, USN

VOCAL SOLO .... "The Kerry Dance" .... Jack BOADWAY
Hospital Apprentice, USN — Class 2-50

PIANO MEDLEY .... Dalton LAWRENCE
Hospital Apprentice, USN — Class 31

INTRODUCTORY REMARKS .... G. W. WIESE
Lt. Commander, Medical Service Corps, USN

VALEDICTORY ADDRESS ....Edgar D. GALBRAITH
Hospital Apprentice, USN

COMMENDATORY MAST .... Hugo O. WAGNER
Captain, Medical Corps, USN

PRESENTATION OF CERTIFICATES .... Gwenevere WOODALL
Lieutenant, Nurse Corps, USN
Arthur J. BINSFELD
Hospital Corpsman, First Class, USN

BENEDICTION .... C. A. HEROLD
Lt. Commander, Chaplain Corps, USN

STAR SPANGLED BANNER ....

HONOR STUDENT

Edgar D. GALBRAITH 97.44

HONOR ROLL

Robert S. R. SMITH	97.00
Dalton B. LAWRENCE	96.77
Kenton E. HULL	96.44
George B. LINCOLN	96.00
Dalton B. LAWRENCE	95.88
Rudolph MASARYK, Jr.	95.88
George R. ROSWELL	94.88

ROSTER OF CLASS 31-49

Edward C. BENFOLD	HA	Camden, New Jersey
Gligor (n) CHORBA	HA	Clifford, Michigan
Larry V. CLAXTON	HN	Cairo, Illinois
Stanley F. DEMPSKI	HA	Fort Atkinson, Wisconsin
Richard A. DICKERSON	HN	Akron, Ohio
Carl J. FICKES	HA	Lansing, Michigan
Kenneth E. FRYE	HA	Pittsburgh, Pennsylvania
Edgar D. GALBRAITH	HA	Waynesboro, Pennsylvania
Delbert T. HARRISON	HN	Irvine, Kentucky
Kenton E. HULL	HA	Butler, Pennsylvania
Roman L. JACOBSON	HA	Shell Lake, Wisconsin
William H. JOHNSON	HA	Bronxville, New York
William K. JORDAN	HA	Mount Jackson, Virginia
George M. KOKINCHAK	HA	Hawthorne, New York
William E. LAMBERT	HA	Newburgh, New York
Dalton B. LAWRENCE	HA	Milwaukee, Wisconsin
George B. LINCOLN	HN	Union Grove, Wisconsin
Rudolph (n) MASARYK, Jr.	HA	Binghamton, New York
Herbert V. MC KINSTRY	HN	Mt. Vernon, Ohio
Marvin J. MEREDITH	HN	Dunnville, Kentucky
Edward C. MYERS	HA	Biddeford, Maine
Richard F. NELSON	HA	Dedham, Massachusetts
George R. ROSWELL	HA	Scranton, Pennsylvania
Edward P. SARGELIS	HA	Brockton, Massachusetts
Cecil B. SCRUGGS	HN	Woodruff, South Carolina
Arnold C. SLEEPER	HA	Manchester, New Hampshire
Robert S. R. SMITH	HA	West Hartford, Connecticut
Richard W. STONE	HA	Lynn, Massachusetts
George A. TIRABASSI	HA	Niagara Falls, New York
John G. WHITFORD	HN	St. Louis, Missouri

Class Average 91.76

Captain T. F. COOPER, MC, USN
Commanding Officer

Captain HUGO O. WAGNER, MC, USN
Executive Officer

Lieutenant Commander G. W. WIESE, MSC, USN
Senior Instructor
Administrative Assistant

LT C. D. MOSS, MSC, USN
Assistant Instructor
Instruction Training Officer

CWO C. H. WALKER, HC, USN
Assistant Instructor
Regimental Commander

WO R. W. RICKER, HC, USN
Assistant Instructor
Personnel Officer

NAVY NURSE CORPS STAFF

LCDR Evelyn V. PARKER, NC, USNR
Instructor (Nursing Section)

LT Gwenevere WOODALL, NC, USN
LT Myrtle G. O'HARA, NC, USN

LT Pearl I. M. HEBERT, NC, USN
LT Lillian SCHOONOVER, NC, USN

LT Mary M. VAN HUSS, NC, USNR
Assistant Instructors (Nursing Section)

ASSISTANT INSTRUCTORS

J. V. CHASE, HMC, USN
L. C. GILLEY, HMC, USN
W. J. JOCHUM, HMC, USN
L. A. MILSTEAD, HMC, USN
T. E. SCHEELER, HMC, USN
V. F. STRETCH, HMC, USN
W. V. SULLIVAN, HMC, USN

A. J. BINSFELD, HM1, USN
J. E. CLARK, HM1, USN
H. G. LASALLE, HM1, USN
R. PARMER, Jr., HM1, USN
L. SHELL, HM1, USN
T. R. TALIAFERRO, HM1, USN
P. A. NEIMI, HM2, USN

W. T. WUNSCH, HM2, USN

RECORD OFFICE

E. B. WOMACK, HMC, USN
Miss Lucia HECHIMOVICH, GS-2

W. W. WOLFE, HM1, USN
Mrs. Dolores CLARK, GS-2

CHIEF MASTER AT ARMS
M. WEAVER, HMC, USN

ASSISTANT MASTER AT ARMS

G. L. PROPER, HM1, USN

W. E. SCOTT, HM2, USN

INFORMATION DESK, OFFICER OF THE DAY'S OFFICE
J. P. KING, HM1, USN

VISUAL TRAINING AIDS, MOTION PICTURE AND MIMEOGRAPH OPERATOR
H. J. RYAN, HM1, USN

SICK BAY
A. F. PUTZ, HM2, USN

MISSION

The mission of the U. S. Naval Hospital Corps School is to train naval enlisted personnel, so assigned, in the various subjects pertaining to naval medicine to the extent that they will have a fundamental knowledge sufficient to assist the medical officer in his professional duties, and that with further in-service training may advance in rating.

1950:

(cont)   After graduation from the Hospital Corps School in Great Lakes, Illinois, Edward was stationed for a while at the Philadelphia Naval Hospital and at Camp Le Jeune in North Carolina. His mother had moved into Fairview where she resided on Constitution Road. The photos shown on the next three pages provide a photographic collage of Edward, at home, on his motorcycle, with his mother and with several of his navy buddies. They need no detailed explanation. The photo below of Edward standing along the railroad tracks evokes an image of the uncertainty that awaits in the future . . . . . Where will the tracks lead?

Edward with his mother Glenys
outside her Fairview home.

Edward with wife Dorothy on a
park bench in Dudley Grange.

Edward and wife Dorothy outside their
East 32nd Street home in Camden.

1951:

(cont)   On June 9th, Edward and Dorothy were married in St. Joseph's Catholic Church in Camden, New Jersey. (See the wedding photo on preceding page and the photo at the reception on the next page).

Edward was stationed at Camp Pendleton in California and, following the wedding, the couple lived at Camp Pendleton. As part of the research for this book, we asked Dorothy (now Mrs. Waida) to tell us a little about life with Edward. She gave us some insight in the following statement:

"Ed and I were married in June, 1951, and we went to live in California, as Ed was stationed at Camp Pendleton. Ed was a wonderful person and fun to be with. He loved to dance and take walks on the beach and talk about our life together after the war and about our son, who was born in May of 1952. He was so happy."

1952:   On May 1st, Edward participated in the Atom Bomb Test on the Yucca Flat testing grounds in the Nevada Desert. In a news article published following the blast, Edward stated that he "could have been as close as a mile to 'ground zero' and lived through the explosion". He added: "But that would have to be in a foxhole about six or eight feet deep." Other Marines were not so sure . . . . (The photos and articles on pages 175, 176, 177 and 178 focus on this May Day event in 1952)

On May 15th, Dorothy Benfold gave birth to the couple's only child, Edward Joseph Benfold. Two weeks later, Edward saw his wife and son for the last time while on leave from his assignment at Camp Pendleton.

In mid-July, Edward was informed that he was to be sent to Korea where he would be assigned as a medic to the 1st Marine Division at Bunker Hill. When he wrote to his wife to tell her about his new assignment, he enclosed the poem on page 174 entitled *"Loving A Marine"* . . .

LOVING A MARINE

Loving a Marine is not always gay,
For with the price you must pay,
It's mostly loving, but not to hold,
It's being young and feeling old,
It's sending a letter with an upside-down
  stamp,
To a far away lover in a far away camp;
Being in love with merely your dreams
Brings thoughts of heaven where love-
  light gleams.

You wish it were possible for him to
  phone,
You want him to say, "I'm on my way
  home."
And when he comes in, the laughing
  together—
Unconscious of people, of time and
  weather.

It's having him whisper his love for
  you—
It's whispering back that you love him
  too.
Then comes a kiss, a promise of love,
Knowing you're watched by God above.
Reluctantly, painfully, letting him go;
While you're crying inside, wanting him
  so.

Days go by, no mail for a spell,
You wait for a word that he is well,
And when the letter comes, you shiver
  with joy,
And act like a child with a shiny new
  toy.
It's loving a Marine, the boy you adore.
And hating the world, yourself and the
  war.

And it's going to church to kneel and
  pray,
And really meaning all the things that
  you say,
And though you know that he's far
  away,
You love him more and more each day.

Loving a Marine is bitterness and tears,
It's loneliness and tears, sadness and
  unfounded fears,
No, loving a Marine is really no fun,
But it's worth the price when the battle
  is won.

by Miss Beverly Regan

174

Before the Big Blast

Five Marines play cards while waiting to participate in Atom Bomb test yesterday on Nevada desert. From left: Staff Sergeant Edward Speck, of Tuckerton; Private First Class Philip Andrew, of Winsted, Conn.; HM3C Edward Benfold, of Camden; Corporal Ralph Gonzales, of New York City, and Corporal Robert H. Brown, of Garden City, N. Y.

Marines Get Baptism Of Atom Bomb Warfare, Seize 'Island' in Test

MOUNT CHARLESTON, Nev., May 1 (UP). — Two thousand battle-hardened U. S. Marines got a May Day baptism of atomic warfare today on the Yucca Flat testing grounds.

An Air Force bomber at 9:30.36 A. M. (PDT) dropped a medium-sized atomic bomb over the Nevada proving grounds for the benefit of the Leathernecks huddled in foxholes only 7000 yards from the "ground zero" target.

Seconds after the now-familiar fireball shot up into the clear sky, the marines, with cool, professional alertness, jumped from their foxholes and simulated an advance on "Yucca Island," their theoretical objective in the make-believe atomic amphibious attack.

BRILLIANT SPECTACLE

Even from the depth of the foxholes, the marines saw a brilliant red flash, one of the brightest of the series of nuclear detonations held

The marines and 250 Army observers felt a blast of heat immediately following the explosion.

For a few moments they were enveloped by a gust of dirt, pebbles and debris hurled at them as the air suddenly became turbulent.

Today's explosion was the 16th set off at the Nevada testing grounds.

BOMB AWES MARINES

The marines came through the maneuvers with nothing but respect and awe for the A-bomb.

"I think that all our men know now that the atomic bomb can be one of their best friends in a tight situation," Brig. Gen. Joseph C. Burger said. "The bomb is an outstanding weapon, but it still hasn't taken the place of the rifleman."

Several marine infantrymen gave a graphic picture of seeing an M-7 tank thrown through the air 70 or 80 feet.

One, a Korea veteran, Staff Sgt. Edward L. Speck, of Tuckerton, N. J., said he saw six planes set on fire near "ground zero" and that dummies were "burned to a crisp and thrown 150 yards."

Edward Penfold, of Camden, N. J., said he felt he could have been as close as a mile to "ground zero" and lived through the explosion. "But that would have to be in a foxhole about six or eight feet deep," he added. Others were not so sure.

The Marines and 250 Army observers felt a blast of heat immediately following the explosion. As they scrambled out of their foxholes they braced themselves on the ground above for the shock wave that came seconds later.

CHECK FOR RADIATION

For a few moments they were enveloped by a gust of dirt, pebbles and debris hurled at them as the air suddenly became turbulent.

While the Marines looked curiously at the cloud overhead, scientists quickly checked the area for radiation and on their signal the Marines moved into the blasted area to check the effect of detonation on their equipment and conclude their simulated attack on "Yucca Island."

Today's explosion was the 16th set og at the Nevada testing grounds. Aside from indicating that today's explosion was not as powerful as that set og last week in a public demonstration for press, radio and television, atomic scientists would not give details on the intensity of the explosion.

BRIGHTEST EXPLOSION

From a spectator's standpoint, today's flash was called "the brightest yet seen." The explosion, however, did not form an ice cap like last week's blast.

The explosion was clearly visible in Las Vegas, 70 miles southwest of the blast area. It was even reported seen from a mountain top 150 miles northeast of St. George, Utah. Ham radio operators received reports that a gentle shock was felt below Parker Dam, on the Colorado River, about 120 miles south of the test area. Atmospheric conditions, however, sent the shock wave away from Las Vegas itself.

A-Bomb Blast Jolts Marines, Some Equipment Destroyed

Las Vegas, Nev., May 2—(AP)—A new tactical A-bomb of fiery intensity gave 2,150 entrenched marines a solid jolt in their first nuclear maneuvers, but there were no casualties.

The brilliant bomb burst about 2,000 feet above Yucca Flat, less than 4 miles from two picked combat battalions from Camp Pendleton, Calif., and Camp Lejeune, N. C., yesterday.

The weapon selected for the test came from the Atomic Energy Commission's top secret drawer, and it was perhaps the brightest bomb seen in a daylight test here.

Newsmen, not permitted on the test site this time, saw from the distance a fire ball that lasted a full 10 seconds and continued to flicker in the subsequent nuclear cloud for perhaps another 5 seconds.

There was no concussion on Mt. Charleston, the news observation point 50 miles away, but the rumble of the blast and its echo were heard five minutes after the flash.

The marines were in foxholes and trenches, most of them 4½ feet deep. Two hours later they proceeded toward Yucca Island, the mythical enemy-held "atoll" centered on Ground Zero which was the objective of their maneuver.

The detonation level of 2,000 feet put the marines closer to an atomic burst than any troops had been before. The 1,500 Army troops in last week's maneuvers were the same distance from Ground Zero, but the bomb exploded at 3,500 feet.

Battalions Charge

The blast yesterday decimated much of the marines' equipment within 900 yards of Ground Zero, but the two battalions came charging out of their foxholes on signal from their maneuver commander, Brigadier General Joseph C. Burger.

While high ground radiation kept the troops from moving to Ground Zero, Gen. Burger said that "in a battlefield situation we would have had no fear of going through."

The advance was halted within 500 yards of the target, which was surrounded with burning planes, trucks and smashed machineguns—showing graphically what would have happened to the enemy.

Tank Blown 80 Feet

One M-7 tank was blown 80 feet and flipped on its back, General Burger said.

But he pointed out to his men that dummies placed in close-up foxholes received very slight damage, whereas dummies placed upright above ground farther back were completely destroyed.

Staff Sgt. Edward L. Speck, 34, Tuckerton, N. J., said he saw stand-up dummies blown 150 yards and burned to a crisp a half mile from the target.

Speck, a Korea veteran in charge of a machinegun company from Camp LeJeune, said some of the guns were still usable, but "200 yards from Ground Zero they were smashed to bits."

He added: "I think it would be a good idea to try a few of these bombs in Korea."

Gen. Burger said only: "It is an outstanding weapon, but it still has not taken the place of the rifleman."

1952:

(cont)   Edward J was born in Camden, New Jersey, since Dorothy had moved back to the East Coast after staying with her husband for only a short time in an apartment in Long Beach, California, near Camp Pendleton.

On September 5th, Edward was killed in action in Korea, sacrificing his life to save two wounded Marines.

Initially, Edward was reported as "wounded in action", but on September 8th, Dorothy received a telegram reporting his death.

The items on the next several pages pertain to Edward's death. To the right is the Medic patch worn by Edward while in Korea. The next page shows two newspaper articles reporting his death. On pages 182 and 183 is the letter sent to Dorothy on September 9th from the Captain of the 92nd Battalion, 1st Marines of the US Marine Corps. Page 181 is taken from the Commissioning book of the USS BENFOLD (DDG-65) and summarizes the events of September 5th.

Camden Sailor Killed in Korea

Was Medic Attached To the Marines

Edward C. Benfold, of 224 N. 32d st., Camden, a sailor, was killed in action in Korea, September 8, a Defense Department casualty list disclosed yesterday.

Benfold, a hospital corpsman 3d class, was the husband of Mrs. Dorothy A. Benfold, of the Camden address.

He enlisted in May, 1949, and had been in Korea about three weeks. He wrote his wife that he was attached as a "medic" to the 1st Marine Division at Bunker Hill.

His father, Edward S. Benfold, was killed in World War II. He

Edward C. Benfold

was a merchant marine officer on a troop transport that was torpedoed.

The younger Eenfold also is survived by a son, Edward J., who was two weeks old when his father left for Korea, and his mother, Mrs. Gladys Benfold, 2868 Constitution road, Camden.

Camden Sailor Killed in Korea; Marine Is Hurt

Hospital Corpsman Had Participated In A-Bomb Tests

A Camden Navy man was killed while serving as a hospital corpsman in the Korean area, his wife has been informed.

The name of Edward Clyde Benfold apeared as "wounded in action" on the Department of Defense casualty list 658 released last night, but his wife received a telegram Sept. 8 reporting his death. The telegram, signed by Vice Adm. L. T. Dubose, Chief of Naval Personnel, said nfold died ept. 5 "as a result of action in the Korean area."

Benfold, who was 21, lived at 224 N. 32d st., Camden. In

EDW. C. BENFOLD

addition to his wife, Dorothy, also 21, he is survived by a 4-month-old son, Edward Joseph, whom he saw while home on leave June 1, and his mother, Mrs. Glenys Benfold, of 2868 Constitution rd., Camden.

His father, Edward S. Benfold, a Merchant Marine officer, was killed in the Second World War while transporting troops.

STATIONED AT HOSPITAL

Benfold had been in the Navy since 1949. After attending Great Lakes Naval Training Station, he was stationed here at the Naval Hospital for a short time. He left the West Coast for duty in Korea in mid-July.

He attended Audubon High School. Benfold was a member of the school's senior choir and he was a color guardsman in the band. For two years he served in the Camden wing of the Civil Air Patrol.

While serving as a hospital corpsman, Benfold participated in the Nevada atom bomb test, his wife said.

Service with the First Marine Division

Bunker Hill was located on the western end of an 8000 meter United Nations front near the 38th parallel in Korea. Official communiques state that the enemy began probes along the front in early September, testing the strength of Bunker Hill prior to the ensuing battle. The full assault on Bunker Hill began in the predawn hours of September 5, 1952. The evening before, the First Marine Division began taking incoming rounds. "Bombardment with heavy artillery began several hours earlier" according to Sgt. Michael L. Crnkovich.

Throughout the night Benfold had been moving rapidly between positions in the platoon, medically treating those in need and encouraging all others with his supportive attitude. It was when Benfold approached a crater near the middle of the platoon and was treating the two men there that the grenades were thrown. Sgt. Crnkovich said "it was not until Benfold was killed from behind that the platoon was first alerted that it was completely enveloped by the enemy." Sgt. Crnkovich was one of the two Marines in the crater when Benfold picked up the grenades and hurled himself at the onrushing troops. When Crnkovich crawled out he saw the enemy crawling everywhere. Fierce hand to hand combat ensued. Sgt. Crnkovich, one of the men saved by the courageous Hospitalman, laid his jacket over Benfold as he was carried away. As he described it, "the entire platoon knew that we owed our lives to Benfold."

The Korean War is often referred to as "the forgotten war." For the men and women who fought there and for the families and friends of those who died there it will never be forgotten.

- Kenneth N. Jordan, Sr.

1952:

(cont)   In late September, two letters were sent to 224 N. 32nd Street in Camden, where Dorothy Benfold and her son were residing at the time of Edward's death. One was from the Chaplain of the US Navy, Gerald E. Kuhn, dated September 27th. (See letter on the following page). The second letter, dated September 26th, was the first of two to be received from Senator Robert C. Hendrickson of New Jersey. This letter was addressed to Edward, extending sincere wishes for a quick recovery from wounds suffered in action. The letter resulted from the Department of Defense casualty list (#658) that was released on September 6th. (See letter on page 186).

      On October 24th, a second letter from Senator Hendrickson arrived, addressed to Dorothy. Condolences were extended to the family. (See letter on page 187).

      On October 26th, a Memorial Service was held in honor of US Marine Corps and US Navy Personnel who had served in the field in Korea and who had been killed in action between July 26th and October 12th of 1952. Pages 188, 189 and 190 show the program cover for the Service, the program format and the list of those men of the Second Battalion, First Marines who had died. This list, which includes the name of Edward C. Benfold, was read by Lt. Col. C.E. Warren as part of the Roll Call of the Dead.

      Lt. Col. Warren forwarded a copy of the Memorial Program to Dorothy several days following the Service. (See letter on page 191).

      On November 4th, a telegram was sent to Dorothy, advising her that the remains of Edward would be arriving by train to Philadelphia on Monday, November 10th. (See telegram on page 192).

      On Saturday, November 8th, the Courier-Post published the death notice about Edward, with details on the service that had been arranged. (See Death notice on page 193).

Office of the Regimental Chaplain,
1st Marines, 1st Marine Division, Fleet Marine Force,
c/o Fleet Post Office, San Francisco, California

27 September 1952

Mrs. Edward Benfold
224 North 32nd St.
Camden, N.J.

My dear Mrs. Benfold:

As the Protestant Chaplain of the regiment in which your
husband faithfully served his country, it is my desire to
convey to you my deepest sympathies for the great loss
which you have sustained. We of the 1st Marines also feel
keenly the departing of Edward, in that we have lost a friend
and comrade who can never be replaced. In giving his life
for the cause of justice and morality, the honor of our
country and the United States Marine Corps has been preserved
in a manner characteristic of the illustrious traditions of
both.

It is not easy for us at times to understand the full meaning
of all that is happening in our world today, especially here
in Korea. When we suffer the loss of one whom we love greatly, deep, personal sorrow is added to the confusion of our
minds. Sometimes we are called upon to sacrifice much in life.
Now we have to struggle for the preservation of our liberties,
our way of life and our great principles of freedom. Some
have to lay down their lives that we and others in days to
come may live in such freedom. Your husband has given his
life with others in the service of our country for this cause.

I join with you in a prayer that the life of Edward, along
with the lives of others who have made this great sacrifice
in Korea, has not been in vain and that he has made it possible for a better world in the near future.

Sincerely in Christ,

GERALD E. KUHN
Chaplain, U. S. Navy

185

United States Senate

COMMITTEE ON THE JUDICIARY

September 26, 1952

My dear Mr. Benfold:

I have just learned from the Department of Defense of the
heroic contribution you have made in foreign fields, that
liberty and justice may continue in this great land of ours.

As a veteran of two wars, I know something of the pain and
suffering, not to mention the anguish, which accompany battle
wounds. I sincerely trust that the injury you have sustained
will heal with all due speed.

In the meanwhile, you have my deepest sympathy, as well as my
profound gratitude for the service you have rendered for your
country and for all of us who are privileged to live within
its borders.

With every good wish for your early recovery, I am

Sincerely yours,

Robert C. Hendrickson

Edward C. Benfold, HM3
224 N. 32nd Street
Camden, New Jersey

186

United States Senate

COMMITTEE ON THE JUDICIARY

October 24, 1952

My dear Mrs. Benfold:

It is with profound sorrow that I have learned of the great tragedy which has befallen your family in the death of your husband, Edward.

I realize that, at such a time, mere words have little meaning but, as a veteran of two wars and as a parent, I wanted you to know that my sympathies are with you in this trying hour.

Moreover, I wanted to indicate to you, as a citizen, the deep sense of gratitude which I feel for the heroic sacrifice which your husband so freely made in the defense of our beloved liberties.

I would that there were some way by which I might bring some measure of comfort to all who have been saddened by this great and irreparable loss, for I know from personal experience how difficult it is to accept a situation of this kind and do so with a show of courage.

May God in His wisdom guide your thoughts through the difficult days ahead and bring you to tranquility through the knowledge that your husband rests peacefully and well with those heroic comrades who have given their all that America may continue to be a haven of liberty and justice for all.

Very respectfully yours,

Robert C. Hendrickson

Mrs. Dorothy A. Benfold
224 North 32nd Street
Camden, New Jersey

187

Memorial Service
in honor of
U.S. Marine Corps and U.S. Navy
personnel who served with the
First Marine Regiment of the
First Marine Division F.M.F.

In The Field   Korea   26. October 1952

```
**************************************
```

MEMORIAL SERVICE

CHURCH CALL   Bugler

THE NATIONAL ANTHEM   Division Band

THE INVOCATION   Catholic Chaplain
                                    Patrick Adams

INTRODUCTION OF THE COMMANDING GENERAL
                    Colonel Walter F. Layer

THE MEMORIAL ADDRESS
                    Major General E. A. Pollock

THE MARINE HYMN   Division Band

*** HONORS ***

ROLL CALL OF THE DEAD

1stBn,	1st Marines	LtCol M. A. LaGrone
2ndBn,	1st Marines	LtCol C. E. Warren
3rdBn,	1st Marines	LtCol S. J. Altman
AT-Co,	1st Marines	1stLt B. C. Kearns
3rdBn,	11th Marines	LtCol C. O. Rogers
"C"Co,	1st Tank Bn	Capt. G. M. McCain

MINUTE OF SILENT TRIBUTE   Assembly

THE MEMORIAL PRAYER   Protestant Chaplain
                                    Oscar Weber

RIFLE SALUTE   Honor Guard

TAPS   Bugler

THE BENEDICTION   Jewish Chaplain
                                    Samuel Sobel

```
**************************************
```

```
*******************************************************
```

Second Battalion, First Marines

Wilfred E. Hall	Raymond L. Hergert
Robert E. Stafford	Phillip N. Hobson Jr.
Joseph L. Francomano	Alber E. Drummond Jr.
Billy Seals	Warren E. Christian
Donald A. Sorrentino	George M. Matthews
Vernon Mahan	E. Pomales-Santiago
Bobby Canterberry	Roger L. Desclos
Donald C. Trausch	John M. Juilien Jr.
Olie J. Belt	Carl M. Burke
Arthur G. Choquette	Sidney M. White
Edward R. Belardi Jr.	James W. Buddenberg
G. Cruhigger-Rodriguez	Earl D. Stoll
James J. Carlson	John J. Dopazo
Floyd F. Cox	Alefandro Gonzales
James A. Naour	William R. Haralson
Robert M. Ellars	George R. King
Owen A. Norton	Edward W. Breutzmann
Larry D. Turner	Donald R. Jackson
Thomas R. Cook	Thomas A. Janelle
Roy L. Griffin	Harold L. Piesik
Merlyn Johnson	James L. Gillam
French Mounts Jr.	William W. Lewis
John J. Boyle	Brian B. Thornton
Donald D. Miner	Donald L. Fish
Henry V. Camire	John T. Hoenes
Juan B. Cordova	Edward Schmitt
Arnold R. Tobias	Frank W. Halley
Harold E. Reins	Floyd Cooper Jr.
Jose M. Linares-Ortiz	Horace Hayes
David E. Halverson	✷ Edward C. Benfold
Alfredo P. Charles	Richard C. Willmann
William A. McGinnis	Cecil A. Snodgrass
Mason C. Hazard	Gerald L. Haerr
Kenneth F. Wolf	Richard W. Kountz
Bill E. Johnson	Vincent Calvanico

```
*******************************************************
```

                    Headquarters
              2d Battalion, 1st Marines
           1st Marine Division (Reinf), FMF
           c/o FPO, San Francisco, California

Mrs Ed Benfold
224 No. 32d St.
Camden, N. J.

Dear Mrs. Benfold:

        On 26 October, I attended, with the Commanding General
of the First Marine Division and the Commanding Officer,
First Marine Regiment, the memorial service held for those
gallant Marines who gave their "last full measure of devotion".

        It is my desire to enclose this memorial program to you
on behalf of your husband, Edward, who lived his life and gave
his life in a spirit that won for him the high esteem of the
men of his company. He has brought honor to the Marine Corps
and to our country.

                    Sincerely yours,

                    CHARLES E. WARREN
                    LtCol   USMC
                    Commanding

WESTERN UNION

1220

W. P. MARSHALL, PRESIDENT

The filing time shown in the date line on telegrams and day letters is STANDARD TIME at point of origin. Time of receipt is STANDARD TIME at point of destination

PNC118 LONG GOVT NL PD=BNA BROOKLYN NY 4= 1952 NOV 4 PM 12 19

MRS DOROTHY AGNES BENFOLD=

244 NORTH 32 ST CAMDEN NJER=

=IN REPLY REFER TO TCNYP 8250 QM AGRB (NAVY) PLEAEE BE
ADVISED REMAINS OF HN3 EDWARD CLYDE BENFOLD ESCORTED BY
BTG 1/C CHRISTIAN W WOERNER DEPARTS NEW YORK VIA PRR
TRAIN 109 AT 840 AM MON 10 NOV ARRIVES PHILADELPHIA PA
(30TH ST STA) VIA PRR TRAIN 109 AT 1034 AM MON 10 NOV=
COST OF TRANSPORTATION OF REMAINS TO CAMDEN NEW JERSEY
TO BE PAID FROM GOVERNMENT FUNDS= LETTER TO UNDERTAKER
WILL FOLLOW=

RICHARD G HOPKINS US NAVY ESCORT UNIT NY
PORT OF EMBARKATION=

8250 HN3 1/C 109 840 10 30 109 1034 10=.

THE COMPANY WILL APPRECIATE SUGGESTIONS FROM ITS PATRONS CONCERNING ITS SERVICE

192

Camden   NOV 8 1952.

(1)   DEATH NOTICES

BENFOLD—Suddenly at Korea on September 5, H.N.3, Edward C., husband of Dorothy Benfold (nee Groff), of 224 N. 32nd St., Camden, N. J., and son of Glenys and the late Edward S. Benfold, age 21 years. Relatives and friends of the family are invited to attend the funeral services on Wednesday at 10.30 a. m. at the Harry Leonard Funeral Home, 2850 Federal St., Camden, N. J. Interment at U. S. National Cemetery, Beverly, N. J., with full military honors. Friends may call Tuesday evening,

EDWARD C. BENFOLD

Services for Edward C. Benfold, of 224 N. 32nd st., Navy hospitalman third class, who was killed in Korea Sept. 5, will be held Wednesday at 10.30 a. m. in a funeral home at 2850 Federal st., where friends may call Tuesday night. Burial with military honors will be in U. S. National Cemetery, Beverly. Benfold, who was 21, was born in New York City and lived in this area 14 years prior to enlisting in the Navy in 1949. He served in Korea with the First Marine Division. Benfold's company commander said the corpsman gave his life in order to save the lives of two men he was treating by grabbing a grenade which landed nearby and leaping from his position. Benfold attended Audubon High School before enlisting. Surviving are his wife, Dorothy; a son, Edward Jr., five months, and his mother, Mrs. Glenys Benfold, all of Camden.

1952:

(cont)   On Wednesday, November 12th, services were held at the Harry Leonard Funeral Home on Federal Street in Camden. Interment was with full military honors in the U.S. National Cemetery in Beverly, New Jersey. (See the photos taken at the Beverly Cemetery in February and May, 1999 on pages 195, 196, 197 and 198).

Note: A special section of the cemetery (shown on the map on page 1936 with the oval area outlined at the far left) was designated for Medal of Honor recipients.

Note: In 1976, year of our Nation's Bicentennial, a tree was planted at the Medal of Honor site and dedicated to the memory of military heroes. The tree and the special plaque containing the dedication are shown on page 197.

Note: The last page of photos taken at the Beverly Cemetery shows the grave marker for Edward. In the background can be seen the marker for one of Audubon's other Medal of Honor recipients, Nelson V. Brittin, who was also killed in action in Korea in 1951.

On November 21st, Dorothy received a letter from the U. S. Naval Supply Depot Clearfield in Ogden, Utah. The letter addressed the personal effects of her husband, Edward. (See the letter on pages 199 and 200).

1953:   Edward C. Benfold was honored posthumously with three medals that were presented to Dorothy: The Purple Heart, The Medal of Honor and The Order of Military Merit, WHARANG with a Gold Star. The last of these honors was awarded by the Republic of Korea.

On January 14th, Dorothy received a letter and a Purple Heart Certificate from the Department of the Navy, signed by Lt. A. C. Thompson. (See the letter and the certificate on pages 201 and 202).

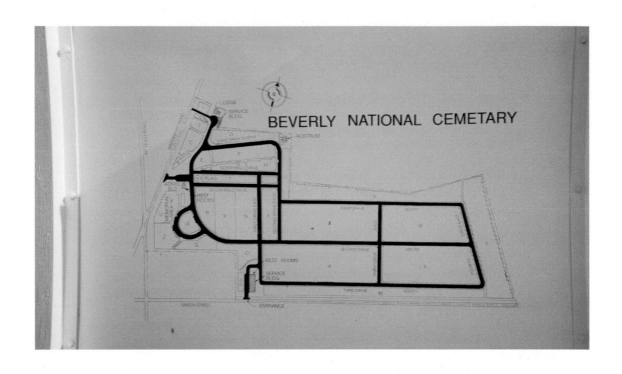

THIS TREE
DEDICATED BY THE VETERANS
ADMINISTRATION IN 1976 TO
AMERICA'S MEDAL OF HONOR
RECIPIENTS WHO HELPED
MAKE THIS BICENTENNIAL
OBSERVANCE POSSIBLE
"BY GALLANTRY ABOVE AND
BEYOND THE CALL OF DUTY"

198

Address Reply To:
COMMANDING OFFICER
And Refer To:

NT4-63/PE-11
Case V-1282-52
Ser

35196

NOV 21 52

Mrs. Dorothy Agnes Benfold
224 N. 32nd Street
Camden, New Jersey

My dear Mrs. Benfold.

We have received personal effects classified as valuables belonging
to your husband, Edward Clyde BENFOLD, HM3, 416 82 34, United States
Navy, from the U. S. Fleet Marine Force, Pacific, Far East Command.

We have no information as yet concerning the bulk effects belonging
to your husband but as soon as we do receive any information concerning them, you will be advised.

In order that we may be able to expeditiously handle these effects
when they are received, please inform us if an administrator or
executor of the estate of your husband has been appointed. If so,
please have that person forward us certified copies of the appropriate
letters of appointment. The effects would be shipped to that person
so appointed, under the authority of those letters.

If none has been appointed, the valuables already received, and the
bulk effects to be received in the future will then be forwarded to
you as the next of kin of your husband, upon our receipt of the
original of the enclosed form, completed before a notary public.
The duplicate copy may be retained by you for your own information.
The enclosed envelope, which requires no postage, is for your convenience
in reply.

This form provides for a mailing and a shipping address, in the event
that they are different.

The valuables already received, consisting of a religious medal, a
pen, and a cigarette lighter, will be forwarded via registered mail.
The bulk personal effects, when received here, will be forwarded via
Railway Express Agency, Inc. All shipments are made at government
expense. The bulk effects consist of clothing and miscellaneous items

Delivery of personal effects into the custody of other than the owner
thereof, by the Department of the Navy, does not in any way vest title

199

NT4-63/PE-11
Case V-1282-52

to the effects in the recipient. Delivery of the effects to the recipient is made in order that distribution of the effects may be made in accordance with the laws of the State in which the owner of the effects was legally domiciled.

Our very deepest sympathy is extended to you in the great loss of your husband.

Sincerely yours,

T. R. COCHRAN
By direction of
Commanding Officer

Encl:
(1) Form 752 (in duplicate)
(2) Return envelope

DEPARTMENT OF THE NAVY
BUREAU OF NAVAL PERSONNEL
WASHINGTON 25, D. C.

IN REPLY REFER TO
Pers-E314-BRH:sp
416 82 34
14 Jan 1953

Mrs. Dorothy Agnes Benfold
224 N. 32nd Street
Camden, New Jersey

Dear Mrs. Benfold:

The Purple Heart Medal is awarded to your husband, the late Edward Clyde Benfold, Hospital Corpsman, third class, United States Navy, in the name of the President of the United States, for wounds received in action against an enemy of the United States on 5 September 1952 while attached to the First Marine Division.

The Purple Heart Certificate is enclosed.

The Purple Heart Medal is being forwarded to you by registered mail, under separate cover.

By direction of Chief of Naval Personnel:

Sincerely yours,

A. C. Thompson

A. C. THOMPSON
Lieutenant, USNR
Head, Branch ONE
Enlisted Services
and Records Division

Encl:
(1) Purple Heart Certificate

201

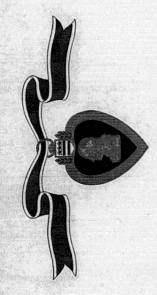

THE UNITED STATES OF AMERICA

TO ALL WHO SHALL SEE THESE PRESENTS, GREETING:

THIS IS TO CERTIFY THAT

THE PRESIDENT OF THE UNITED STATES OF AMERICA

HAS AWARDED THE

PURPLE HEART

ESTABLISHED BY GENERAL GEORGE WASHINGTON
AT NEWBURGH, NEW YORK, AUGUST 7, 1782

TO

Edward Clyde Benfold, Hospital Corpsman Third Class, United States Navy

FOR WOUNDS RECEIVED
IN ACTION

September 5, 1952

GIVEN UNDER MY HAND IN THE CITY OF WASHINGTON
THIS 14th DAY OF January 1953

CHIEF OF NAVAL PERSONNEL

202

1953:

(cont)   A citation was prepared by Son Won Ill, the Minister of National Defense of the Republic of Korea, stating that Edward was to receive the Order of Military Merit, WHARANG with Gold Star for "exceptionally Outstanding and Meritorious Service". (See the citation on pages 204 and 205 in English and in Korean).

A citation was prepared and signed by President Dwight David Eisenhower, stating that Edward was to be the recipient of the Nation's highest honor, the Medal of Honor. (See the signed copy of this citation on page 206).

Note: Dorothy told us that she had been notified of the Medal of Honor by Secretary of the Navy H. Lawrence Garrett III from the Navy Department in Washington, DC. She did not meet with the President. (The Medal of Honor was presented to her at the Philadelphia Naval Base in July).

Note: Edward's son, Edward Joseph, has all three medals displayed in a special frame at his home. He provided us a photo of the display case for this tribute. (See page 207).

Following Edward's death in Korea, his wife Dorothy became a member of the South Jersey Gold Star Wives of America, an organization whose members are widows of servicemen killed in action in wartime. The organization sponsors various community events, while serving as a support group. On March 28th, the group held its annual Easter Party and one of the youngsters entertained was 10-month old Edward J. Benfold. (See photo and caption on page 208).

Office Of The Minister Of National Defense

In recognition and appreciation of his exceptionally outstanding and meritorious service, I take great pleasure in accordance with the authority delegated to me by the Order of the President of the Republic of Korea No. 2 in awarding the Order of Military Merit, WHARANG with Gold Star to

HOSPITAL CORPSMAN THIRD CLASS EDWARD C. BENFOLD
4168234 UNITED STATES NAVY

for services as set forth in the following

CITATION;

"For gallantry and intrepidity at the risk of his life, above and beyond the call of duty and without detriment to the mission of the unit of which he was a member in combat with the enemy in Korea on 5 September 1952. Serving as a company corpsman, Hospital Corpsman Third Class BENFOLD displayed incredible courage and devotion to duty when the company was subjected to heavy artillery and mortar barrages, followed by a determined assault by an estimated battalion strength enemy. With complete disregard for his personal safety, he moved from position to position, treating the wounded and offering words of encouragement. Later, the platoon area in which he was working received numerous attacks from both front and rear. Despite the intense enemy fire, he left the protection of his position and moved to the exposed ridgeline where he saw two Marines in a large crater. He unhesitatingly moved down into the crater to determine the condition of the men but as he approached them, an enemy soldier threw two grenades into the position while two other enemy charged. Displaying unparalleled valor, he picked up a grenade in each hand and hurled himself against the two charging enemy. Pushing the grenades against their chests, he killed the two attackers, whereby saving the lives of his comrades. In committing this act of selfless devotion to his fellow men, he was mortally wounded, gallantly giving his life for his country. Hospital Corpsman Third Class BENFOLD's outstanding courage and disregard of his personal safety were an inspiration to all who observed him. His incredible heroism was in keeping with the highest traditions of the United States Naval Service."

SON WON ILL
Minister of National Defense
Republic of Korea

THE WHITE HOUSE
WASHINGTON

The President of the United States in the name of The Congress takes pride in presenting the MEDAL OF HONOR posthumously to

EDWARD C. BENFOLD
HOSPITAL CORPSMAN THIRD CLASS
UNITED STATES NAVY

for service as set forth in the following

CITATION:

"For gallantry and intrepidity at the risk of his life above and beyond the call of duty while serving as a Hospital Corpsman, attached to a Company in the First Marine Division during operations against enemy aggressor forces in Korea on 5 September 1952. When his company was subjected to heavy artillery and mortar barrages, followed by a determined assault during the hours of darkness by an enemy force estimated at battalion strength, BENFOLD resolutely moved from position to position in the face of intense hostile fire, treating the wounded and lending words of encouragement. Leaving the protection of his sheltered position to treat the wounded when the platoon area in which he was working was attacked from both the front and rear, he moved forward to an exposed ridge line where he observed two Marines in a large crater. As he approached the two men to determine their condition, an enemy soldier threw two grenades into the crater while two other enemy charged the position. Picking up a grenade in each hand, BENFOLD leaped out of the crater and hurled himself against the onrushing hostile soldiers, pushing the grenades against their chests and killing both the attackers. Mortally wounded while carrying out this heroic act, BENFOLD, by his great personal valor and resolute spirit of self-sacrifice in the face of almost certain death, was directly responsible for saving the lives of his two comrades. His exceptional courage reflects the highest credit upon himself and enhances the finest traditions of the United States Naval Service. He gallantly gave his life for others."

206

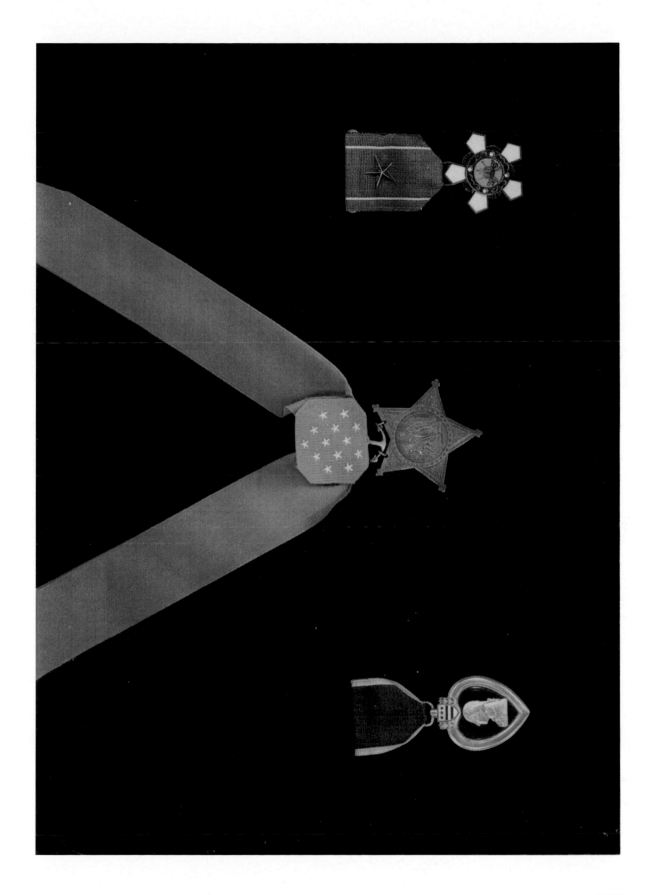

—Courier-Post Photo

ADMIRING PRESENTS at the annual Easter Party of Camden County Chapter, Gold Star Wives, held Saturday in the Townsend C. Young American Legion Post Home, Gloucester City, are five of the youngsters who were entertained. Left to right, they are Geraldine Thinnes, Diane Dickson, George Braun, Gail Dickson, and 10-month-old Edward Benfold.

1953:

(cont)　　　On June 16th, a letter was sent to Mrs. Glenys Benfold, Edward's mother, from Murray-Troutt American Legion Auxiliary of Post #262 in Audubon. The Audubon Auxiliary had donated a book in memory of Edward to the Audubon High School Library. (See the letter below).

American Legion Auxiliary

MURRAY-TROUTT UNIT NO. 262

AUDUBON, NEW JERSEY

June 16, 1953

Mrs. Glenys Benfold
2868 Constitution Road
Camden, New Jersey

Dear Glenys:

　　　The book the Unit placed in the High School Library in honor of your son Edward is entitled "Realties of World Power" - by John E. Kieffer. We felt sure you would be interested in having this information.

　　　With kindest personal regards,

　　　　　　Sincerely yours,

　　　　　　Frances Naylor
　　　　　　Secretary

333 Chestnut St.,
Audubon, N. J.

1953:

(cont)   On July 6th, Edward's mother received an invitation from the U.S. Navy to attend the ceremony at the Philadelphia Naval Base, during which Edward's wife Dorothy would receive the Congressional Medal of Honor - - - given posthumously to her son Edward C. Benfold. (See letter below).

COMMANDANT, 4TH NAVAL DISTRICT
U. S. NAVAL BASE
PHILADELPHIA 12, PA.

6 July 1953

Dear Mrs. Benfold:

On Thursday, July 16, at 3:00 p.m., at the Naval Base Philadelphia, the Commandant of the Fourth Naval District will present a Congressional Medal of Honor to Mrs. Dorothy A. Benfold of Camden, New Jersey.

This Medal was won by your son, the late Edward C. Benfold, Hospital Corpsman Third Class, United States Navy, in action in Korea on 5 September 1952, for gallantry and intrepidity at the risk of his life above and beyond the call of duty.

You are cordially invited to be present. If you can accept this invitation, you will be admitted at the Main Gate of the Naval Base and directed to the ceremony. Please let me know if you will attend.

Sincerely yours,

J. H. BROWN, Jr.
Rear Admiral, U. S. Navy
Commandant, Fourth Naval District

Mrs. Glenys Benfold,
2868 Constitution Road,
Camden 4, New Jersey.

210

1953:

(cont) On July 16th, the presentation of the Medal of Honor took place. The event received attention around the state and was covered by the Courier-Post, the East Camden News, The Philadelphia Inquirer, The Philadelphia Bulletin and other papers, including the Newark Evening News.

The articles and photos that are presented on the following pages provide some interesting insights into the coverage of the event. The headlines focus on the history of the family, on the hero's wife and young son and on the background of Edward's mother, as well as the Medal of Honor itself. The photos focus attention on the 14-month old Edward Joseph Benfold in the days prior to the ceremony, on the morning of the ceremony and, most especially, at the ceremony - - - at 3:00 pm at the Philadelphia Naval Base.

The presentation of the Medal of Honor was made by Rear Admiral John H. Brown, Jr., Commandant of the Fourth Naval District. (See the items on the next 7 pages).

A very special tribute to Edward appeared in an issue of Charlton Comics soon after the Medal of Honor Ceremony. Edward's heroism was depicted in in a five page documentary. We are honored to be able to include this documentary as part of the chapter on the life of Hospital Corpsman, Third Class Edward C. Benfold, U.S.N. #4168234. (See pages 219 - 223).

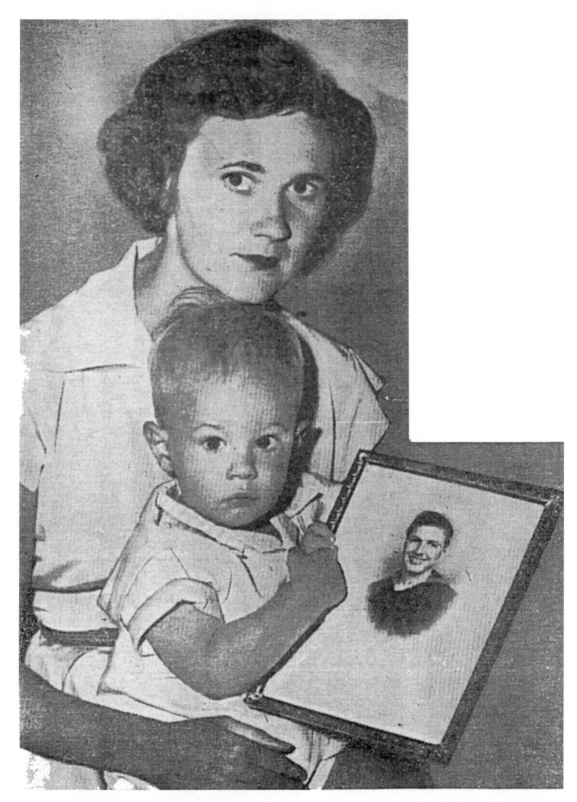

(Associated Press Wirefoto)

Memory Honored. Edward Benfold Jr., 14 months old, sits on lap of his mom, Dorothy, and holds picture of his hero dad, Navy Corpsman Edward Benfold, in family's Camden, N. J. home. Edward Jr. will receive Medal of Honor his late dad won when he saved two wounded marines in Korea.

Father Killed Saving 2 in Korea:

Baby Here to Get Medal of Honor

A Camden mother said today she wanted her 14-month-old son to receive the Congressional Medal of Honor which a grateful Government is awarding to her heroic husband, who gave his life in Korea to save his comrades.

The presentation of the nation's highest military honor to Hospital Corpsman Edward C. Benfold, who was killed on Sept. 5, 1952, five days after his arrival on the Korean front from the United States, will take place at 3 p. m. Thursday at ceremonies at the Philadelphia Naval Base.

The hero's widow, the former Dorothy Groff, of 224 N. 32nd st., and the son, Edward Joseph Benfold, who was born May 15, 1952, will receive the medal from Rear Adm. John H. Brown, commandant of the Fourth Naval District, acting for President Eisenhower and the members of Congress.

"I want the medal given to the baby," Mrs. Benfold said today. "I'm sure that's the way his father would have wanted it."

Relatives to Attend

Benfold's mother, Mrs. Gladys Benfold, of 2868 Constitution rd.; Mr. and Mrs. Clarence G. Groff, of 224 N. 32nd st., parents of the widow, and her brother, Joseph Groff, also will attend the ceremony.

Congressman Wolverton and other national, state and local officials have been invited to be present.

Corpsman Benfold, attached to the First Marine Division,

was killed while treating wounded in the front lines under heavy enemy fire—just about a month after bidding Mrs. Benfold and Edward Joseph, then only about 2½ months old, farewell at Camp Pendleton, Calif.

According to his widow, he was giving aid to two marines in a crater on the battlefront when the enemy tossed two grenades into the pit. At the same time, two enemy soldiers charged the position.

Picking up a grenade in each hand, Benfold leaped out of the crater and hurled himself against the two onrushing soldiers, pushing the grenades against their chests and holding the explosives there until they went off.

EDWARD C. BENFOLD

213

Camden Widow to Get Hero's Medal of Honor

The Congressional Medal of Honor, the highest military award of the United States, will be presented tomorrow to the young widow of Hospital Corpsman Edward C. Benfold, of Camden, who lost his life defending two marines in Korea.

E. C. BENFOLD

The presentation will be made at the Philadelphia Naval Base at 3 P. M. to Mrs. Dorothy Benfold, of 224 N. 32d st., Camden, and her 14-month-old son, Joseph, who was born four months before his father sacrificed his life on Sept. 5, 1952.

The ceremony will be marked by a full battalion review, which is expected to be witnessed by Gov. Alfred A. Driscoll of New Jersey, Sens. Robert C. Hendrickson and H. Alexander Smith, Rep. Charles A. Wolverton, Mayor George Brunner of Camden and high ranking Navy officers. The medal will be presented by Rear Adm. John H. Brown, Jr., commandant of the 4th Naval District.

Benfold was attached to a company of the First Marine Division when it bore the brunt of an artillery and mortar barrage and assault by a battalion of enemies on the night of Sept. 5.

LEFT PROTECTED AREA

While ministering to the wounded, his citation stated, he left the protection of a sheltered position for a platoon area which was attacked front and rear.

He saw two marines in a large crater on an exposed ridge line and moved forward to see if they needed his medical help. The attacking force lobbed two grenades into the crater and two of the enemy charged the position.

Benfold, the citation declared, grasped a grenade in each hand and leaped forward to meet the attackers. He thrust the grenades against their chests and held them there until they exploded. The two enemies were killed and Benfold was mortally wounded. The marines he had defended escaped fatal injuries.

AUDUBON SCHOOL GRADUATE

Benfold was born in Staten Island, N. Y., in 1931. He was graduated from the Audubon, N. J. High School. Edward S. Benfold, his father, was killed in the torpedoing of the merchant ship, Castilla, during the Second World War. His family received the posthumous award of the U. S. Merchant Marine Mariner's Medal.

In addition to his widow and son, Benfold is survived by his mother, Mrs. Gladys Benfold, of 2968 Constitution rd., Camden, the parents of his widow, Mr. and Mrs. Clarence G. Groff, and a brother-in-law, Joseph, all of the 32d st. address.

Sailor's Baby To Receive His Medal of Honor

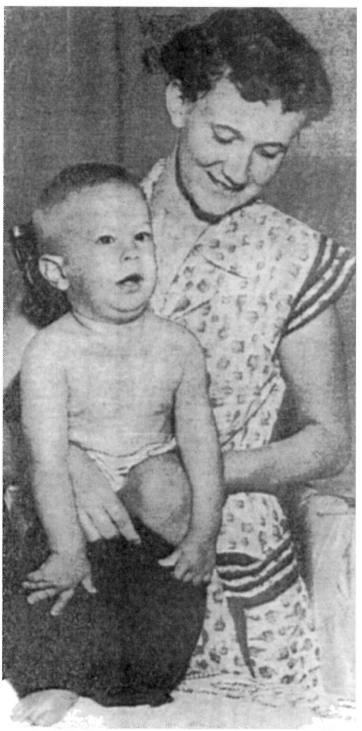

—Courier-Post Photo

CARRYING ON FOR HERO-FATHER, Edward Joseph Benfold, 14 months, climbs into his dress shorts today, guided by his mother, Mrs. Dorothy Benfold, of 224 N. 32nd st., as they prepare to leave for the Philadelphia Naval Base to receive the Congressional Medal of Honor, awarded posthumously to Edward's parent, Hospital Corpsman Edward Clyde Benfold, who sacrificed his life in Korea to save two comrades.

The star-speckled blue ribbon with the shiny medal on the end may seem like a bright plaything to 14-month old Edward Joseph Benfold this afternoon.

But to his mother, the former Dorothy Groff, of 224 N. 32nd st., the Congressional Medal of Honor is a symbol of a grateful nation's gratitude for the heroic action of her husband Hospital Corpsman Edward C. Benfold, who was killed in Korea on Sept. 5, 1952.

The nation's highest military honor will be presented to the sailor's son at 3 p. m. today by Rear Adm. John H. Brown, commander of the Fourth Naval District, at ceremonies at the Philadelphia Naval Base.

"I want the medal given to the baby," Mrs. Benfold said. "I'm sure that's the way his father would have wanted it."

Corpsman Benfold was killed while treating wounded of the First Marine Division in the front lines under heavy fire. He had been in Korea only five days when the action took place.

Benfold was aiding two wounded marines in a battlefront shellhole when the enemy tossed two grenades into the pit. Simultaneously two enemy soldiers charged the position.

Leaping out of the crater with a grenade in each hand, Benfold hurled himself against the two onrushing soldiers and pushed the grenades against their chests until the explosives fired.

Both the enemy soldiers were killed and Benfold was fatally wounded but the two marines in the crater were saved.

The Benfolds were married in St. Joseph's R. C. Church on June 9, 1951, after a five months courtship.

At the time of the wedding, Benfold, who had enlisted in the Navy in June, 1949, was stationed at the Philadelphia Naval Hospital. A native of Staten Island, N. Y., where he was born Jan. 15, 1931, Benfold also served at Camp LeJeune, N. C., and at Camp Pendleton before being ordered to Korea.

215

COURIER-POST, Camden, N. J., Friday, July 17, 1953

—Courier-Post Photo

'GREATER LOVE HATH NO MAN' than that displayed in Korea by Hospital Corpsman Edward Clyde Benfold of Camden, who died to save two comrades. This was asserted Thursday at the Philadelphia Naval Base where the fallen hero's son, Edward Joseph, 14 months old, shown in the arms of his mother, Mrs. Dorothy Benfold of 224 N. 32nd st., received the Congressional Medal of Honor. The award was given in the name of President Eisenhower and the Congress by Rear Adm. John H. Brown, right, commandant of the Fourth Naval District.

Daddy's Medal of Honor

Medal of Honor, awarded posthumously to Navy Corpsman Edward C. Benfold, of Camden, N. J., becomes the proud possession of his widow, Mrs. Dorothy C. Benfold, and their 14-month-old son, Edward, after a presentation ceremony at the Philadelphia Naval Base. Corpsman Benfold was killed in Korea while saving the lives of two wounded marines.

Medal of Honor Of Camden Hero Given to Son

Award for Valor In Korea Presented At Naval Base

By WALTER W. RUCH

The heroism of the Benfolds was accorded the nation's highest honor Thursday afternoon on the hushed and sunswept Marine barracks area of the Philadelphia Naval Base.

The Congressional Medal of Honor, reserved for only the greatest of the country's military heroes, was awarded posthumously to Hospital Corpsman Edward C. Benfold of Camden, who gave his life without hesitation in Korea to save two comrades.

As his father before him, young Benfold died in the service of his country, and just as he, as a child of 12, had received the Mariner's Medal in the name of his father in War II, so was the corpsman's son on hand Thursday to receive the Medal of Honor.

Proud Young Widow

Blond and handsome, 14-month-old Edward Joseph Benfold sat alert and unsmiling in the arms of his pretty mother, Mrs. Dorothy Benfold, of 224 N. 32d st., as the star-shaped medal of gold, suspended from a light blue ribbon, was placed about his neck by Rear Adm. John H. Brown, commandant of the Fourth Naval District.

Stars of pride glistened in the young widow's eyes as the full meaning of the honor was brought home to her by the marching battalion of marines and the words of Adm. Brown and the prayer of Capt. Roy E. Bishop, Navy chaplain.

Although, in accordance with regulations, the medal had first to be given to Mrs. Benfold, Adm. Brown, in keeping with her wish, then transferred it to the neck of the son, who was born in Camden on May 15, 1952.

Saved Two Comrades

That was less than four months before his father died in a display of gallantry and courage above and beyond the call of duty, on Sept. 5, 1952, to save two marines pinned down in a Korean shell crater.

Corpsman Benfold's act, Capt. Bishop said in his prayer, was the exemplification of what Jesus, according to St. John, meant when He said: "'Greater love hath no man than this, that a man lay down his life for his friends.'"

In the citation, read by Adm. Brown for President Eisenhower and in the name of the Congress, Benfold's heroic deed was summed up:

"Leaving the protection of his sheltered position to treat the wounded when the platoon area in which he was working was attacked from both the front and rear, he moved forward to an exposed ridge line where he observed two marines in a large crater.

Felled Enemy Attackers

"As he approached the two men to determine their condition, an enemy soldier threw two grenades into the crater, while two other enemy charged the position.

"Picking up a grenade in each hand, Benfold leaped out of the crater and hurled himself against the onrushing hostile soldiers, pushing the grenades against their chests and killing both the attackers.

"Mortally wounded while carrying out this heroic act, Benfold, by his great personal valor and resolute spirit of self-sacrifice in the face of almost certain death, was directly responsible for saving the lives of his two comrades."

In Korea Only Five Days

The ceremonies at the base took little more than a half-hour. Most of the officers were on hand with Adm. Brown to do honor to Corpsman Benfold, who was only 21 years old when he met his death, only five days after arriving in Korea.

Mrs. Benfold, wearing a straw hat, dress and shoes of the same dark blue shade, with the solid color broken only by white trim at the neckline and a white bow, was in the seat of honor, separated only by the aisle on the front row from the Admiral.

To her right sat Lt. Cmdr. Robert Rogers, her official escort. Then came Mrs. Glenys Benfold, of 2863 Constitution rd., mother of the fallen hero, holding little Edward; Clarence G. Groff and his wife, of 224 N. 32d st., parents of the widow, and Mr. and Mrs. Joseph Groff, brother and sister-in-law of Mrs. Benfold.

Review of Honor

Following the preliminary maneuvers by the battalion and the presentation of the colors, Capt. Bishop offered prayer and the admiral presented the medal. A review in honor of Corpsman Benfold followed before Mrs. Benfold was taken on an automobile tour of the entire base.

Adm. Brown pointed out that Benfold was only the fourth Navy recipient of the Medal of Honor since the start of the Korean action.

"There is little than can be said or done as recompense for the grief to his family and loved ones," Adm. Brown said. "But they may always cherish in their hearts the quiet pride which is only for those who have lost a dear one through acts so valiant and courageous.

Skilled Horseman

"May (this medal) serve to remind you always that your husband's name will be revered by his country as one of its most gallant men who gave his life in the cause of freedom."

Corpsman Benfold was born the son of Edward E. and Glenys M. Benfold at Staten Island, N. Y., Jan. 15, 1931. The first few years of his life he spent with relatives in Liverpool, Nova Scotia and London.

By the time he was five, he knew how to swim, ice skate, handle a canoe and a bobsled.

He was brought to Haddon Heights in 1937, where he became a skilled rider, winning several ribbons in horsemanship.

Father Lost at Sea

In June, 1942, his father, an officer in the Merchant Marine, was lost at sea when the SS Castilla was torpedoed. Edward received the Mariner's Medal and a letter of citation in honor of his father's bravery.

While in high school, he became interested in music and the amateur theatre, joining the choir and participating in school plays.

He enlisted in the Navy in June, 1949, and received his basic and hospital corpsman training at Great Lakes, Ill. Before leaving for Korea, he served in Rhode Island, the Philadelphia Naval Hospital, Camp LeJeune, N. C., and Camp Pendleton, Calif.

Albert J. Gifford, deputy director of the Camden County Department of Veterans' Affairs, represented Mayor Brunner at the ceremonies, attended also by Joseph Zucchi, director of the department, and representatives of veterans' organizations in Camden County and by many friends of the dead hero.

Congressman Wolverton and Senators Hendrickson and Smith were unable, because of press of affairs in Washington, to be present.

IN WORLD WAR I, MEN FOUGHT FOR THEIR IDEALS... THEY BELIEVED THEY WERE MAKING THE WORLD SAFE FOR DEMOCRACY AND WORLD WAR II SAW THE MARINES AND THE REST OF THE ARMED FORCES FIGHTING FORCES OF EVIL THEY KNEW AND RECOGNIZED: HITLER AND NAZIS NAZISM; TOJO AND TREACHERY...BUT THIS WAS KOREA IN THE YEAR 1952!

THEY BEEN PEACE-TALKIN' AT PANMUNJOM FOR A YEAR, BENFOLD! HOW COME WE KEEP FIGHTIN' WHILE THEY KEEP TALKIN'?

NOBODY CARES ABOUT KOREA! MY FOLKS WRITE ASKIN' ME WHAT'S DOIN' OVER HERE! THEY DON'T EVEN KNOW THERE'S A WAR ON! THIS PLACE AIN'T WORTH A FIST-FIGHT, LET ALONE A WAR!

I GUESS WE HAD TO COME HERE! WE TOLD THE COMMIES TO STAY PUT ON THEIR SIDE OF THE LINE BUT THEY WOULDN'T STAY...NOW, WE'RE GOING TO SHOVE THEM BACK! IF WE DON'T STOP 'EM SOMEWHERE, THEY'LL KEEP COMING ALL OVER THE WORLD!

YES, AT PANMUNJOM THEY WERE HAGGLING OVER THEIR TRUCE, QUIBBLING ON MINOR POINTS WHILE IN THE KOREAN MOUNTAINS HARSHER DECISIONS WERE REACHED...

MEDIC! MEDIC!

MEDIC! MEDIC!

CHARLTON COMICS GIVE YOU MORE!

THE FIRST MARINE DIVISION COMPANY BENFOLD WAS ATTACHED TO WAS UNDER HEAVY FIRE SEPT. 5, 1952/ AN ENEMY ARTILLERY AND MORTAR BARRAGE WAS FOLLOWED IN THE PREDAWN DARKNESS AN ENEMY ATTACK IN BATTALION STRENGTH...

BLAST IT, MEDIC, TAKE COVER!

GO CUSS OUT THE MARINES, SARGE, I GOT A JOB TO DO!

NO ONE COULD MAKE THE MEDIC TAKE COVER/ HE MOVED FREELY IN THE RAIN OF ENEMY STEEL, IGNORING THE DANGER TO HIS OWN LIFE...

I KNEW IT'D BE YOU WHO'D COME, BENFOLD/ DOESN'T ANYTHING EVER SCARE YOU?

ZING ZING

I'M SCARED HALF TO DEATH RIGHT NOW, FRIEND/ BUT BEING SCARED DOESN'T MEAN I CAN'T DO MY WORK/ BEING SCARED DOESN'T KEEP YOU MARINES FROM FIGHTING...AND I KNOW FOR A FACT SOME MARINES ARE SCARED MOST OF THE TIME/

YOU GOT HIM... LUCK FOR US BOTH!

KRAK

WHEN DAYLIGHT CAME, IT WAS EVEN WORSE FOR BENFOLD...THE ENEMY COULD SEE HIM NOW AND THE MEDICAL CORPS INSIGNIA MEANT NOTHING!

ZIP ZIP ZIP ZIP

CONTINUED AFTER FOLLOWING PAGE

THE COMMIES ATTACKED THE COMPANY'S POSITION FROM THE FRONT AND THE REAR! BENFOLD HAD WOUNDED TO TEND IN A SHELTERED POSITION...

STICK HERE WITH THEM, BENFOLD! DON'T STICK YOUR NECK OUT NOW... THEY'RE SHOOTING FROM BOTH DIRECTIONS!

VOOM

BUT THE NAVY CORPSMAN ADMINISTERED WHAT AID HE COULD TO THE WOUNDED NEARBY THEN HE WAS ON HIS WAY...

I'M NOT TOO BAD OFF, BENFOLD! LOWERY AND COMMACK ARE OUT THERE... BOTH OF THEM TOOK BAD HITS IN THE GUTS!

WHAM

TWO MARINES THERE... GOT TO TAKE A LOOK AT THEM!

WHAM

ZING ZING ZING

DIDN'T THINK ANYONE'D BE NUTS ENOUGH TO COME OUT HERE FOR US!

BE QUIET UNTIL I PATCH THAT HOLE, MACK!

BENFOLD, AS USUAL, CONCENTRATED COMPLETELY ON THE WORK AT HAND! IT WAS THE ONE WAY TO FIGHT OFF THE EVER-PRESENT FEAR...

WATCH IT, MEDIC! COMMIE GRENADES!

THE MEDIC TURNED...HE HAD BEEN TAUGHT TO SAVE THE MEN AND HIS BRAIN COOLLY WEIGHED THEIR CHANCES NOW/ BOTH MARINES WERE TOO BADLY WOUNDED TO MOVE...IF HE COULD RETRIEVE THE GRENADE AND THROW IT BACK...

HE TURNED...SAW THE OTHER GRENADE, HIS HEART KNOWING THE SMALL CHANCE THEY HAD NOW...HE LUNGED FOR THE SECOND ONE/

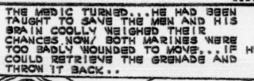

ANOTHER ONE MEDIC/ WATCH OUT/

WE HAD IT NOW, MEDIC/ WE'RE GONNA GIT IT ONE WAY OR THE OTHER/

BENFOLD KNEW EXACTLY WHAT THE CONSEQUENCES OF WHAT HE WAS ABOUT TO DO WOULD BE... HE CAME ERECT, THEN LEAPED AT THE ENEMY, A GRENADE IN EACH HAND/

NO, BENFOLD... THROW THE GRENADES/

HE...HE STOPPED THAT PAIR, ALL RIGHT/ POOR GUY/

KVOOM

THE TWO MARINES LIVED...EDWARD C. BENFOLD DIED THERE IN KOREA...IN A WAR THAT NO ONE REALLY WANTED VERY MUCH AT ALL!

END

1953:

(cont)   On Tuesday evening, July 21st, Dorothy made an appearance on the CBS TV program "Wheel of Fortune". According to the producers of the program, its purpose is that of paying tribute to those who have performed good or heroic deeds. Nominations for those who appear on the show normally come from citizens in the community, but in the case of Dorothy Benfold, the nomination came from the Navy PIO. Sgt. Close was chosen to sponsor Dorothy and he had to answer questions on the show. Dorothy won a total of $2300.00 and son Edward won a cocker spaniel, a supply of dog food and "enough toys to keep him busy for a year". The money was awarded in defense bonds and was accompanied by a 'secret desire' award which included a mahogany dining room set, a set of chinaware and a set of sterling silver. (See the news article about the appearance on page 225).

A week following the Medal of Honor ceremony, on Thursday, July 23rd, George E. Brunner, Mayor of Camden, New Jersey, issued a special resolution 'for valor', detailing the heroism of Edward C. Benfold. (See the resolution on page226).

On Wednesday, August 19th, Mayor George E. Brunner of Camden presented a framed copy of the resolution for valor (issued by his office on July 23rd) to Dorothy and 15-month old Edward J. Benfold. The presentation took place at City Hall in Camden. (See the photo published by the Philadelphia Inquirer on page 227).

On November 11th, Dorothy represented the Gold Star Wives at the Armistice Day ceremonies in City Hall Plaza, Camden. 18-month old Edward Joseph Benfold helped his mother place a wreath of remembrance on the War Memorial Marker. (See photo with caption on page 228).

Note: The name Armistice Day was changed by Congress to Veterans Day in 1954.

Lady Luck Smiles Double:

$2300 Won on TV Quiz by Widow Of Congressional Medal Hero

Other Prizes Awarded To Mrs. E. C. Benfold And Young Son

By GEORGE MAWHINNEY

Lady Luck emptied her brimming cornucopia Tuesday night into the hands of a Camden mother whose husband last week posthumously was awarded the Congressional Medal of Honor.

Summoned to New York, for the CBS Wheel of Fortune TV program, Mrs. Edward C. Benfold, of 224 N. 32d st., won $2300 in defense bonds, plus a "secret desire" award which included a mahogany dining room set, a set of chinaware, and a set of sterling silver.

Her 14-month-old son, Edward Joseph Benfold, who last Thursday received the medal in the name of his father at the Philadelphia Naval Base, will be sent a cocker spaniel, a supply of dog food, and enough toys to keep him busy for a year.

He remained at home in Camden while his mother appeared on the program, which was broadcast locally by WCAU-TV, but his mother carried his picture with her.

The Wheel of Fortune is a CBS sustaining program. Its purpose, as its producers explained, is to pay tribute to those who have performed good or heroic deeds.

In the case of Mrs. Benfold, the tribute was for her husband, a hospital corpsman, who gave his life in Korea to save the lives of two marines pinned down in a shellhole. Ordinarily, the rank and file of citizens make nominations for appearances on the program.

But the Navy PIO nominated Corpsman Benfold. And since the two men whose lives were saved were not available for the program—one is in Korea and the other in a West Coast hospital—the Navy assigned Sgt. Kenneth Klose, a Philadelphia-born marine who lives in Flushing, N. Y., to sponsor Mrs. Benfold.

Under the rules of the program, Sgt. Klose answered the questions which won Mrs. Benfold the prizes.

The Wheel of Fortune, which in appearance is much like a carnival wheel, was spun to designate the prize of $800 for the correct answers to four questions. But, in the spinning, it also hit the jackpot, and made possible the winning of an extra $1500 for the answer to a single additional riddle.

Answers Questions

The questions Sgt. Klose answered were:

A family in a fight against privation, caused by midwestern drought and dust storms, became characters in a book. What was the name of the book? (The answer is "Grapes of Wrath.")

In Gentlemen Prefer Blondes who co-stars with Marilyn Monroe? (The answer is Jane Russell.)

What is the name of the song used as a title for a film for Judy Garland? (The answer is "For Me and My Gal.")

What composer is called the

MRS. EDW. C. BENFOLD

Waltz King? (The answer is Johann Strauss.)

The riddle that won the jackpot was:

A statesman, a real man of
    might;
Almanac and others he did
    write;
A scientist as he grew older,
With discoveries to make us
    bolder.
His name in our jackpot you'll
    sight.
(The answer is Benjamin Franklin.)

The program ran from 8.30 to 9 p. m.

The "secret desire" awards were chosen by Mrs. Benfold from a roomful of prizes.

For Valor

Whereas, Hospital Corpsman Edward Clyde Benfold of the City of Camden, New Jersey, has made the supreme sacrifice while serving our country; and

Whereas, Hospital Corpsman Edward Clyde Benfold in the most gallant display of heroism and selflessness gave his life in order to save the lives of his comrades; and

Whereas, his heroism, self-sacrifice and personal valor over and beyond the call of duty has been signally recognized by awarding to him the Congressional Medal of Honor;

Now, Therefore, Be it Resolved by the Board of Commissioners of The City of Camden, New Jersey, that it hereby records and acknowledges its respect and honor of the late Edward Clyde Benfold;

And Be it Further Resolved that the City of Camden hereby expresses its sympathy and understanding to his widow and son in the loss that they have sustained and trusts that this spirit will be an ever source of comfort and pride to them; and

Be it Further Resolved that a certified copy of this resolution be forwarded to his family.

CITY OF CAMDEN

Dated: July 23, 1953.

George E Brunner
_____
MAYOR

_____
COMMISSIONER

Frank A. Abbott
_____
COMMISSIONER

William Dorshimer
_____
COMMISSIONER

_____
COMMISSIONER

226

Mayor George E. Brunner, of Camden, presents Mrs. Dorothy Benfold, of 224 N. 32d st., Camden, and her son, Edward J. Benfold, 3d, 15 months, with a copy of a resolution by the city honoring her late husband, Medical Corpsman 3d Class Edward J. Benfold, Jr., who received the Congressional Medal of Honor posthumously for heroic action in Korea. The Navy man's mother, Mrs. Glenys Benfold, is in center.

227

ARMED FORCES. At the Service of the Holy Communion this Wednes-
day the following names will be especially remembered
  Edgar H. Mullin. serving with the Navy
  John J. Breen, serving with the Navy. Great Lakes. Ill.
  Wallace McPherson, serving with the Army at Fort Benj.
                 Harrison. Indiana
  Also to be remembered - Edward Benfold who was killed in
     Korea in September, 1952. May he rest in peace.
We commend these names to the prayers of the Congregation.

A WREATH OF REMEMBRANCE is placed on the War Memorial marker in City
Hall Plaza by little Edward Benfold, 18-month-old son of Mrs. Dorothy Benfold,
representing the Gold Star Wives, at Armistice Day ceremonies today.

SPECIAL NOTE: Shortly after the Medal of Honor ceremony, Dorothy was presented a recording of the events that took place on July 16th by the members of the Camden Lions Club. (See the article and photo on this page).

Widow Is Present As Lions Give Hero Tribute

Mrs. Dorothy Benfold relived on Wednesday with members of the Camden Lions Club the stirring moments of July 16, when she received the Congressional Medal of Honor in the name of her hero husband, Hospital Corpsman Edward Clyde Benfold.

All of the moving events that occurred that afternoon at the Philadelphia Navy Yard, reduced to a single recording, were played back as they happened for the 100 club members as they paid tribute to Camden's fallen hero.

Benfold was killed in Korea on Sept. 5, 1952, when he went to the rescue of two trapped Marines. Seizing two grenades tossed toward them by advancing North Koreans, Benfold leaped at two enemy soldiers to hold a grenade against the chest of each as it exploded.

Mrs. Benfold, of 224 N. 32nd st., with her parents, Mr. and Mrs. Clarence Groff, sat at a table near the record player. Both women were moved repeatedly to tears as the more stirring words were repeated, particularly the reading of the citation by Rear Adm. John H. Brown, commandant of the yard, who made the presentation.

Only Edward Joseph Benfold, 14-month-old son of the medal recipient, was absent from the ceremonies held at Kenney's. But he was not forgotten. The club presented to Mrs. Benfold a pen-and-pencil set, to be held for him against the day he can use it in school.

Russell C. Heimert, president of the club, and Robert Harmer, program chairman, were in charge of the affair, climaxed by the presentation of the recording and a large basket of flowers to Mrs. Benfold and an orchid corsage to her mother.

The recording was made by the staff of radio station WKDN, whose president, L. N. Maxwell, a club member, arranged its preparation.

Hero's Widow Is Honored

Mrs. Dorothy A. Benfold, widow of Edward C. Benfold, winner of the Congressional Medal of Honor, was honored by the Camden Lions Club yesterday at a luncheon at Kenny's Restaurant, 521 Market st. Russell C. Heimert (left), president, and Robert H. Harmer, chairman of the program, present her with a record of the actual ceremony held at the Philadelphia Navy Yard when she received her husband's medal.

1954: On Friday, January 29th, Rear Admiral John H. Brown, Jr. retired as commandant of the Fourth Naval District. Rear Admiral Brown presented the Medal of Honor to Dorothy Benfold on July 16th, 1953. (See the photo and short article on the following page).

On Sunday, September 26th, at a special service at St. Mary's Episcopal Church in Haddon Heights, a new stained-glass window was dedicated to the memory of Edward C. Benfold. The right section of the Baptismal window contains his name and a replica of the Medal of Honor. (See articles, cover of the Service bulletin and the stained-glass window on pages 233, 234 and 235).

1961   -   1970

1963: Lyndon B. Johnson, the 36th President of the United States, took office on November 22, 1963, following the assassination of John F. Kennedy and served as the country's leader until 1969. President Johnson honored the memory of Edward C. Benfold by issuing a special certificate "in recognition of devoted and selfless consecration to the service of our country . . . ". (See the certificate, signed by President Johnson, on page 235).

1970: The US Naval School Command at Mare Island, California, requested permission from the family of Edward to name one of the two Bachelor Enlisted Quarters the "Benfold Hall". The Dedication Ceremonies took place on September 4th.

Several weeks prior to the dedication, an article appeared in one of the local newspapers which focused on the special stained-glass window at St. Mary's Episcopal Church in Haddon Heights. (See the photo and article on page 236 and the cover of the dedication Ceremonies' program on page 237).

Edward is honored in several locations across the country. His photograph, along with the citation issued from the office of President Eisenhower, can be seen at the Medal of Honor Corridor of the San Diego Naval Hospital and in the Medal of Honor Hall at the office of Medicine and Surgery in Washington, DC (see photo on page 238).

Note: As we did the research for this chapter, we found it Interesting that the citations that are on display with Medal of Honor recipients are NOT signed copies. The wording is also slightly different from the signed copy presented on page 206 (see page 239 for the unsigned citation that is displayed with the photo of Edward).

Adm. Brown Retires Today, Expects to Sit and Rock

Grid Hero Won Many Honors on Submarine Duty

By FREDERIC G. HYDE

The life of a Naval officer, as he moves up toward the goal of flag rank, is a long succession of successions. Giving up one command, taking over another —until the day comes when a Rear Admiral hauls down his two-star flag, and furls it for good instead of transferring it to another ship or installation.

As it has happened so many times before, that is happening again this morning at the Philadelphia Naval Base. But the tall, athletically built officer who steps aside then with the salutes to his successor booming in his ears, is one whose links with this city are of an especial and enduring kind.

Rear Adm. John H. Brown, Jr., who retires today as commandant of the Fourth Naval District and of the Philadelphia Naval Base, strolls the dockside there on a final tour of inspection. In background is the destroyer tender Yosemite.

231

COURIER-POST, Camden, N. J., Saturday, September 25, 1954

Life Hereabouts

By Jake Weiner

TRIBUTE TO A HERO: Two years ago in Korea a young hospital corpsman went to the rescue of two trapped marines. Seizing two grenades tossed toward the marines by advancing North Koreans he leaped at two enemy soldiers. And he held a grenade against the chest of each as they exploded.

The hospital corpsman, just turned 21, was killed.

That hero—who gave his life to aid his buddies—hailed from Camden. He was Edward Clyde Benfold, whose wife and son still live in East Camden.

For his heroism. Edward Clyde Benfold was posthumously awarded the Congressional Medal of Honor—reserved for only the greatest of our country's military heroes.

And Sunday at St. Mary's Episcopal Church in Haddon Heights, the Camden hero will be honored again. That's when the parish will dedicate a church window in his memory.

Among those who will participate in the solemn ceremony will be the mother who lost a son when Edward gave his life. His mother, Mrs. Benfold, of Fairview.

Church to Bless 40 Memorials

Forty new memorials will be blessed at a special service Sunday at 11 a. m. at St. Mary's Episcopal Church in Haddon Heights.

The memorials, given by members and friends of the parish. include pews for the nave, hymn boards, nave and vestibule lights. memorial windows, a new bulletin board, missal stand and prayer book for the children's altar and a children's altar in the children's chapel in the church basement.

At 10 a. m., the altar of the children's chapel will be dedicated. The Rev. Peter M. Sturtevant. rector, has invited all donors. their friends and families to attend.

Tribute To A Hero

(Courier-Post, **Camden, N. J.**)

Two years ago in Korea, a young hospital corpsman went to the rescue of two trapped marines. Seizing two grenades tossed toward the marines by advancing North Koreans he leaped at two enemy soldiers, and held a grenade against the chest of each as they exploded.

The hospital corpsman, just turned 21, was killed.

That hero—who gave his life to aid his buddies—hailed from Camden. He was Edward Clyde Benfold, whose wife and son still live in East Camden.

For is heroism, Edward Clyde Benfold was posthumously awarded the Congressional Medal of Honor—reserved for only the greatest of our country's military heroes.

And Sunday at St. Mary's Episcopal Church in Haddon Heights, the Canadian hero will be honored again. That's when the parish will dedicate a church window in his memory.

Among those who will participate in the solemn ceremony will be the mother who lost a son when Edward gave his life: His, mother, Mrs. Benfold, of Fairview, was formerly Glenys Adams of Liverpool, Nova Scotia.

(Edward (Teddy) was at one time a schoolboy in Liverpool).

A SPECIAL MEMORIAL SERVICE

AT

St. Mary's Episcopal Church

HADDON HEIGHTS, N. J.

Sunday, September 26, 1954

MEMORIAL WINDOWS

Mrs. Ernest W. Clark, Jr.

Young People's Fellowship

Ernest W. Clark, Jr.

Edward Benfold—killed in Korea—The Congressional Medal of Honor posthumously awarded.

233

234

The United States of America

honors the memory of

EDWARD C. BENFOLD

This certificate is awarded by a grateful nation in recognition of devoted and selfless consecration to the service of our country in the Armed Forces of the United States.

Lyndon B. Johnson

President of the United States

235

In Haddon Heights:

Unusual Church Window
Memorializes Dead Hero

In St. Mary's Episcopal Church in Haddon Heights there is a stained glass window that is a little different from the other windows which commemorate the memory of some former member of the church.

This window has a facsimile of the Congressional Medal of Honor in the lower right hand corner. The window is dedicated to the memory of Edward Clyde Benfold who was killed in Korea Sept. 5, 1952 when he was 21 years old.

Benford was a member of the Young People Fellowship of the church and it was this society which remembered him by placing a Baptismal Memorial window in the church.

He was attached to the First Marine Division and was awarded the Congressional Medal of Honor posthumously by Commander Brown at the Philadelphia Naval Shipyard. Later the Korean Government awarded him the Korean Medal of Honor. Now the U. S. N. .. Schools Command at Mare Island, Calif., has requested the permission of the family to name one of the two Bachelor Enlisted Quarters the "Benfold Hall" for which the family have given permission.

Benfold's Mother is Mrs. Glenys Benfold Flaherty, his widow, Mrs. Dorothy A. Waide lives in Camden and his son Edward J. Benfold will be 18 in June and has been accepted for entrance to the University of Miami this fall. Mrs. Glenys Benfold Flaherty lives in Cherry Hill.

GLASS MEDAL: A new addition to the St. Mary's Episcopal Church in Haddon Heights is this stained glass memorial window portraying the Medal of Honor awarded to Edward C. Benfold, who was killed during the Korean conflict.

236

DEDICATION CEREMONIES
4 September 1970

Benfold Hall

Freund Hall

Halford Hall

Thompson Hall

Truett Hall

The President of the United States in the name of The Congress takes pride in presenting the MEDAL OF HONOR posthumously to

HOSPITAL CORPSMAN THIRD CLASS
EDWARD C. BENFOLD
UNITED STATES NAVY

for service as set forth in the following

CITATION:

For conspicuous gallantry and intrepidity at the risk of his life above and beyond the call of duty while serving as a Hospital Corpsman attached to a company in the 1st Marine Division during operations against enemy aggressor forces in Korea on 5 September 1952. When his company was subjected to heavy artillery and mortar barrages, followed by a determined assault during the hours of darkness by an enemy force estimated at battalion strength, Petty Officer Benfold resolutely moved from position to position in the face of intense hostile fire, treating the wounded and lending words of encouragement. Leaving the protection of his sheltered position to treat the wounded when the platoon area in which he was working was attacked from both the front and rear, he moved forward to an exposed ridge line where he observed two Marines in a large crater. As he approached the two men to determine their condition, an enemy soldier threw two grenades into the crater while two other enemy charged the position. Picking up a grenade in each hand, Petty Officer Benfold leaped out of the crater and hurled himself against the onrushing hostile soldier, pushing the grenades against their chest and killing both the attackers. Mortally wounded while carrying out this heroic act, Petty Officer Benfold, by his great personal valor and resolute spirit of self-sacrifice in the face of almost certain death, was directly responsible for saving the lives of his two comrades. Petty Officer Benfold's exceptional courage, personal initiative, and selfless devotion to duty reflected great credit upon himself and were in keeping with the highest traditions of the United States Naval Service. He gallantly gave his life for others.

The photos on these final pages of this chapter reflect the pride that
the community of Audubon has in Medal of Honor recipient Edward C. Benfold

IN HONOR OF
THOSE WHO SERVED
OUR NATION

KOREA
JUNE 1950 — JAN. 1955
KILLED IN ACTION

• NELSON V. BRITTIN   EDWARD A. HELMES
WILLIAM J. CONNELLY, JR.   JAMES E. OPIE, JR.
• EDWARD BENFOLD
• CONGRESSIONAL MEDAL OF HONOR

VIETNAM
DEC. 1961 — MAY 1975
KILLED IN ACTION
GUY P. GUADAGNO

HEROES LIVE BEYOND THE TOMB...
DEDICATED MAY 28, 1994

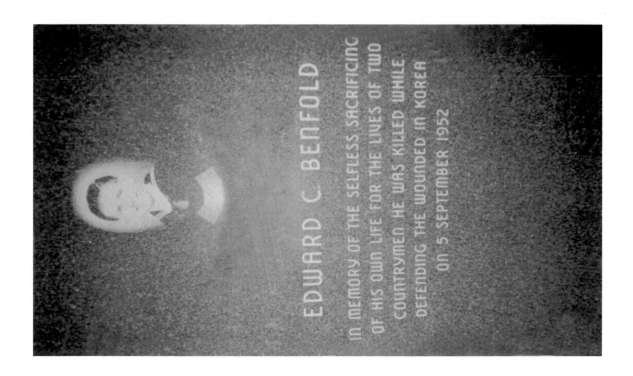

EDWARD C. BENFOLD

IN MEMORY OF THE SELFLESS SACRIFICING
OF HIS OWN LIFE FOR THE LIVES OF TWO
COUNTRYMEN HE WAS KILLED WHILE
DEFENDING THE WOUNDED IN KOREA
ON 5 SEPTEMBER 1952

THE KOREAN WAR VETERANS' MEMORIAL   WASHINGTON, C. C.

Chapter III
The History of the
USS BENFOLD (DDG-65)

ONWARD WITH VALOR

USS BENFOLD (DDG-65)

Official ship's painting by retired Aegis artist Vince Piecyc.

"The American's Creed"

I believe in the United States of America as a Government of the people, by the people, for the people; whose just powers are derived from the consent of the governed; a democracy in a republic; a sovereign Nation of many sovereign States; a perfect union, one and inseparable; established upon those principles of freedom, equality, justice, and humanity for which American patriots sacrificed their lives and fortunes.

I therefore believe it is my duty to my country to love it; to support its Constitution; to obey its laws; to respect its flag, and to defend it against all enemies.

William Tyler Page, circa 1917

Tribute To Benfold

I am the United States Ship BENFOLD
Because of my namesake, I carry a burden of a load.
Edward Benfold was born a common man - - -
Unknown to him, he would be a hero in his native land.

Today in Audubon, New Jersey, where he was raised,
They talk of him with respect, honor and praise.
He joined the Navy after high school, 1949 was the year:
He was known as a Hospital Corpsman who showed no fear.

He served with the First Marine Division during the Korean War:
He needed no reason for what he was fighting for.
He fought for freedom and a grateful nation.
For two Marines under attack, he was their salvation.

2 grenades were thrown into the crater where they lie:
With the grenades, he leaped toward the enemy so that his comrades would not die.
He received the Medal of Honor for sacrificing his life:
Back at home he left behind a child and a young wife.

Because of his heroics and his fame,
I sail the seas, protecting the free, bearing his name.
I stand for freedom, I live by a code:
ONWARD WITH VALOR, I'M THE USS BENFOLD.

With these stirring words by Petty Officer 1st Class Danny K. Edgar, we begin our journey into the history of the USS BENFOLD (DDG-65), a naval destroyer in the Pacific Fleet equipped with the Aegis Weapons System and carrying the name of Audubon hero and Medal of Honor recipient Edward C. Benfold. Construction of the ship began on Columbus Day, October 12, 1992, in Pascagoula, Mississippi. We proudly present an historical summary of major milestones and key events leading up to the ship's Commissioning on March 30, 1996 . . . .

Construction of BENFOLD

The story of BENFOLD begins on October 12, 1992 when Ingalls Shipbuilding began construction in Pascagoula, Mississippi. The ship's keel was laid on September 27, 1993. During the construction of DDG 65, hundreds of subassemblies were built and outfitted with piping sections, ventilation ducting, and other shipboard hardware. These subassemblies were joined to form dozens of assemblies, which were then joined to form three hull modules. They were then outfitted with larger equipment items, such as electrical panels, propulsion equipment, and generators. The ship's superstructure, or "deckhouse," was lifted atop the midbody module early in the assembly process, facilitating the early activation of DDG 65's electrical and electronic equipment.

The separately-constructed modules, each weighing thousands of tons, were joined together on land to form the completed ship hull. DDG 65 was then moved, as a completed ship, over land via Ingall's wheel-on-rail transfer system, and onto the shipyard's launch and recovery dry-dock.

On November 9, 1994, the dry-dock was ballasted down, and DDG 65 floated free. She was then moved to an Ingalls outfitting berth in preparation for her traditional christening ceremony on November 12, 1994.

Construction of BENFOLD

Outfitting of the ship continued through 1995 with the crew moving aboard and taking custody of the ship on December 4, 1995. BENFOLD sailed from Pascagoula, MS on February 28, 1996 en route to San Diego, California for her Commissioning and new homeport. The following is a list of major milestones and key events during BENFOLD's construction:

27 September 1993	Keel Laid
09 November 1994	Float Off
12 November 1994	Christening
04 April 1995	Generator Light Off
10 April 1995	Aegis Weapons System Light Off
27 June 1995	Main Engine Light Off
18 September 1995	Combined Alpha/Bravo Trials
17 October 1995	Navy Acceptance Trial
04 December 1995	Custody Transfer
30 March 1996	Commissioning

STEPPING THE MAST --- In a ceremony aboard BENFOLD, Commander Mark Ferguson, and Lieutenant Susan Fortney placed three pennies (two dated 1931 and 1952, representing the dates of the ship's namesake's birth and death, and one dated 1965, honoring the ship's hull number) along with a button from the Navy peacoat of HM3 Benfold provided by his family. These items will remain in the mast as long as DDG 65 sails.

The first key event in the history of the USS BENFOLD (DDG-65) took place in Pascagoula, Mississippi, at one of the Ingalls' outfitting berths, on November 12, 1994. On this date, the new DDG-65 was christened in a traditional naval ceremony. Members of the Benfold family who took part in the ceremony were: Mrs. Dorothy Waida, the ship's Sponsor and Widow of Edward C. Benfold; Mr. Edward J. Benfold, Edward's son; Miss Nicole and Miss Alexandra Benfold, daughters of Edward J. and Maids of Honor. (See the photographs below)

Pages 249 - 253 show information from the Christening book and two photos taken during the ceremony.

MRS. DOROTHY WAIDA

Mrs. Dorothy Waida
Ship's Sponsor, BENFOLD (DDG 65)

MR. EDWARD J. BENFOLD

Mr. Edward J. Benfold
Son of DDG 65's namesake

MISS NICOLE BENFOLD

Miss Nicole Benfold
Maid of Honor

MISS ALEXANDRA BENFOLD

Miss Alexandra Benfold
Maid of Honor

Christening

BENFOLD (DDG 65)
Aegis Guided Missile Destroyer
November 12, 1994

STEM TO STERN

BENFOLD (DDG 65) is the 15th ship in the ARLEIGH BURKE (DDG 51) Class of Aegis guided missile destroyers — the U.S. Navy's most powerful destroyer fleet. DDG 65 is the seventh Aegis destroyer to be launched and christened of 14 ships contracted or allocated to Ingalls Shipbuilding division of Litton Industries in Pascagoula, Mississippi.

Ingalls' first two Aegis destroyers, USS BARRY (DDG 52) and USS STOUT (DDG 55), were commissioned in December 1992 and August 1994, respectively. MITSCHER (DDG 57) has been delivered and is being prepared for commissioning in December. RUSSELL (DDG 59), RAMAGE (DDG 61) and STETHEM (DDG 63) precede DDG 65 in predelivery outfitting and testing at Ingalls.

Destroyers continue to be the workhorse of the Navy's surface fleet. The modern naval threat dictates that Aegis destroyers be prepared to conduct simultaneous operations in multi-threat environments that include air, surface and subsurface targets. Aegis destroyers are equipped and capable of conducting a variety of missions, from peacetime presence and crisis management to sea control and power projection, around the clock and around the world in support of the Nation's military strategy.

The 504-foot, 8,300-ton BENFOLD will operate with aircraft carriers and battle groups in high-threat environments and will also provide essential escort capabilities to Navy and Marine Corps amphibious forces, combat logistics ships and convoys. The ship will be operated by a crew of approximately 340 officers and crewmembers.

DDG 65's Aegis Combat System, the world's foremost naval weapons system, includes the AN/SPY ID phased array radar, which scans in all directions simultaneously to detect, track and engage hundreds of aircraft and missiles while continuously watching the sky for new targets from wavetop to the stratosphere. The ship is equipped with the MK 41 Vertical Launching System (VLS), which fires a combination of up to 90 Standard surface-to-air, Tomahawk surface-to-land and surface-to-surface and VLA antisubmarine missiles; and the AN/SQQ 89 Antisubmarine Warfare System, with a bow-mounted AN/SQS 53C sonar and AN/SQR 19 towed array.

BENFOLD will have deck-mounted Harpoon antiship missile launchers and MK 32 torpedo tubes, MK 15 Phalanx Close-In Weapon Systems and a five-inch, rapid-firing deck gun. DDG 65 also has the LAMPS MK III Control System, with helicopter landing and replenishment facilities.

Aegis destroyers match maximum survivability with potent offensive capability. Extensive topside armor is placed around vital combat systems and machinery spaces, and a new large-waterplane-area hull form significantly improves seakeeping ability.

Acoustic, infrared and radar signatures have been reduced, and vital shipboard systems are hardened against electromagnetic pulse and over-pressure damage. A comprehensive Collective Protection System guards against nuclear, chemical or biological agents. State-of-the art propulsion and damage control are managed by an all-new data m ing system.

Truly multimission surface ants, Aegis destroyers are the m anced surface warships ever built, ing the weapons, ics, helicopter supp ities, and propulsio iary and survivabi tems to carry out Nav sion and next

SHIPBUILDER'S LOG

Christening DDG 65 "BEN-FOLD" writes the newest chapter in the ship's history. Construction of the ship began on October 12, 1992, and DDG 65's keel was September 27, 1993.

[In]galls Shipbuilding builds Aegis [destroy]ers using modular techniques pio-[neered] by the shipyard in the 1970s, and [...] during two decades of assembly [...]nstruction of destroyers, cruisers [and am]phibious assault ships.

[Th]e ships also benefit from Ingalls' [ongo]ing efforts to integrate advanced [compu]ter technology into ship design [and co]nstruction. The design process for [ships] built at Ingalls is accomplished [with] a three-dimensional Computer-[Aided Design] (CAD) system, which is [linked] with an integrated Computer-[Aided Manufacturing] (CAM) produc-[tion] network of host-based computers [and lo]calized minicomputers throughout [the ship]yard.

[In]galls' system produces digital data [for] the CAM equipment to electroni-[cally d]irect the operation of numerically-[control]led manufacturing equipment cut-[ting ste]el plates, bending pipe and laying [out she]etmetal assemblies, and supporting [other m]anufacturing processes.

This technology significantly enhances design efficiency, and reduces the number of manual steps involved in converting design drawings to ship components, improving productivity and efficiency.

During the construction of DDG 65, hundreds of subassemblies were built and outfitted with piping sections, ventilation ducting and other shipboard hardware. These subassemblies were joined to form dozens of assemblies, which were then joined to form three hull modules, which were outfitted with larger equipment items, such as electrical panels, propulsion equipment and generators. The ship's superstructure, or "deckhouse," was lifted atop the midbody module early in the

assembly process, facilitating the early activation of DDG 65's electrical and electronics equipment.

The separately-constructed modules, each weighing thousands of tons, were joined together on land to form the completed ship hull. DDG 65 was then moved — as a completed ship — over land via Ingalls' wheel-on-rail transfer system, and onto the shipyard's launch and recovery drydock.

On November 9, 1994, the drydock was ballasted down, and DDG 65 floated free. She was then moved to an Ingalls outfitting berth in preparation for her traditional christening ceremony.

Upon completion of post launch outfitting, as well as dockside and at-sea testing and crew training, DDG 65 will be commissioned USS BENFOLD in early 1996, and will be assigned to the U.S. Pacific Fleet, homeported in San Diego, California.

BENFOLD...A SEAWORTHY NAME

DDG 65 is named in honor Hospitalman Third Class Edward Clyde Benfold, USN, who was posthumously awarded The Medal of Honor for extraordinary heroism during the Korean War.

Born January 15, 1931, Hospitalman Benfold enlisted in the U.S. Navy as a Hospital Recruit in June 1949. In July 1951, he was designated a Field Medical Technician, and assigned to Fleet Marine Force, Pacific. HM3/c Benfold was killed in action September 5, 1952, while serving with the First Marine Battalion in Korea.

His Medal of Honor citation reads "...When his Company was subjected to heavy artillery and mortar barrages, followed by a determined assault during the hours of darkness by an enemy force estimated at battalion strength, Benfold resolutely moved from position to position in the face of intense hostile fire, treating the wounded and lending words of encouragement. As he approached two Marines in a large crater on an exposed ridge line, an enemy soldier threw two grenades into the crater. Picking up a grenade in each hand, Benfold leaped out of the crater and hurled himself against the onrushing enemy soldiers — killing both of the attackers.

"Mortally wounded," the citation continues, "Benfold, by his great personal valor and resolute spirit of self-sacrifice in the face of almost certain death, was directly responsible for saving the lives of his two comrades. He gallantly gave his life for others."

The Order of the Day

MUSICAL HONORS   *To The Honorable Paul G. Kaminski*

PRESENTATION OF COLORS   *Pascagoula High School NJROTC Color Guard*

THE NATIONAL ANTHEM   *Pascagoula High School Band*

INVOCATION   *Commander Doug Palmer, CHC, USN*
Chaplain, Naval Station Pascagoula

WELCOME   *Mr. Jerry St. Pe´*

REMARKS   *Mr. Edward J. Benfold, son of DDG 65's namesake*

Captain Joseph A. Carnevale, USN

Rear Admiral Philip J. Coady Jr., USN

Rear Admiral George A. Huchting, USN

The Honorable Nora Slatkin

PRINCIPAL ADDRESS   *The Honorable Paul G. Kaminski*

CHRISTENING OF BENFOLD (DDG 65)
Mrs. Dorothy Waida, Sponsor
Miss Nicole Benfold, Maid of Honor
Miss Alexandra Benfold, Maid of Honor

Following the Christening ceremony, much work still needed to be completed before the ship was ready to make her way from Pascagoula to her home port in San Diego, California. It was more than a year before the outfitting was finished, trials were conducted and custody of the ship was transferred to the crew (on December 4, 1995).

During the trials, the USS BENFOLD performed magnificently and was a source of pride to all of the employees and craftsmen at Ingalls Shipbuilding. The photograph below shows Commander Mark E. Ferguson III presenting a plankowner plaque to Ingalls in thanks for its excellence in workmanship.

Ingalls featured the USS BENFOLD in its September 21, 1995 newsletter. This special article is shown on pages 255 - 256

Thank You

Craftsmen of Ingalls Shipbuilding

It All Starts With Me!

Ingalls News

Volume 25. Number 39

September 21, 1995

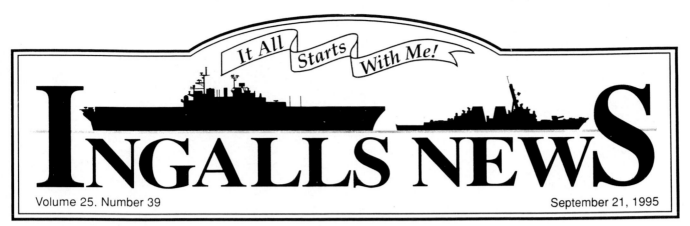

Benfold's performance *'magnificent... memorable'* for namesake's son

In its truest test to date, BENFOLD (DDG 65) successfully accomplished its missile firing exercise Tuesday -- scoring two direct hits -- during her Combined Alpha/Bravo (COAB) Trial, conducted in the Gulf of Mexico Monday through Wednesday.

Ed Benfold, son of Navy Hospitalman Third Class, and Medal of Honor winner, Edward Clyde Benfold, the ship's namesake, described DDG 65's performance as "magnificent. It's hard to put into words my impression of this sea trial, because nothing can describe my elation and wonder of this event," he said. "This is a great ship; and it's clear to me what makes this ship so great is the sense of team work and professionalism of Ingalls employees. They not only did their jobs well, but did

them with pride in serving their country. 'Thank you' to all the trial crew who made my stay aboard very memorable, and

BENFOLD at sea

a job 'well done' to a very friendly Ingalls team."

"DDG 65 was extremely clean and was well presented for her COAB Trial. The performance of the ship was exceptional and both missile shoots were

impressive. Equally impressive was the professionalism of the Ingalls/Navy trial team."

-- Rear Admiral George A. Huchting, USN
Aegis Program Manager

"BENFOLD's COAB trial was another tribute to the SupShip, Ingalls and ship's force team. Ingalls ran as smooth a trial as I've ever witnessed. The exceptional performance by DDG 65's crew during the two successful missile shots was noted with pleasure."

-- Captain Joseph A. Carnevale, USN
**Supervisor of Shipbuilding,
Conversion and Repair**

"These trials have once again proven that the Ingalls/SupShip team builds the finest warships in the world. It's an honor for my crew to sail in a ship that is ready now to fight and win -- anywhere, anytime. 'Well done' to General Ship Superintendent Tommy Johnson and the pros at Ingalls for building such an outstanding ship. Our perfect record on the missile exercise -- two missiles, two kills -- is a tribute to the exceptional professionals who con-duct these sea trials, including the Aegis Test Team, Ingalls employees and SupShip."

-- Commander Mark Ferguson. USN
**BENFOLD's Prospective
Commanding Officer**

"Once again. Ingalls employees have demonstrated their shipbuilding expertise, skills and talents as BENFOLD gave us an awesome display of power during COAB. Having Ed Benfold aboard ship during this sea trial made it an even more spectacular event honoring his father, because he exemplifies what this ship is about -- the American spirit. All our

(See BENFOLD...back)

255

Benfold...*from page one*

shipbuilders from every craft should be proud of this outstanding ship."

-- Jerry St. Pe'
Ingalls President

"DDG 65, Ingalls' seventh Aegis destroyer, performed exceptionally during her COAB Trial. Congratulations to all the men and women of Ingalls and the plank-owner crew, for achieving this important milestone in BENFOLD's history. It's another great Ingalls-built ship from 'America's Shipyard' -- on time and on budget."

-- Pat Keene
Operations/Engineering Vice President

"Ed Benfold's assessment is a fitting tribute to the combined Ingalls/Navy team that brought together thousands of separate components, equipment and people to fashion it all into this state-of-the-art ship. DDG 65 and others like her will serve our country well into the 21st Century as a protector of peace or, if necessary, a potent weapon well prepared to sail into harm's way."

-- Jess Brasher
Quality Assurance Vice President

"BENFOLD's COAB Trial was an overwhelming success. I never cease to be amazed that it takes three years to build an

Aegis destroyer, and yet on the first time away from the pier, the ship is put through as severe a propulsion, steering and habitability trial as it will ever see. And for the ship to fire its weapons systems flawlessly is indeed a credit to the thousands of men and women who build, test and support Ingalls-built Aegis ships."

-- Bat Robinso
Aegis Program Manag

Trial Charlie for DDG 65 is scheduled for next month, and commissioning is set for next March in San Diego, California.

Below is a photo of the crew of the USS BENFOLD,
taken in July of 1995 while the members were completing team training.

On pages 258 - 265, we present a photographic summary of the early days in the life of the USS BENFOLD (DDG-65). The first set of photos show her during construction, basking in the brilliance of the setting sun (that gives a golden aura to her hull) and aglow in the evening, radiating in the reflection of spotlights. Following are some dramatic photos of the ship in action, taken during testing and trials of the Aegis weapons system. Also shown is a practice drill at the helipad at the stern of the vessel. We begin the summary with the photo shown below.

The small white building hides the sonar dome Sonar is used to find submarines.

Notice the two large propellers. The blades can change their angle so the ship can go backwards.

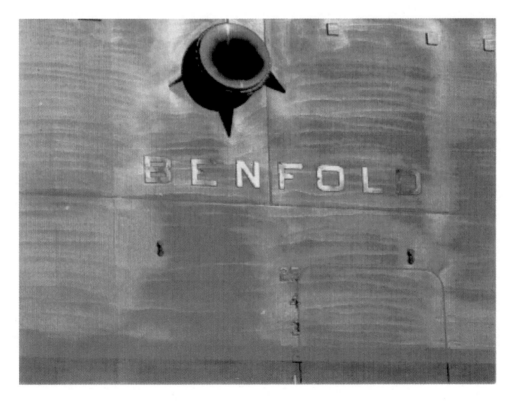

The stern (back). The round hole above the ship's name is for a sonar that is towed behind BENFOLD to locate submarines

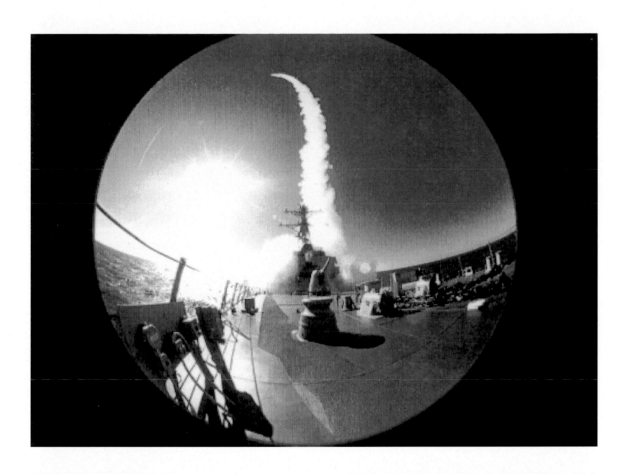

SHELL

High-speed photography catches a 5" shell leaving BENFOLD's gun,
possibly shooting a target over 10 miles away!

A destroyer is a lovely ship, probably the nicest fighting ship of all.

Battleships are a little like steel cities or great factories of destruction. Aircraft Carriers are floating flying shields. Even Cruisers are big pieces of machinery, but a Destroyer is all boat.

In the beautiful clean lines of her, in her speed and roughness, in curious gallantry, she is completely a ship, in the old sense.

- John Steinbeck

BENFOLD launches a standard missile used for shooting planes or other missiles.

A Sea King Helicopter prepares to land. The two rigid hull inflatable
boats (RHIBs) are ready to be used.

In late 1995, a mother of one of the sailors on board the USS BENFOLD composed a special poem for the new ship. The poem was included in the Commissioning Book and we take pride in presenting it here. The selection is a perfect way to salute the life of the ship during pre-commissioning trials.

"The USS BENFOLD"

See her glide into the water
Colors and numbers bold
Behold the might and splendor
Of the USS BENFOLD

With her maiden voyage before her
She sits primed and ready to go
As we ponder on her future
What adventures will she know

What missions will she make
Which war zones will she see
As she goes about the business
Of protecting the land of the free

Glistening in the sunlight
Spotlessly from stem to stern
How many heroes will she foster
Which medals will they earn

We may never see her again
The way she is today
But we want her taken care of
So in a prayer we say

God save the honorable captain
And all the illustrious crew
Make them superior and victorious
Over what they sail into

When they travel unfamiliar oceans
On starless and stormy nights
Keep the BENFOLD on her course
Til she returns to the light

Whether on native or foreign shores
Whether on waters warm or cold
Please look over this ship forever
God protect the USS BENFOLD

- Margaret H. Oliver, 1995
  Mother of a BENFOLD Sailor

The proud new member of the Navy's Pacific Fleet showed herself prepared for active duty and, on February 28, 1996, sailed from Pascagoula. Prior to her departure, the officers and crew received several congratulatory letters from high - ranking officials - - - including the President of the United States. We present these letters on pages 266 - 270.

A newsletter for families and friends of the crew of the USS BENFOLD is published three times a year in an effort to keep everyone up-to-date on events and activities. The newsletter, called *"Bold Defender"*, also contains articles on special ceremonies, awards presented to crew members and other pertinent information. In the January - March, 1996 issue, Commander Ferguson wrote a letter, thanking all those who helped make the Commissioning of the USS BENFOLD a reality. (See this letter on page 271.) Also included in this issue was an updated schedule of activities leading up to the Commissioning Ceremony on March 30, 1996. (See the schedule on this page.)

SHIP'S SCHEDULE

EVENT	DATE & TIME
Sailaway from Pascagoula, MS	28 February, 0900
Arrival Panama Canal Zone (Atlantic)	4 March, 0600
Departure Panama Canal Zone (Pacific)	5 March, 0900
Arrival San Diego, CA	16 March, 1330
Berthshift to Broadway Pier	25 March, TBD
Commissioning at Broadway Pier	30 March, 1100
Post-Commissioning Reception	30 March, Following Commissioning
Dependents Day Cruise (Depart Broadway Pier, Arrive NAVSTA)	1 April, TBD

THE WHITE HOUSE

WASHINGTON

November 28, 1995

        Greetings to all those gathered for the
commissioning of BENFOLD (DDG 65).

        This ceremony celebrates a great new symbol
of American excellence -- a ship that exemplifies
our nation's technological skill and creativity,
as well as our resolve to ensure that freedom
continues to flourish. BENFOLD will strengthen
and sustain the invaluable contributions the Navy
makes to America's leadership in global affairs.
Ready for any contingency, her combat power,
mobility, and flexibility will help to promote
the cause of liberty and protect our national
security. This fine ship stands as a noble
reminder of our steadfast commitment to maintaining a democratic world for the generations
to come.

        To all who will serve aboard BENFOLD, I wish
you every success in your mission as you stand
resolute in defense of freedom.

                    Bill Clinton

THE SECRETARY OF DEFENSE

WASHINGTON, THE DISTRICT OF COLUMBIA

2 5 OCT 1995

Commander Mark E. Ferguson III, USN
Prospective Commanding Officer
BENFOLD (DDG 65)
P.O. Box 7003
Pascagoula, MS 39568-7003

Dear Commander Ferguson:

Congratulations to you and your crew on the commissioning of
BENFOLD (DDG 65).

BENFOLD's commissioning is the culmination of a planning and
construction effort that combines American technology with talent
and innovation. She provides a significant increase in our joint
military capability.

Yet, she can only be effective with a skilled and highly-
trained crew. It is your challenge to develop the teamwork and
professional skills that will make full use of her capabilities
in achieving your mission. I know this is a challenge that the
crew of BENFOLD is dedicated to meeting.

I wish you and the crew of BENFOLD the greatest success on
your voyage toward excellence.

Sincerely,

William J. Perry

267

THE SECRETARY OF THE NAVY
WASHINGTON, D.C. 20350-1000

Commander Mark E. Ferguson, III, USN
Prospective Commanding Officer
BENFOLD (DDG 65)
P.O. Box 7003
Pascagoula, MS 39568-7003

Dear Commander Ferguson:

Congratulations on your new command and best wishes to you and your crew on the commissioning of BENFOLD (DDG 65).

BENFOLD, the newest guided missile destroyer in the Fleet, incorporates the latest technology and the most modern capabilities our nation can produce. I know that your professionalism and skill will establish a tradition of excellence which will be the standard for all who serve in this ship for years to come.

As you assume your place in the Fleet, those who serve in BENFOLD are charged with the heavy responsibility of making her an instrument of peace through strength. I wish you every success in meeting the challenges which lie ahead.

Sincerely,

John. H. Dalton

A MESSAGE TO THE OFFICERS AND CREW OF
BENFOLD (DDG 65)

I am pleased to extend my best wishes to the officers and crew of BENFOLD (DDG 65), our newest guided missile destroyer, on the occasion of her commissioning.

BENFOLD is a most impressive new addition to our Fleet. Like her sister ships of the ARLEIGH BURKE class, BENFOLD is entrusted with the mission of defending battle groups against threats in the air, on the surface and under the sea well into the 21st century. I expect those who sail her to live up to the spirit of commitment that has always been a hallmark of the American Sailor. While her technological capabilities make her a fine ship, BENFOLD's true strength comes from the dedicated officers, chiefs and sailors who proudly walk her decks.

As you assume an active role in the Fleet, you are charged with the responsibility of making BENFOLD a ready instrument of seapower in our nation's defense.

I wish you every success, fair winds and following seas as you bring BENFOLD into the Fleet.

J. M. BOORDA
Admiral, U.S. Navy

Commander in Chief
United States Pacific Fleet

13 November 1995

Dear Commander Ferguson,

On behalf of the men and women of the United States Pacific Fleet, I extend my sincerest congratulations on the commissioning of USS BENFOLD (DDG 65).

BENFOLD now assumes the important responsibility of living up to the same heroic and determined standards of excellence of its namesake, Hospitalman Third Class Edward C. Benfold, USN, who gallantly gave his life for others while serving in Korea. While embarking on the exciting journey ahead, you will be responsible for more than just the operational readiness of one of the Navy's most capable guided missile destroyers. You will also set the standard for future crewmembers who will serve onboard well into the 21st century.

I am confident you will answer well the demand for our Navy's presence throughout the Pacific region. As you carry out your duties as valued members of the world's most modern force, USS BENFOLD will serve as an important instrument in support of U.S. national security interests.

From everyone in the Pacific Fleet, welcome to the operating forces!

Sincerely,

R. J. ZLATOPER
Admiral, U.S. Navy

Commander Mark E. Ferguson, III, USN
Prospective Commanding Officer
PCU BENFOLD (DDG 65)
Pascagoula, MS 39568-7003

January - March 1996   Volume 2.1

BOLD DEFENDER

NEWSLETTER FOR THE FAMILIES AND FRIENDS OF
USS BENFOLD (DDG 65)

COMMISSIONING EDITION

ALMOST HOME...

FROM THE BRIDGE

As our time winds down here in Mississippi, we bid a fond farewell to our friends in the Magnolia State, and hello to our families and friends in our new homeport of San Diego, California. After move-aboard on 4 December, it has been a torrid pace of inspections, certifications, and training evolutions to prepare to join the world's finest Navy. It is no easy task to take 300 individual sailors, and mold them into a fighting team - but your BENFOLD Sailors have shown their drive to succeed at every opportunity. Keep charging!

CDR MARK E. FERGUSON III

I want to offer a special thanks to the people of Ingalls Shipbuilding who have built this fine ship - your spirit of excellence and dedication will be with us each day as we sail around the world in defense of this great country.

I also want to recognize members of the USS BENFOLD Commissioning Committee, specifically Chairman Mr. Morris Wax and LTGEN Jack Godfrey, USMC (Ret.). With their leadership, the people of San Diego are projected to raise over $70,000 to support the purchase of plankowner plaques for each crew member and the sponsorship of a reception for the crew and their families immediately following the commissioning ceremony. The Navy League of San Diego will also sponsor a homecoming party for the ship when it arrives at the Naval Station at 1330 on Saturday, 16 March.

On behalf of the entire crew - THANK YOU to all of you who have worked so hard to make our arrival and commissioning special events for the officers and crew of BENFOLD.

And lastly, thank you to all of our family members who have endured the long separations of pre-commissioning duty. We will be home soon - keep us in your prayers as we sail for San Diego.

DO YOU KNOW ANYONE WHO WANTS A PERSONAL COPY OF THE

BOLD DEFENDER?

If someone you know has read your Bold Defender and would like to start receiving their own copy, send their name and address to: Public Affairs Officer, USS BENFOLD (DDG 65), FPO AP 96661-1283

The ship arrived at her homeport in San Diego on Saturday, March 16, 1996, two weeks prior to the Commissioning Ceremony at the Broadway Pier.

The Commissioning Ceremony was attended by more than 4600 members of the U.S. Navy, families of the crew members and special guests. What a fine "Welcome Aboard" to a new ship in the Pacific Fleet. Following the ceremony, guests were taken on a tour of the vessel and had an opportunity to meet members of the crew. Pages 274 - 288 present highlights of the Commissioning, special proclamations presented by the County, and the city of San Diego, congratulatory letters from Ingalls Shipbuilding, and from the ship's sponsor, Mrs. Dorothy Waida and a letter of welcome from Commander Ferguson.

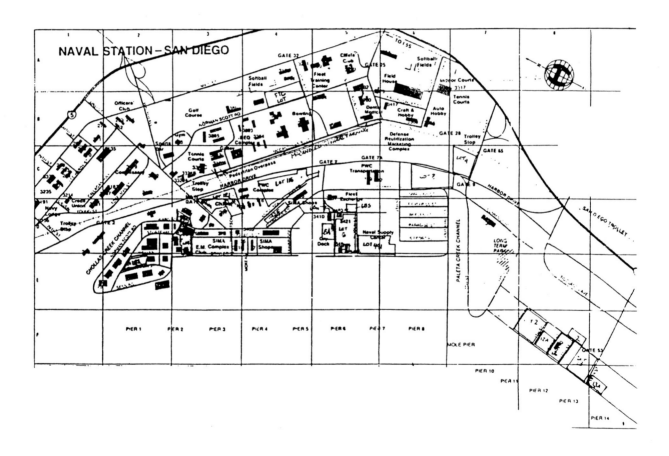

BENFOLD's new home: Naval Station, San Diego.

United States Ship
BENFOLD (DDG 65)
Commissioning Day

March 30, 1996
San Diego, California

Tradition of Commissioning a Warship

The breaking of the commissioning pennant marks the formal entrance of BENFOLD into the active service of the United States Navy whom she will so proudly serve. The commissioning pennant is a red, white, and blue streamer with seven stars representing the seven seas. As the distinctive mark of a ship in commission, the pennant is flown at all times except when displaced by the personal flag of an embarked officer or official.

The origin of the commissioning pennant stems from the first ships that sailed for our Navy. At that time the United States did not have a shipbuilding program; therefore, when in need of warships the Navy would contract merchant vessels. To distinguish between those ships which were or were not naval warships, naval vessels were authorized to fly a special pennant. Since that time, the commissioning pennant has been the unique mark of a warship.

Sign on and sail with me. The stature of our homeland is not more than the measure of ourselves. Our job is to keep her free. Our will is to keep the torch of freedom burning for all. To this solemn purpose we call the young, the brave, the strong and the free. Heed my call, come to the sea.

- John Paul Jones

274

Mrs. Dorothy Waida   Ship's Sponsor

The ship christening ceremony is a tradition whose origin can be traced back to when ships first put to sea. This custom still survives today and is practiced in some form by all seafaring nations. Until the 19th century, U.S. ships were christened by men. In 1846, Mrs. Lavina Watson Fanning became the first women to sponsor a United States warship as she christened the sloop GERMANTOWN in Philadelphia, PA. Since that occasion, the honor has always been bestowed upon a woman. Tradition holds that the spirit of the sponsor enters the ship at the christening and remains forever.

BENFOLD is honored to have Mrs. Dorothy Waida as her sponsor. She is the former wife of the ship's namesake, HM3 Edward Benfold, USN.

As the American flag waves proudly on the stern of the USS BENFOLD,
the ship's officers and special officials from the US Navy stand
at attention and salute the American Flag as the Color Guard marches by.

One of the key moments of the Commissioning Ceremony is the Setting of the First Watch. In this photo, Edward J. Benfold, son of the DDG-65's name-sake (l.) prepares to give the ceremonial spyglass to the officer who will be in charge of the first watch.

When the ship's sponsor gives the command to the crew to Man the Ship and bring her to life, crew members run along the pier and board the vessel.

Following the ceremony, those in attendance are invited to come aboard.
The special plaque shows photos of the Commander (CO), Executive Officer (XO), Command
Master Chief CMC and the six other top officers of the ship.

THE BOROUGH OF AUDUBON
YOUR SECOND HOMETOWN

Wednesday, June 16, 1999

To : The officers and crew members of the USS BENFOLD (DDG-65)

From : All the members of your second family in the Borough of Audubon, New Jersey

As you make your final preparations for deployment, please know that our thoughts and prayers will be with you during the coming six months. May fair winds and calm seas be with you.

We are sending you a special poetic 'farewell', composed by Robert Sweet, an 11-year old in town.....

FRIENDSHIP

The rainbow is nice, just like the star,
But no one can beat how nice you are.
The rainbow is far, as well as the star,
But you are the closest to our hearts.

No one will change that ...
Not even the cutest kitty cat.
We'll miss you when you are away,
But in our hearts you will stay.

Robert Sweet

Robert Sweet

ONWARD WITH VALOR ! We shall keep in touch by mail and by E-mail while you are away.

Craig E. Burgess

Mr. Craig E. Burgess
Liaison from Audubon
to the USS BENFOLD

County of San Diego California

PROCLAMATION

CELEBRATING THE CHRISTENING OF
THE USS BENFOLD

WHEREAS, the USS Benfold is the 15th ship in the United States Navy's most powerful destroyer fleet; and

WHEREAS, named after Hospitalman Third Class Edward Clyde Benfold, USN; this ship represents the great personal valor and self sacrifice demonstrated by Mr. Benfold during the Korean War when he saved the lives of two fellow servicemen; and

WHEREAS, this 504-foot, 8,300-ton work of art is an excellent addition to the Aegis Class, offering the latest technology and finest materials; and

WHEREAS, carrying its crew of 340, the USS Benfold will operate with aircraft carriers and battle groups in high-threat environments, providing essential escort service to Navy and Marine Corps amphibious forces, combat logistics ships and convoys; and

WHEREAS, the USS Benfold will support the nation's military strategy around the world, throughout peace time and in crisis situations; and

WHEREAS, on March 30, 1996, the USS Benfold's Commanding Officer Mark E. Ferguson III will be joined by military officials, relatives of Mr. Benfold, friends, and community members who have gathered to celebrate the christening of this fine ship; NOW THEREFORE,

BE IT PROCLAIMED by Chairman Ron Roberts and all members of the San Diego County Board of Supervisors on this 29th day of March 1996, that they congratulate the United States Navy, Commander Ferguson and the fine USS Benfold crew on the christening of the USS Benfold and join in the two-day celebration by officially declaring March 29-30, 1996 to be USS BENFOLD DAYS throughout San Diego County.

Gregory R. Cox
Supervisor 1st District

Supervisor 2nd District

Pamela Slater
Supervisor 3rd District

Supervisor 4th District

Supervisor 5th District

The City of San Diego

Proclamation

USS BENFOLD

WHEREAS, the Aegis Destroyer USS Benfold (DDG 65) was launched and christened in November, 1994, at the Ingalls Shipbuilding Division of Litton Industries in Pascagoula, Mississippi; and

WHEREAS, the USS Benfold, and her sister ships in the Arleigh Burke (DDG 51) Class of Aegis guided missile destroyers, benefit from the pioneering modular techniques and integration of computer technology into ship design and construction developed by Ingalls; and

WHEREAS, the USS Benfold is named in honor of Hospitalman Third Class Edward Clyde Benfold, United States Navy, who, while serving with the First Marine Battalion in Korea on September 5, 1952, gallantly gave his own life to save the lives of two of his comrades; and

WHEREAS, Hospitalman Benfold was posthumously awarded the Congressional Medal of Honor for his selfless act; and

WHEREAS, the USS Benfold will be commissioned with appropriate ceremonies in the City of San Diego on Saturday, March 30, 1996, and will commence active service; and

WHEREAS, San Diego is proud to be the home port for the USS Benfold; and

WHEREAS, Commander Mark E. Ferguson, III, United States Navy, will serve as the first Commanding Officer of the USS Benfold;

NOW, THEREFORE, I, SUSAN GOLDING, the Thirty-second Mayor of the City of San Diego, do hereby proclaim March 30, 1996, to be **"USS BENFOLD DAY"** in San Diego, and commend all those involved in the construction and operation of this magnificent vessel.

IN WITNESS WHEREOF, I HAVE HEREUNTO SET MY HAND, THIS DAY, AND HAVE CAUSED THE SEAL TO BE AFFIXED HERETO:

SUSAN GOLDING
MAYOR

March 30, 1996

DATE

Proclamation

WHEREAS, guided missile destroyers are a special class of fighting ships which have modernized and strengthened our surface Navy to cope with potential threats through the year 2010; and

WHEREAS, the USS BENFOLD (DDG 65), a guided missile destroyer, will be commissioned on March 30, 1996 and join the Pacific Fleet; and

WHEREAS, the ship's namesake, Hospitalman Third Class Edward Clyde Benfold, from Audubon, New Jersey, was posthumously awarded the Congressional Medal of Honor during the Korean War, "for gallantry and intrepidity at the risk of his life above and beyond the call of duty while serving as a Hospital Corpsman, attached to a Company in the First Marine Division during operations against enemy aggressor forces in Korea on 5 September 1952..."; and

WHEREAS, New Jersey defense firms played a major role in the construction of the ship, which makes the USS BENFOLD the finest, most modern warship in the world; and

WHEREAS, it is important and appropriate that the citizens of the State of New Jersey recognize and commend the crew of the USS BENFOLD, who represent a special and dedicated group of sailors, for their supreme devotion to duty;

NOW, THEREFORE, I, CHRISTINE TODD WHITMAN, Governor of the State of New Jersey, do hereby proclaim

MARCH 30, 1996

as

USS BENFOLD DAY

in New Jersey.

GIVEN, under my hand and the Great Seal of the State of New Jersey, this twentieth day of March in the year of Our Lord one thousand nine hundred and ninety-six and of the Independence of the United States, the two hundred and nineteenth.

GOVERNOR

BY THE GOVERNOR:

LONNA R. HOOKS, SECRETARY OF STATE

Litton

Ingalls Shipbuilding

P.O. Box 149
Pascagoula, Mississippi
39568-0149

601-935-3643

Jerry St. Pe'
President

March 30, 1996

Commander Mark E. Ferguson III, USN
Commanding Officer
USS BENFOLD (DDG 65)

Dear Commander Ferguson:

On behalf of my fellow employees of Ingalls Shipbuilding,
I congratulate you and your fine crew on the occasion of
the commissioning of the U.S. Navy's seventh Ingalls-built
Aegis guided missile destroyer, USS BENFOLD (DDG 65).

Our work force of highly skilled, patriotic shipbuilders
is proud of its team efforts in transforming individual
pieces of steel and other raw materials into a formidable
surface combatant -- one of America's very best. We are
equally proud to have worked alongside you, your officers
and sailors as we prepared DDG 65 for Fleet duty.

We congratulate you and your commissioning Plankowners for
being selected for this prestigious and historic
assignment. Best wishes for calm seas as you sail the
world's oceans in service to our Navy, our Nation and the
free world.

Bravo Zulu!

Sincerely,

Jerry St. Pe'
Senior Vice President, Litton Industries
President, Ingalls Shipbuilding

COMMANDER DESTROYER SQUADRON TWENTY-ONE
UNIT 25072
FPO AP 96601-4720

30 March 1996

Commanding Officer and Crew of USS BENFOLD (DDG 65)

It is with great pleasure I extend my congratulations on the commissioning of USS BENFOLD, the newest addition to America's force from the sea.

The commissioning ceremony marks the point at which the ship comes to life. A warship takes on the personality of her Commanding Officer and crew, and this is already evident from the strong spirit and dedication exhibited by you and your crew. Keep this spirit strong and pass it on to those who will follow. By doing this, the memory of Hospitalman Third Class Edward C. Benfold could receive no higher tribute.

I, and the Rampant Lions of Destroyer Squadron TWENTY ONE, welcome you to the Pacific Fleet. I look forward to working with you at sea for a long time to come.

Sincerely

C. I. Lundquist
Captain   USN

Commander Mark E. Furguson III, U. S. Navy
Prospective Commanding Officer
PCU BENFOLD (DDG 65)
Pascagoula, MS 39568-7003

SUPERVISOR OF SHIPBUILDING
PASCAGOULA, MISSISSIPPI 39568-7003

30 March 1996

Dear Commander Ferguson,

On this occasion of the commissioning of BENFOLD (DDG 65), I offer my personal congratulations along with those of the men and women of SUPSHIP Pascagoula.

USS BENFOLD is truly a magnificent warship. She is equipped with the most sophisticated weapons and survivability systems ever developed. Her name memorializes the service of a modern day hero, Hospitalman Third Class Edward C. Benfold, USN. The strength, courage, and perseverance of Petty Officer Benfold is what America is all about. His firmness of purpose, unwavering loyalty to country and bravery in facing extreme difficulty and danger without fear exemplifies the ships motto, "ONWARD WITH VALOR."

Your selection as the first Commanding Officer of BENFOLD is a great honor and privilege of which you should be quite proud. I am confident you and the crew of BENFOLD will meet every challenge that lies ahead with the same gallantry and intrepidity of the ship's namesake.

On behalf of the men and women of SUPSHIP Pascagoula, I wish you and your crew good luck and Godspeed.

Sincerely,

J. A. CARNEVALE
Captain, U.S. Navy

Commander Mark E. Ferguson III, U.S. Navy
Prospective Commanding Officer
PCU Benfold (DDG 65)
Pascagoula, MS 39568-7003

Dorothy A. Waida

30 March 1996

Dear Commander Ferguson,

On behalf of myself and the Benfold Family, I extend congratulations and best wishes to the officers and sailors of the USS BENFOLD as you commission this ship into naval service.

We are all proud of this ship which will most certainly be one of the Navy's state of the art tools in the years to come. But I am also proud of the fine crew you have assembled. I am confident that this ship and crew will be able to serve our country well in the years to come.

I know that Edward must be looking on with great pride at this ship. I hope that in times of need his spirit may be with you and the crew. Most of all I pray that God will be with you and all the Benfold crew in the years to come.

Sincerely,

Dorothy A Waida

Mrs. Dorothy A. Waida

Commander Mark E. Ferguson III, U.S. Navy
Prospective Commanding Officer
PCU Benfold (DDG 65)
Pascagoula, MS 39568-7003

Dear Families and Friends,

Thank you for joining us for this historic event. Today the Benfold name returns to the Navy in defense of America, this time as a commissioned warship.

This commissioning of the fifteenth destroyer of the Arleigh Burke class again demonstrates America's commitment to the preservation of freedom, equality, and justice throughout the world. We are grateful to the thousands of our fellow citizens in government and industry whose genius and craftsmanship have created this mighty ship.

We also thank those who knew and loved Hospitalman Third Class Edward Clyde Benfold, USN. Their efforts on our behalf and presence here today are an inspiration to all of us. Our wonderful sponsor, Mrs. Dorothy Waida, the Benfold family, the veterans of the Second Battalion, First Marine Division, and his fellow Navy Corpsmen may rightly take pride in this ship named for one of their own. We will always strive to be worthy of the Benfold legacy of courage and devotion to duty.

Today is also a day to recognize the true hero of our Navy, the American Sailor. USS BENFOLD is particularly blessed. No captain ever led a finer crew, and I ask you to join me in saluting each of our men and women for their dedication and patriotism in bringing this ship to life. Their pride and spirit will truly make BENFOLD a ship to remember.

To our families, we thank you for your encouragement and steadfast support as we worked to ready our ship for sea. We could not have done it without you.

USS BENFOLD is ready to join the Fleet and do our country's work. Thank your for sharing this special day with us.

Onward With Valor,

M. E. FERGUSON III
Commander, U.S. Navy
Commanding Officer

A SPECTACULAR SPLASH -- Mrs. Dorothy Waida breaks a bottle of champagne across the bow of a new U.S. Navy Aegis guided missile destroyer, naming the ship "BENFOLD" (DDG 65) in honor of Hospitalman Third Class Edward Clyde Benfold, USN, who was posthumously awarded The Medal of Honor for extraordinary heroism during the Korean War. Mrs. Waida, of Audubon, New Jersey, is Hospitalman Benfold's widow. More than 700 guests attended the November 12, 1994, christening ceremony at Ingalls Shipbuilding division of Litton Industries in Pascagoula, Mississippi. Mrs. Waida is assisted by A. C. Weeks, Ingalls' Director of Public Relations.

USS Benfold reports for U.S. Pacific Fleet duty

Ingalls Shipbuilding's seventh Aegis guided missile destroyer

The San Diego
Union-Tribune.

Special Edition   March 30, 1996   *Special Edition*

At San Diego's Broadway Pier

Aegis destroyer USS Benfold, Pacific Fleet's newest, commissioned this morning

DDG 65, the seventh DDG 51 Class Aegis guided missile destroyer to be built for the U.S. Navy by Ingalls Shipbuilding division of Litton Industries in Pascagoula, Mississippi, was commissioned USS BENFOLD, and reported for Pacific Fleet duty during ceremonies this morning at Broadway Pier in downtown San Diego.

Vice Admiral Philip M. Quast, USN, Commander, Military Sealift Command, delivered the ceremony's principal address. Vice Admiral David B. Robinson, USN, Commander, Naval Surface Force, U.S. Pacific Fleet, placed the new ship in commission. Mrs. Dorothy Waida, widow of the ship's namesake and Ship's Sponsor for the new destroyer, gave the traditional order to "Man our ship and bring her to life." Edward J. Benfold, son of the ship's namesake, also participated in the commissioning ceremony.

Commander Mark Ferguson III, USN,

USS BENFOLD JOINS THE FLEET -- USS BENFOLD (DDG 65), the seventh U.S. Navy Aegis guided missile destroyer to be built by Ingalls Shipbuilding division of Litton Industries in Pascagoula, Mississippi, sailed from the shipyard on February 28, 1996, and was commissioned this morning at Broadway Pier in downtown San Diego. Assigned to the U.S. Pacific Fleet and homeported here in San Diego, DDG 65 is named to honor the life and service of Hospitalman Third Class Edward Clyde Benfold, USN, who was posthumously awarded The Medal of Honor for extraordinary heroism during the Korean War.

assumed command of the new ship, which will be homeported here in San Diego. Lieutenant Commander Sinclair Harris, USN, is Commissioning Executive Officer. ENCM(SW) Robert Scheeler, USN, is Commissioning Command Master Chief.

Other ceremony participants included Vice Admiral Conrad C. Lautenbacher Jr., Commander, Third Fleet; Rear Admiral George A. Huchting, USN, Aegis Program Manager, Office of the Assistant Secretary of the Navy; Rear Admiral Rodney P. Rempt, USN, Director of Theater Air Defense, Office of the Chief of Naval Operations; Rear Admiral Wayne E. Meyer, USN (Ret.), Father of Aegis; Captain Carl I. Lundquist, USN, Commander, Cruiser/Destroyer Group 21; Captain David J. Vogel, USN, Deputy Supervisor of Shipbuilding, Conversion and Repair, Pascagoula; Jerry St. Pe', Senior Vice President of Litton Industries and President of Ingalls Shipbuilding; and Commissioning Committee Co-Chairmen Morris Wax and Lieutenant General Jack Godfrey, USMC (Ret.).

The U.S. Navy's Aegis program, of which

USS BENFOLD is the newest ship, is one of the most important shipbuilding programs in America today. Aegis ships are designed to provide primary protection for the Navy's battle forces. Aegis destroyers are 505 feet long, with a beam of 66 feet. Four gas turbine engines power the 8,600-ton ships to speeds in excess of 30 knots.

DDG 65's Aegis Combat System, the world's foremost naval weapons system, includes the AN/SPY-1D phased array radar; the MK 41 Vertical Launching System (VLS), which fires a combination of up to 90 Standard surface-to-air, Tomahawk surface-to-land and VLA antisubmarine rockets; and the AN/SQQ-89 Antisubmarine Warfare System, with a bow-mounted AN/SQS-53C sonar and AN/SQR-19 towed array. USS BENFOLD has Harpoon antiship missile launchers and MK 32 torpedo tubes, both mounted on the ship's deck, as well as two MK 15 Phalanx Close-In Weapon Systems and a five-inch, rapid-firing deck gun. DDG 65 also features the LAMPS MK III Antisubmarine Warfare Control System, with landing and replenishment facilities for the SH-60B antisubmarine

warfare helicopter.

Aegis destroyers have been designed to match maximum survivability with potent offensive capability. In the Aegis destroyer program, the Navy returns to all-steel construction, and extensive topside armor is placed around vital combat systems and machinery spaces. Acoustic, infrared and radar signatures have been reduced, and a comprehensive Collective Protection System guards against nuclear, chemical or biological agents.

Ingalls brings to the destroyer program a wealth of experience in the Aegis program. As lead shipbuilder for the Navy's first Aegis shipbuilding program, the TICONDEROGA (CG 47) Class of Aegis guided missile cruisers, Ingalls built and delivered into Fleet service 19 of the 27 ships in the cruiser program. Lead shipbuilder for five of the newest classes of Navy surface combatants, Ingalls, the premier shipyard for naval surface combatants ships, has delivered 71 major surface warships into the U.S. Navy's Fleet since 1975 — more than any other shipyard.

Commander Ferguson assumes command of U.S. Navy's newest Aegis destroyer

Commander Mark Ferguson III was born in Newfoundland, Canada. Raised in Maryland, he is a distinguished graduate of the United States Naval Academy, where he earned a Bachelor of Science degree in Systems Engineering. Upon graduation, he received the National Society of the Sons of the American Revolution awards for the highest standing in weapons systems studies and required military courses.

Following graduation, Commander Ferguson completed naval nuclear propulsion training. His sea assignments have been to both the Atlantic and Pacific fleets, with tours on the nuclear-powered guided missile cruiser USS SOUTH CAROLINA (CGN 37), the aircraft carrier USS DWIGHT D. EISENHOWER (CVN 69), and the destroyer USS FIFE (DD 991). His operational deployments included participation in Operations Desert Shield and Desert Storm.

Ashore, he has served in the Bureau of Naval Personnel as the Surface Nuclear Assignment Officer (PERS-412N) and as the Assistant Surface Captain Assignment Officer (PERS-41A). His most recent assignment was to the Secretary of the Navy's Office of Legislative Affairs, where

he was responsible for providing liaison to the House and Senate Armed Services Committees for all surface warfare, sealift, and shipbuilding programs.

In 1984, Commander Ferguson graduated with distinction from the Naval Postgraduate School, earning a Master of Science degree in Computer Science. He is also a graduate of the United States Air Force Command and Staff College.

His decorations include the Meritorious Service Medal, the Navy Commendation Medal, the Navy Achievement Medal, and various unit awards and campaign ribbons.

Commander Ferguson is married to the former Laure' Elizabeth Durbin of McLean, Virginia. They have two children, Andrew and Elaine.

Commander Mark Ferguson III, USN
Commanding Officer
USS BENFOLD (DDG 65)

Benfold...A seaworthy name

DDG 65 is the 15th destroyer in the DDG 51 Class, and the seventh to be delivered by Ingalls, of 14 ships under contract. Fabrication work for the ship began in October 1992, and DDG 65's keel was laid in September 1993. Following launch on November 9, 1994, DDG 65 sailed into the Gulf of Mexico for her first sea trials on September 19, 1995, and was delivered to the U.S. Navy by Ingalls on December 4, 1995.

DDG 65 is named to honor the life and service of Hospitalman Third Class Edward Clyde Benfold, USN, who was posthumously awarded the Medal of Honor for extraordinary heroism during the Korean War. Born January 15, 1931, Hospitalman Benfold enlisted in the U.S. Navy as a Hospital Recruit in June 1949. In July 1951, he was designated a Field Medical Technician, and assigned to Fleet Marine Force, Pacific. HM3/C Benfold was killed in action September 5, 1952, while serving with the First Marine Battalion in Korea.

His Medal of Honor citation reads "...When his Company was subjected to heavy artillery and mortar barrages, followed by a determined assault during the hours of darkness by an enemy force estimated at battalion strength, Benfold resolutely moved from position to position in the face of intense hostile fire, treating the wounded and lending words of encouragement. As he approached two Marines in a large crater on an exposed ridge line, an enemy soldier threw two grenades into the crater. Picking up a grenade in each hand, Benfold leaped out of the crater and hurled himself against the onrushing enemy soldiers -- killing both of the attackers:

"Mortally wounded," the citation continues, "Benfold, by his great personal valor and resolute spirit of self-sacrifice in the face of almost certain death, was directly responsible for saving the lives of his two comrades. He gallantly gave his life for others."

Co-author Burgess was one of the individuals invited to the Commissioning Ceremony. For him, the ceremony was a memorable occasion. He served as liaison from Audubon and extended greetings to the officers from the ship's second hometown.

A copy of the official invitation to the Commissioning is shown on this page, followed by a map of the Broadway Pier area of San Diego (p. 291) and two photos taken of Burgess at the ceremony (p. 292).

The Commanding Officer,
Officers and Crew
request the honor of your presence
at the commissioning of
UNITED STATES SHIP BENFOLD *(DDG 65)*
at Broadway Pier
San Diego, California
on Saturday, the thirtieth of March
nineteen hundred and ninety-six
at eleven o'clock.

RSVP

Participants:	*Full Dress Blue*
Military:	*Service Dress Blue*
Civilian:	*Informal*

GETTING AROUND SAN DIEGO

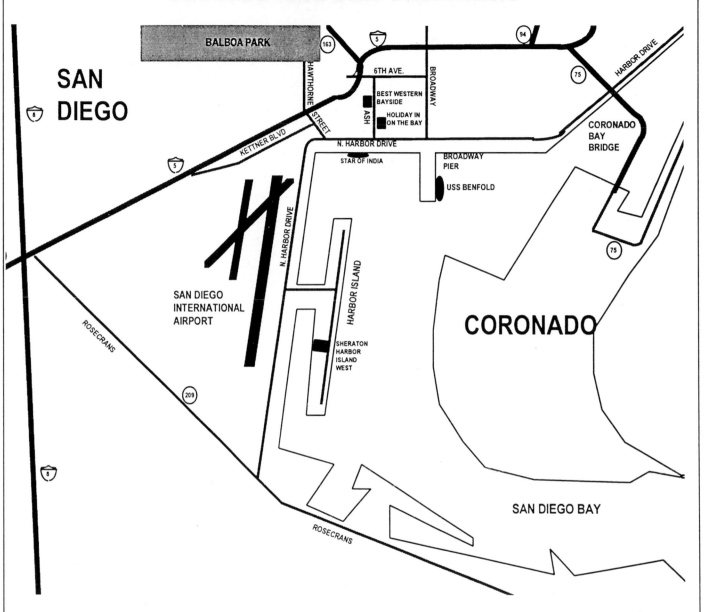

Southbound on I-5, take the airport exit, follow Kettner Avenue until Hawthorne Street, turn right, take Hawthorne to North Harbor Drive, turn left. Pass the China Clipper Star of India, the America's Cup Museum, and the cruise ship terminal (B Street Pier) on the right. The pier following B Street Pier is Broadway Pier, the site of BENFOLD's commissioning.

Heading north on I-5, take the 6th Avenue exit, stay in the left lane on the off-ramp. Follow 6th Avenue into Downtown San Diego to Broadway, turn right. Follow Broadway to North Harbor Drive. In front of you will be Broadway Pier. Parking will cost $3.00, and will be in the Naval Supply Center Parking Lot SE of Broadway Pier.

292

Following the Commissioning Ceremony, the USS BENFOLD spent more than sixteen months preparing for her first deployment, under the capable leadership of Commander Mark E. Ferguson, III and his two top officers: Lieutenant Commander Sinclair M. Harris, the Executive Officer and ENCM (SW) Robert J. Scheeler, Jr., the Command Master Chief. (See close-ups on the careers of these three officers on pages 290 - 292.)

On July 20th and 21st, 1996, the USS BENFOLD (DG-65) was the guest ship at the San Diego Naval Station and was open to the public for tours. (See the photo and caption on this page.) It was a proud day in the post-commissioning life of the ship.

Open house aboard *USS Benfold*

Navy Compass / **JO1 Sheri Crowe**

USS Benfold (DDG 65) is this weekend's guest ship at Naval Station. The ship will be open to visiting public from 1 to 4 p.m. tomorrow and Sunday, and is moored at Pier 7. An *Arleigh Burke*-class guided-missile destroyer, *Benfold* is among the newest and most technologically advanced ships in the Navy's inventory. It was the the first Aegis guided-missile destroyer to be designed from the keel up to accommodate the needs of a mixed-gender crew. The ship was commissioned at the Broadway Pier earlier this year.

Commanding Officer

Commander Mark E. Ferguson III

Commander Ferguson was born in New-foundland, Canada. Raised in Maryland, he is a distinguished graduate of the United States Naval Academy, where he earned a Bachelor of Science degree in Systems Engineering. Upon graduating, he received the National Society of the Sons of the American Revolution awards for the highest standing in weapons systems studies and professional military courses.

Following graduation, Commander Ferguson completed naval nuclear propulsion training. His sea assignments have been to both the Atlantic and Pacific fleets, with tours on the nuclear-powered guided missile cruiser USS SOUTH CAROLINA (CGN 37), the aircraft carrier USS DWIGHT D. EISENHOWER (CVN 69), and the destroyer USS FIFE (DD 991). His operational deployments included participation in Operations Desert Shield and Desert Storm.

Ashore, Commander Ferguson has served in the Bureau of Naval Personnel as the Surface Nuclear Assignment Officer (PERS-412N) and as the Assistant Surface Captain Assignment Officer (PERS-41A). His most recent assignment was to the Secretary of the Navy's Office of Legislative Affairs, where he was responsible for providing liaison to the House and Senate Armed Services Committee for all surface warfare, sealift, and shipbuilding programs.

In 1984, Commander Ferguson graduated with distinction from the Naval Postgraduate School, earning a Master of Science degree in Computer Science. He is also a graduate of the United States Air Force Command and Staff College.

His decorations include the Meritorious Service Medal, the Navy Commendation Medal, the Navy Achievement Medal, and various unit awards and campaign ribbons.

Commander Ferguson is married to the former Laure' Elizabeth Durbin of McLean, Virginia. They have two children, Andrew and Ellie.

Executive Officer

LCDR Sinclair M. Harris

A native of Washington D.C., Lieutenant Commander Harris graduated from James Madison University in May 1981, earning a Bachelor of Science degree in Economics. He was selected for Officer Candidate School and commissioned in June 1982.

His sea assignments include tours in the nuclear-powered guided missile cruiser USS LONG BEACH (CGN 9), commissioning crew of the guided missile cruiser USS VINCENNES (CG 49), guided missile frigate USS JARRETT (FFG 33), and Commander Third Fleet Flagship USS CORONADO (AGF 11).

LCDR Harris has received Master of Science degrees from the Naval Postgraduate School in Operations Analysis, and from India's Defense Services Staff College in Defense and Strategic Studies.

His decorations include the Navy Commendation Medal (with a Gold Star), Navy Achievement Medal, Combat Action Ribbon, and various unit awards and campaign ribbons.

Lieutenant Commander Harris is married to the former Cora Ann Griffiths of Washington, D.C.

The world needs more people:
- Who don't borrow from integrity to pay for expediency.
- Who are honest in small matters as in large.
- Whose ambitions are big enough to include others.

In short, the world needs more leaders.

295

ENCM (SW) Robert J. Scheeler Jr.

Master Chief Scheeler is a native of Casper, Wyoming. After graduation from Kelly Walsh High School, he enlisted in the U.S. Navy. He completed Recruit Training in Orlando, Florida and Engineman Class A School at the Naval Training Center, Great Lakes, Illinois.

His sea tours include assignments on USS JOHN RODGERS (DD 983) and USS LAKE CHAMPLAIN (CG 57).

He has served ashore at the Naval Ocean Systems Center San Diego, California, Naval Air Station Sigonella, Italy, Recruiting District Boston, Massachusetts, and Navy Management Systems Support Office Detachment Pacific.

Master Chief Scheeler's personal awards include the Navy Commendation Medal, Navy Achievement Medal (with a Gold Star), and Good Conduct Medal (five awards).

He is married to the former Cheryl D'Amore from Revere, Massachusetts. They have one daughter, Chelsea.

Special Note:

There is a certain amount of friendly competition seen between 'sister ships' in the Naval Fleet. Such is the case with the USS BENFOLD and the USS STETHEM (DDG-63).

The article shown on page 294 reflects something else that these sister ships have in common: efforts to work together on peaceful projects in our world. Operation Project Handclasp, carried out in Mazatlan, Mexico in 1997, is one example of this aspect of Navy life.

The two sister ships, sailing side by side, were photographed by the Navy Department for Ingalls Shipbuilding in 1996 and we have been given permission to present this photo to illustrate the article.

In the September-December 1996 issue of the "Bold Defender", Commander Ferguson provided an update on some of the early successes of the ship. Also, he thanked those who provide ongoing support for the crew members. One of the individuals mentioned was Mrs. Donna Tyson, the President of the Spouse Support Group (SSG). She and the members of the SSG published a monthly newsletter during 1996 and 1997 and helped organize special events for the crew members and their families. The update from Commander Ferguson is presented on page 299; several pages from the March, 1997 issue of "The Support Group Scoop" are presented on pages 300-301. The article on "Deployment" was the first in a series of 'helpful hints' for family members designed to help them cope with the six-month separation from a loved one.

On March 30, 1997, the officers and crew celebrated the ship's first birthday. Following Naval tradition, the birthday cake was cut with a sword by the oldest and youngest members of the crew. (See the photos on page 302).

In the special note above we presented information showing how the US Navy reaches out to the community in peacetime projects. Another example of how the officers and crew of the USS BENFOLD became involved in the community is reflected in the photos on page 303. On April 14, 1997, a special ceremony was held on the campus of the Hazel Goes Cook Elementary School. The USS BENFOLD became a "partner in Education" with the student body of the school. Among crew members present for the ceremony were (from right to left in the center photo) Commander Ferguson, Command Master Chief Scheeler and the ship's 1996 "Sailor of the Year", STG1 Alfred R. Salamanca. (Seaman Salamanca represented the USS BENFOLD at the 4th of July celebration in Audubon, NJ in 1997.)

BENFOLD AND STETHEM LEND A HAND IN OPERATION HANDCLASP

Mazatlan, Mexico -- Warm sun, palm trees, surf and Mardi Gras. For the majority of the 600 Sailors in USS BENFOLD (DDG 65) and USS STETHEM (DDG 63), a recent port visit to Mazatlan, Mexico meant only that. But for the fourteen Sailors of STETHEM who joined with BENFOLD Sailors and pitched in to help with Operation Handclasp, the weekend also meant a reaching out to the less fortunate in the less popular areas of the city.

The volunteer teams were led by LCDR Sinclair Harris, BENFOLD's Executive Officer, and the Sailors attended to the needs of several orphanages across the city of Mazatlan including the Salvation Army home for children. The work performed included painting the children's dormitories and buildings, fabricating a replacement basketball backboard, clearing dry brush from a nearby hillside, strengthening a swing foundation, and performing minor electrical repairs within the home. Not bad for a day's work. The highlight of the day for the Sailors was playing with the children of the orphanage.

"I had fun with the children and felt like we did something to help them out," said SN Gaylen Frazier of Yakima, WA. "I would love to do it again. Seeing the smiling faces on the children was pretty fun."

Another volunteer who agreed was EW1 (SW) Victor Rivera of Oxnard, CA, STETHEM's event coordinator. "Volunteer work involves a little time and effort, but often pays off with big smiles and warm thank yous. I was very excited about the enthusiasm and support for the Project Handclasp event."

The BENFOLD and STETHEM Sailors found more to the resort town of Mexico than the typical sun and fun. They built a special trust and friendship with the people of Mazatlan.

September - December 1996　　　　　　　　**Volume 2.3**

BOLD DEFENDER

NEWSLETTER FOR THE FAMILIES AND FRIENDS OF
USS BENFOLD (DDG 65)

FALL EDITION

FROM THE BRIDGE

CDR MARK E. FERGUSON III

Greetings from San Diego! It has been quite a summer and fall for your BENFOLD Sailors. The ship has successfully completed nearly all of the training exercises and inspections in preparation for its first deployment. Along the way, the Supply Department earned our first departmental excellence award (the Blue "E"). We also qualified our Combat Systems watch teams in Cruise Missile employment, surface-to-air missile firings, and undersea warfare. Simultaneously, we also successfully completed our Engineering Certification, Financial Audit and several other important inspections. No other crew in the Navy could have done as well in accomplishing these tasks in such a short period of time. It was also our pleasure to have Secretary of Defense, Dr. William Perry for a visit. As he told me, "meeting this crew once again reinforces my faith in the future of the Navy."

None of our accomplishments over this intense period could have been done if not for the support of you, our families and friends. All of you have made a special contribution to the nation by allowing our officers and sailors to meet their country's military obligations. I especially want to commend our Ombudsman, Mrs. Kathy Priolo, and the President of the Spouse Support Group (SSG), Mrs. Donna Tyson. Both of them have done an outstanding job in maintaining liaison between the command and our families. Recently, I was fortunate enough to attend the SSG Children's Halloween Party. It was a terrific event. The children had a superb, fun afternoon, and our families had an opportunity to meet and share experiences. If you would like to participate in the activities of the SSG or would like to know more, please contact Donna Tyson at (619) 222-8575. This group is the single group supporting BENFOLD families, and is comprised of both officer and enlisted spouses.

As you can see from our upcoming schedule, we will have quite a bit of work to do in the new year. Fortunately, our underway tempo will not be at the same pace as the past six months. In addition, we have several visits planned to ports on the west coast of the United States and Mexico.

I look forward to seeing many of you at the Command's Christmas Party (December 5th) at the Doubletree Hotel. May God bless you and your families during this holiday season and in the new year.

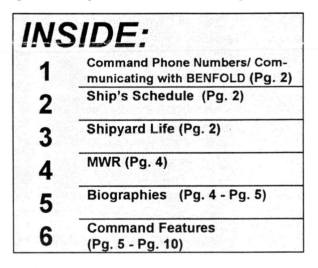

INSIDE:

BOLD DEFENDER is an authorized publication of USS BENFOLD (DDG 65), and is printed in accordance with Navy Publication and Printing Regulations (P-35). It is intended for the information, welfare, and entertainment of the crew, families and friends of USS BENFOLD. Views and opinions are not necessarily those of the Department of the Navy. Send any correspondence and contributions of articles, photos, or artwork to: Public Affairs Officer, USS BENFOLD (DDG 65), FPO AP 96661-1283. If you would like a personal copy of the BOLD DEFENDER sent to your home, send us your address and a short note stating your desire to receive a personal copy of the BOLD DEFENDER

SUPPORT GROUP SCOOP

MARCH, 1997   VOLUME 2, ISSUE 2

FROM THE PRESIDENT'S DESK

With March comes Spring, a time of new beginnings. A new Board of Officers for the Support Group means a fresh start with new ideas and faces. The Support Group elections will take place on April 10. It's not too late to enter the election. If you are interested in a position on the Executive Board, please give me a call. Please look for your ballot in the April issue of Support Group Scoop.

I would like to say "THANK YOU" from the entire Support Group and extend a fond farewell along with our best wishes to LCDR Sinclair Harris and his wife Cora. Good luck in your new position. You will be missed. I would like to take this opportunity to welcome LCDR Jeffrey Harley and his wife Cindy. LCDR Harley is the new Executive Officer for the USS Benfold.

At this time I want to personally invite and encourage all of you to attend our Family Gathering at Gator Beach (Coronado) on March 15, 1997 (for details, read enclosed flyer). This should be a great day for all of us to get together in the sun and sand, play volleyball, swim, basketball or whatever. Hope you can all make it, the day promises to be full of frolic and fun.

Hope to see you there!!
Donna Tyson

SUPPORT GROUP SCOOP is an authorized publication of USS BENFOLD (DDG 65), and is printed in accordance with Navy Publications (P-35). It is intended for the information, welfare, and entertainment of the crew, families and friends of the USS BENFOLD. Views and opinions are not necessarily those of the Department of the Navy. Send any correspondence and contributions of articles, photos, and or artwork to: Benfold Support Group, President, USS BENFOLD (DDG 65), FPO AP 96661-1283. If you would like a personal copy of the SUPPORT GROUP SCOOP sent to your home, send us your address and a short note stating your desire to receive a personal copy of the SUPPORT GROUP SCOOP.

HAPPY BIRTHDAY WISHES!

3-2	FC[1] Robert Connery
3-3	Kathy Priolo
3-10	Michelle Anthony
3-15	Kristina Priolo (10)
3-24	Jonathan Connery (6)
3-29	YN Steve Anthony

ANNIVERSARY WISHES!!!

3-5	MR[2]Chris & Debra Gates (4)
3-13	FCCS Michael & Sylvia Schanche (15)
3-16	HT[1] Bob & Stephanie Zambrana (5)
3-28	SKC Ed & Brenda Regec (10)

300

DEPLOYMENT

In upcoming issues of Support Group Scoop, we will have a "Deployment" section that will deal with different aspects of deployment. **Why is it important to learn about deployment?** Because deployment is a very stressful event! By learning about it and staying **prepared** for it, you can help make it less stressful and a more positive experience.

What is deployment? It is the assignment of military personnel to temporary, unaccompanied tours of duty.

For military families, deployment involves: Separation, when the service member departs on a tour of duty, leaving other family members behind.

Deployment is a FACT of military life. Our nation's military works around the world — and around the clock — to keep us safe and strong. Some military jobs must be performed in remote locations or under conditions that make deployment an absolute necessity.

DID YOU KNOW?

That 190 million gallons used oil are improperly disposed of each year? That only 10% of used motor oil gets recycled? That there are almost 60 certified centers recycling used oil in the San Diego area? That you can get cash for your used oil?

California has initiated a $.04 per quart fee on purchases of motor oil. The State authorizes certified centers to refund this $.04 fee when you bring your used oil or offer a coupon. For more information, call the USED OIL INFOLINE at 235-2105.

TAXES

STG³ George is the Benfold's resident tax "EXPERT." You may contact STG³ George directly for additional information or to prepare your tax return.

The next key event in the ship's history took place on Friday, June 20, 1997: a Change of Command Ceremony. The first Captain of the vessel, Commander Mark E. Ferguson, III, turned over command of the USS BENFOLD to Commander D. Michael Abrashoff in a formal ceremony held on board. Following the ceremony, the two Captains cut the Change of Command cake with a sword. Later, a red carpet was rolled out and an honor guard saluted Commander Ferguson and his family as they departed the vessel.

The following pages include the Change of Command program, a photo summary of the ceremony, an official invitation and parking permit for the ceremony.

A new period in the life of the ship now was beginning, under the leadership of Commander Abrashoff, his Executive Officer, Lieutenant Commander Jeffrey A. Harley and Command Master Chief Scheeler, who remained in his position. Photographs and career profiles of the new CO and XO are presented on pages 316-317.

The Commanding Officer
USS BENFOLD (DDG 65)
requests the pleasure of your company at the
Change of Command Ceremony at which
Commander Mark E. Ferguson III, United States Navy
will be relieved by
Commander D. Michael Abrashoff, United States Navy
on Friday, the twentieth of June
at ten o'clock
on board USS BENFOLD (DDG 65)
Pier Two, United States Naval Station
San Diego, California

R.S.V.P.
Card Enclosed
(619) 556-3826

Uniform: Summer White
Civilian: Informal

DISPLAY ON DRIVER'S SIDE OF DASHBOARD

OFFICIAL GUEST

CHANGE OF COMMAND CEREMONY

Commander Ferguson
will be assigned as a
Federal Executive Fellow
Harvard University

UNITED STATES SHIP BENFOLD (DDG 65)

FRIDAY, 20 JUNE 1997

PIER TWO, NAVAL STATION
SAN DIEGO, CALIFORNIA

USS BENFOLD (DDG 65)
COMMAND EMPLOYMENT
01 DECEMBER 1994 TO 20 JUNE 1997

01 Dec 1994	Established Precommissioning Detachment
04 Dec 1995	Custody Transfer, Ingalls Shipbuilding
04 Dec 1995	Post Delivery Availability
16 Dec 1995	First Christening onboard
16-26 Jan 1996	Tomahawk/Harpoon Material Certification
31 Jan-01 Feb 1996	Aviation Assist Readiness Exam
21-23 Feb 1996	Light-Off Assessment
27 Feb 1996	Departed Pascagoula, MS
04 Mar 1996	Panama Canal Transit
11-12 Mar 1996	Port Visit, Puerta Vallarta, Mexico
16 Mar 1996	Arrived San Diego, CA
30 Mar 1996	Commissioning
01 Apr 1996	Dependents Cruise
22-26 Apr 1996	Command Assessment of Readiness and Training
13-17 May 1996	Anti-Air Warfare Firing Exercise
03-07 June 1996	Logistics & Adminstrative Training Review
19-23 June 1996	Port Visit, Lahaina, Hawaii
06-09 Jul 1996	Missile Exercise
22 Jul-02 Aug 1996	Industrial Hygiene Survey
19-21 Aug 1996	Final Contract Trials
19 Sep 1996	Engineering Certification
30 Sep-16 Dec 1996	Post Shakedown Availability
30 Sep-24 Oct 1996	Drydock Southwest Marine
04-08 Nov 1996	Combat Systems Light-Off
02-06 Dec 1996	Crew Move Aboard
12-13 Dec 1996	Sea Trials
28-30 Jan 1997	Industrial Hygiene Survey
07-09 Feb 1997	Port Visit, Mazatlan, Mexico
13-15 Feb 1997	Joint Task Force Exercise
04-13 Mar 1997	HUNTER WARRIOR/Fleet Battle Experiment Alpha
18-20 Mar 1997	Torpedo Exercises
08-10 Apr 1997	Final Evaluation Problem
16-18 Apr 1997	Naval Surface Fire Support Exercise
28 Apr-09 May 1997	Combat Systems Readiness Review
28 Apr-02 May 1997	Aviation Assist Visit
13-16 May 1997	COMPUTEX
18-21 May 1997	Port Visit, Cabo San Lucas, Mexico
27-28 May 1997	Ship's Explosive Safety Inspection
17-19 Jun 1997	Middle East Force Exercise

PROGRAM OF EVENTS

MUSICAL PRELUDE
United States Navy Band
San Diego, CA

ARRIVAL HONORS
Vice Admiral A. J. Krekich
Commander, Naval Surface Force,
U.S. Pacific Fleet

PARADING OF COLORS

NATIONAL ANTHEM

INVOCATION
Lieutenant James E. West, CHC

REMARKS BY GUEST SPEAKER
Vice Admiral A. J. Krekich

REMARKS AND READING OF ORDERS
Commander Mark E. Ferguson III

READING OF ORDERS AND REMARKS
Commander D. Michael Abrashoff

PRESENTATION OF COMMISSION PENNANT
Master Chief Bfigineman (SW)
Robert J. Scheeler, Jr.
Command Master Chief

BENEDICTION
Lieutenant James E. West, CHC

RETIRING OF COLORS

DEPARTURE OF OFFICIAL PARTY

RECEPTION

306

OFFICERS

Executive Officer	LCDR Jeffrey A. Harley
Chief Engineer	LCDR Clifford A. Pish
Combat Systems Officer	LT Kevin C. Hill
Supply Officer	LT David L. Devlin
Weapons Officer	LT Daniel H. Taylor
Operations Officer	LT Patrick M. Kelly
Nav/Admin Officer	LT Jennifer L. Ellinger
Electronics Material Officer	LT Susan A. Fortney
Main Propulsion Officer	LT Jaime V. Singh
Combat Information Center Officer	LT Kevin M. Brand
Undersea Warfare Officer	LT Andrea L. Lindenberg
Fire Control Officer	LT Leopoldo S. Albea
First Lieutenant	LT Derek J. Nisco
Ordnance Officer	LTJG Brenna B. Embree
Communications Officer	LTJG Brian P. Hansen
Electrical Officer	LTJG Kenneth C. Marshall
Auxiliaries Officer	LTJG James T. Martin
Systems Test Officer	LTJG Gerald R. Olin
Disbursing Officer/Asst Supply	LTJG Pamela S. Theorgood
Damage Control Assistant	ENS Eric W. Rasch
Assistant Operations Officer	CWO2 Gregory W. Horshok

CHIEF PETTY OFFICERS

Command Master Chief   ENCM (SW) Robert J. Scheeler Jr.

FCCM (SW) Christopher V. Vasquez	OSCS (SW) David S. Bludworth
DSCS (SW) Douglas E. Brown	FCCS (SW) Michael D. Schanche
GSCS (SW) John H. Kendrick	GSEC (SW) Thomas O. Darter
FCC (SW) Michael D. Faruq	MAC (SW) John N. Green II
FCC (SW) Kevin C. Hackett	GMC (SW) Foy M. Harris
RMC (SW) Janice F. Harris	BMC (SW) Timothy A. Hartman
DCC (SW) Brian L. Hoch	BMC (SW) Scott B. Moede
EWC (SW) Timothy T. Murphy	ENC (SW) Judy K. O'Brien
GMC (SW) Terry W. Piper	GSMC James M. Priolo
SKC (SW) Edward T. Regec	ETC (SW) Thomas A. Talley
DKC (AW) Yolanda D. Tyler	

Outgoing Captain, Commander Ferguson, with his mother (above)
and wife and two children (both of whom are dressed patriotically) at the
Change of Command Ceremony at Pier Two in San Diego, California.

With the USS BENFOLD in the background, photos are taken with the
flag honor guard and Commander Ferguson and his wife (above)
and Commanders Ferguson and Abrashoff (below).

Commanders Ferguson and Abrashoff (center), take time to talk with some of the guests following the Change of Command Ceremony.

Salute To Commander Mark E. Ferguson, III
First Captain of the USS BENFOLD

This morning on the USS BENFOLD
The Navy honored one of its own:
A Commander who, in all lines of service,
Precision and leadership has shown.
Many friends and associates gathered
To pay tribute to this exceptional man
Who has affected the lives of so many
In ways that few citizens can.

The event that took place on the BENFOLD
Is tradition in Naval routine:
A CHANGE OF COMMAND CEREMONY.
It's a formal, yet emotional scene,
Especially for those who have gathered
To bid farewell to a fabulous friend . . . .
On June 20th, in the year '97
More than 150 did attend !

Who is this special Commander
Who departs from the BENFOLD today
To continue to serve in the Navy
In some new and challenging way?
He was BENFOLD'S first great Captain - - -
He's been with her for more than three years - - -
And D. Michael Abrashoff will now take command
From this man for whom some will shed tears.
His name is Mark E. Ferguson, III
And all those who know him are proud,
For he's more than a Naval Commander
(That's why he stands out in the crowd !!!)
He's sincere, very patient and caring,
As well as considerate and kind.
The citizens of Audubon, New Jersey,
Won't forget what he's now left behind.

Commander Ferguson will now go to Harvard
And the J.F.K. Government School there;
His rank will be that of Captain,
Through a promotion that's revered everywhere !

Yet what residents of Audubon will remember
Are the visits he made to it's schools . . .
And the day the Commander played softball in town:
Those moments will sparkle like jewels !
As he leaves the command of the BENFOLD
To continue his Naval career,
Each time this town learns of his honors
It will stand up and give a big cheer !

Captain Ferguson, thanks for the memories !
We salute you and wish you the best
As you sail off to new destinations
In search of your next Naval quest.
Be assured that our door's always open,
So stop in, when'er you're nearby.
Let us know of your future achievements:
Say "So Long" . . . . but never "Good-bye".

Craig E. Burgess
June 21, 1997

315

COMMANDING OFFICER
COMMANDER D. MICHAEL ABRASHOFF
UNITED STATES NAVY

Commander Donald Michael Abrashoff was born in Altoona, Pennsylvania. He is a 1982 graduate of the United States Naval Academy. His initial sea duty assignment was in USS ALBERT DAVID (FFG 1050) where he served as Communications Officer and Anti-Submarine Warfare Officer. Upon completion of Department Head School, he was ordered to USS HARRY W. HILL (DD 986) where he served as Combat Systems Officer. His second department head tour was as Combat Systems Officer in USS ENGLAND (CG 22). During this tour, he participated in Operation DESERT SHIELD in Southwest Asia. He served as Executive Officer in USS SHILOH (CG 67) which also deployed to Southwest Asia.

Commander Abrashoff served ashore as Aide and Flag Lieutenant to Commander, Naval Surface Group Western Pacific/Commander Surface Combatant Force Seventh Fleet and Commander Logistics Support Force Seventh Fleet in Subic Bay, RP. In Washington, D.C., he served as a Surface Warfare Assignment Officer, Junior Officer Shore Coordinator and Cruiser Destroyer Atlantic Fleet Placement Officer. Additionally, he served as the Military Assistant to the Secretary of Defense, the Honorable William J. Perry.

Commander Abrashoff's personal awards include the Defense Superior Service Medal, the Meritorious Service Medal, four Navy and Marine Corps Commendation Medals, and one Navy and Marine Corps Achievement Medal, various Campaign and Service Medals and four Battle "E" Awards for shipboard excellence.

LCDR Jeffrey A. Harley
Executive Officer,
AKA Executive Warrior

A native of Brooklyn, Michigan, Lieutenant Commander Harley graduated from the University of Minnesota in December 1983 with a Bachelor of Arts degree in Political Science.

His sea assignments include tours in the guided missile frigate USS SAMUEL ELIOT MORISON (FFG 13), destroyer USS DAVID R. RAY (DD 971), and guided missile cruiser USS COWPENS (CG 63). Ashore, Lieutenant Commander Harley served as Fleet Scheduler for Commander in Chief, U.S. Pacific Fleet. He has received Master of Arts degrees from the Naval War College and Fletcher School of Law and Diplomacy.

Lieutenant Commander Harley is married to the former Cynthia Kay Johnson of New Richmond, Wisconsin. They have a daughter, Emily.

317

In presenting a history of a naval vessel, it is important that the reader be able to understand the vessel's 'life' from the perspective of someone sailing with her, not merely from the perspective of an observer. Petty Officer 1st Class Danny K. Edgar now takes us on a poetic journey through the first deployment of the USS BENFOLD, beginning with a selection about the ship itself . . .

Being a sailor on board a warship in today's Navy can be frightening to the public eye. The thought of being far away from home and in harm's way would steer some people away. It takes pride, discipline and dedication to be part of the world's greatest Navy. The warship is not only the sailor's home away from home: it represents peace and freedom in times of need. The ship is an ambassador of goodwill, whether delivering supplies to hurricane victims or giving aid to merchant ships or to refugees in times of hostility. The warship is the protector, or policeman, of the seas and performs its duties with no questions asked. Its presence demands respect. Not only does the crew rely on the warship to get them wherever they need to go, swiftly and safely: the freedom of a nation depends on it.

Pride of the Defender

I'm a mighty warship, I dress in gray.
Any moment I'm relied on to save the day.
I sail in peace time and at war,
I have allies and enemies I can't ignore.
I could be in the Gulf or the Pacific:
Because of my situation, I can't be specific.
My duties are very loud and clear:
I sail for a country, and I have no fear.
My purpose is to protect the seas - - -
From foreign and domestic, if I please.
There may come a time when I must show
My strength to a foe.
For now, my crew relies on me
To be the very best I can be.
I bear my pride by the flag I fly,
Sailors at attention, standing by.
I visit different countries from time to time:
I must be able to leave on the drop of a dime.
I sail for respect and a nation:
The trips I make are no vacation.
So, if you think you're bad, and you dare,
Remember: I am a mighty warship. Beware!!!

This next selection is what has resulted in my many poems about life on board a naval vessel. It was written in August of 1997 for the newly selected Chief Petty Officers. I am indebted to my shipmates for their encouragement and their support of my writing.

318

Hail To The New Chiefs

Congratulations to the new Chiefs
An honor bestowed upon you because of your beliefs
Whether you're an ET or saving lives is your fate
You've always managed to excel in your rate
Long hours in Admin or the Galley
You've always been able to get behind your troops and rally
Working in Sonar around the clock
You proved to be solid as a rock.
So as one journey ends
And another one begins
Remember, from the shine of the sun's rays
A Chief, you will become today.

Congratulations to:

MSC (SW) Danner,   HMC (SW) Olger,   ETC (SW) Schneider,

PNC (SW) Eller   STGC (SW) Salamanca

When I first met Master Chief Scheeler, he was just a Chief Petty Officer on board the LAKE CHAMPLAIN (CG-57). I was a seaman recruit. I knew then that he would someday make Master Chief, for he was known for taking care of his sailors. Scheeler became the first Command Master Chief of the USS BENFOLD: the senior enlisted officer on board. He is the enlisted sailors' voice to the Commanding Officer. He can tell if a sailor is sincere and is always looking out for the welfare of the crew members. Scheeler has been in the Navy for a long time, but, just like fine wine, he has grown fine with time. A typical underway period would find him walking the deckplates, talking to crew members, and, most importantly, listening; taking care of the ship's everyday business; even on the messdecks with the CO playing cards with crew members. At night you could find him working out. The crew's morale plays a big part in the successful completion of a mission and Scheeler was a reason for the morale being so high. He never asked a sailor to do something that he himself wouldn't do. He led by example and told you like it was - - - like it or not. He is what sailors in the Navy would call a sailors' sailor.

C M C (Crusty Old Salt)

I was raised in Casper, Wyoming, near Cheyenne
I'm not rich and I don't own a Benz
I'm not a rancher, and I don't ride a bull
But I can tell you a thing or two about a ship's hull
I've been in the Navy, 22 years to be exact
I still love being out to sea, and that's a fact
There're probably not too many things, I haven't done

But no one can ever tell me, I didn't have fun
As a recruiter in Boston, I met my beautiful wife
On board the LAKE CHAMPLAIN, a newborn child came into my life
I am now on the BENFOLD, where I'm known as the CO's right hand man
To me, I have the best job in the land
I have a crew onboard that can't be outdone
In my opinion they're second to none
As Command Master Chief I'm where I want to be
On board a warship, protecting the free
In life, people don't always do what they like
I'm a sailor, I was born to fight.

When a ship leaves for a six-month deployment - - - as we did on August 19, 1997 on the maiden voyage of the USS BENFOLD - - - all 300 plus crew members' lives (as well as the lives of their families) will change. The spouse or family member no longer has the crew member around to help make decisions. Their only communications are by letters, e-mail and phone calls (when they are in port). That is why the family members back home play such an important role. The Navy wife or husband now has to deal with the everyday hassles on the home front - - - and for those who have children, it's a constant battle to keep everything looking normal without Mom or Dad at home. Questions often asked are: Where is Mommy or Daddy? When are they coming back? Are they coming back? When crew members get ready to leave, they try to make sure everything is ready to go and they take time to explain to the kids where they're going and when they will be back. But once they are gone, the spouses have all the responsibility on their shoulders.

To the spouses and family members and friends who support the American sailor, we salute you for all that you do, for you are the reason we can do our job so well. Without your love and support, we would not be able to get through the hard times.

On the day of departure (see the photos on the following page), emotions are high. Some people show them, while others try to hide them: butterflies doing somersaults in your stomach; tears building up inside; thoughts of family members constantly on your mind. Then come those last minute hugs and kisses, as time swiftly goes by. Watching family members and friends on the pier, waving and crying, leaves a lasting impression in your mind. As the ship pulls away, some crew members can't hold back the tears, while others fight to keep from crying. Most of the crew look teary-eyed . . . like they have just lost their best friend - - - and, for most, they have, temporarily. As the ship goes farther and farther through the bay and they secure the sea and anchor detail, it seems like everybody takes a deep breath and composes him or herself, remembering the faces on the pier and realizing that in six months tears of joy will be falling as the ship returns. That thought brings a smile to most. For those on their first deployment, there are shipmates to help them through the tough times. We're not just shipmates: we're a family, 300 plus strong!

FAREWELL

USS BENFOLD (DDG 65)
ONWARD WITH VALOR

AUG 19th

321

Six Months And Counting

Loved ones filing off the ship;
The IMC sounded in the air, like a whip;
The crane slowly removed the shore power,
Like the removal of a petal from a flower.
Families were waving good-bye on the pier:
Most were trying not to show a tear.
Sailors manned the weather decks;
Department heads were making their last checks;
Underway ships colors was all you heard:
No one said not even a word.
As the ship slowly pulled away,
Everyone knew they would remember this day . . .
For wherever there's a beginning, there comes an end - - -
With a little luck and a strong wind - - -
For the very same ship that leaves today
Will be coming home soon, through the same bay.
At home waiting, counting mile after mile
Like the birth of a newborn child,
Waiting for the sound of these three little words,
"Moored Ships Colors", to be heard.

When there's a fire, disturbance, flooding, injury, mine hit, incoming missiles or torpedoes, who are you gonna call? TEAM BENFOLD is the answer. For a fire or flooding, every member is a firefighter. Damage Control Center (DCC) and repair parties are the BENFOLD's Fire Department. In case of a personal injury the Medical Department is called upon (Hospital Corpsmen): a group consisting of two corpsmen and 6 - 10 stretcher-bearers. The Hospital Corpsman (which is what Edward C. Benfold was) is led by an independent corpsman, who is also the senior medical representative on board - - - usually an E-6 or E-7 on a destroyer - - - , and an E-1 to E-4 assistant. If the ship has females, one of the corpsmen is a female.

In the Navy anything can happen. Through repetitive training, the ship has to rely on the crew to get itself through any ordeal. Out to sea, the ship usually conducts daily training on different drills, like man overboard, general quarters, security drills and riot control; while in port, training involves situations involving loss of power, war games, mass casualties, helo crash and underway replenishment (bringing aboard fuel and provisions at sea is a very dangerous operation). Through training, the ship is prepared for anything . . . because what CAN happen, often does. I know this from personal experience as a stretcher-bearer on board the USS LAKE CHAMPLAIN CG-57. The ship was over in the South China Sea when it got a distress signal from the Chinese Merchant Ship HUAZAH. The ship was sinking and logs they were carrying were tossing violently about in 10-20 foot waves, her crew of twenty in the chilling water. As helicopters from the LAKE CHAMPLAIN and two other warships were pulling the seamen out of the chilling waters and bringing them on board, I, being a stretcher-bearer, was waiting in the helo hanger as bodies started coming in. The first helo had three people on board, all dead: a chilling wake-up call. I had no time to react, for a second helo brought in four more people. With the aid of HMC(SW) Alex Taylor, Independent Corpsman, we treated two of the more critically injured, giving CPR and treating for hypothermia and shock. Of the twenty crew members, fourteen survived. The Captain of the ship was crushed between the logs and we were unable to retrieve him from the sea. The remaining five were put into body bags and into the freezer. The merchants on board were dropped off in the Philippines. As they left, they showed their gratitude by hugging and bowing to us, and repeatedly thanking us through an interpreter.

To this day, I always thank God and the Navy for the training received. "Chief Taylor (who is now a Master Chief), I now understand why we had all those drills. You were a great teacher. That is just one of the reasons I am a firm believer in the training we do."

Danger At Sea

It can happen at any time of the day.
It's part of life and the Navy way.
Sometimes it's called a drill:
In dangerous times, it's for real.
Repair parties and crew hustling around:
A missile from a MIG could be abound.
It could be an oil leak, flooding or fire:
When danger plays, it's down to the wire.
Locker leaders yelling to set Zebra or Yoke.
Remember: this is not a joke.
If you fool around, someone can die.
So go ahead, complain, whine, or even cry.
Out to sea, anything can come up.
You're a warrior, it's time to get tough.
So next time you wonder why we have to train,
Personnel or ship casualties, this is not a game.

My next poem talks about one of the responsibilities of crew members who are part of the VBSS Team . . . and needs no introduction.

Long Arm Of The Law

We are the VBSS Team
We are a lean mean fighting machine
V is for visit
A lot of ships do not wish it
Board is what the letter B stands for
And we're not here for any pleasure tour
Search is how we find out if you're up to no good

So cross your fingers and knock on wood
Seizure is what happens if you break the rules
So just stand by and act real cool
U.N. Sanctions our are just cause
This will be quick if you have no flaws
Dark blue uniform a 9MM at our side
You can try to run you can even hide
Out to sea we are the law
So you might as well come clean and stand tall
We've been compared to John Wayne and Wyatt Earp
Just like them we go after little twerps
It can be anytime day, night or early morning
Violators better heed this warning
Break the rules and you will pay
Go ahead, Make my day!!!

The next poem, "Angels Of Bahrain" was published in a special column of the Gulf Daily News in Manama, Bahrain. It appeared on the "Postbox" page under the heading of "A Tribute To 'My Angels'". The selection describes one of the unexpected emergencies that can come up during a 6-month deployment, as well as the special nurses who attended to me in a time of need.

Angels Of Bahrain

As days go by and years pass
My memory in Bahrain will be just a flash
The buildings and mosques, are a sight to see
There's really only one thing that is important to me

I was a stranger unknown to them
They gave me their help without a thought or a whim
I was in a strange place
I was bleeding and had a bandage on my face

They did not know me or where I was from
These women were professional and not to be outdone
When I was feeling sad they always had a smile
Especially when they would come into my room in a single file

They didn't want anything but to say "hi"!
When they left they always had time to say "bye"
Thankful to say I was not on my deathbed
They were always there whether giving a shot or making sure I was fed.

I will always remember the nurses of Ward 1
Even after I have left and gone
I am a sailor I belong to the seas
But the nurses in Bahrain will always be angels to me.

Singapore is a very beautiful place. You will see no trash or graffiti on the streets. Crime is very, very low, the result of very strict laws. This next poem will give you a much better picture of the Garden City of the East.

Singapore

Downtown is like one you've never seen:
Singapore sidewalks and streets are very clean.
First impression: it's a sight to see.
There's so much more to discover, than in geography.
It's a city of several origins:
It would take all day just to name the religions.
The architecture and tall buildings;
People in the street, at the traffic light yielding;
Different language and different signs;
People at the subway, standing in line.
They have rules that are all their own.
To us, we say it's overblown.
The ways and customs are unique:
Chinatown is what tourists seek.
Temples and shrines are a part of the past;
You can see Merlion as ships go past.
At night, the lights are aglow:
Tis a sight on a moonlight stroll.
The one thing you'll remember, at the least:
Singapore is the Garden City of the East.

During the deployment, Petty Officer Danny Edgar qualified as an Enlisted Surface Warfare Specialist and received a special citation from Commander Abrashoff on November 30, 1997. A photograph of the presentation is shown in the introduction to the book, on page xviii. The official document that accompanies the breast insignia is shown on the next page.

Know all by these presents that

MESS MANAGEMENT SPECIALIST SECOND CLASS
DANNY K. EDGAR

having successfully completed the established personnel qualification standards and having demonstrated the requisite professional skills and competence while serving in

USS BENFOLD (DDG 65)

Has qualified as an

ENLISTED SURFACE WARFARE SPECIALIST

and is authorized to wear the Enlisted Surface Warfare Specialist Breast Insignia

In witness whereof this certificate has been signed and a seal affixed hereunto on this thirtieth day of November 1997

R. J. SCHEELER, ENCM(SW), USN
COMMAND MASTER CHIEF

D. M. ABRASHOFF
COMMANDING OFFICER

An enlisted surface warfare specialist insignia costs anywhere from five to six dollars, but to a United States Sailor it's worth a lot more. In life, anything worth having doesn't come easy. It stands for pride, determination and dedication. Getting the pin is not a given: you have to earn it. You have to have a plan and make time to obtain the pin, while still fulfilling your regular job - - - sometimes working twelve to sixteen hours a day; obtaining signatures from shipmates who are already ESWS qualified; listening and soaking up information like a sponge; giving up a couple extra hours sleep in order to get qualified..

I wish to thank every sailor on board the BENFOLD who helped me attain that goal. When I reported on board the BENFOLD, getting the pin was one of my goals. What sounds better: MS1 Edgar or MS1(SW) Edgar? To all my fellow surface warriors, I salute and challenge you to continue helping our fellow shipmates in fulfilling their goal: to those who have it and to those who want it. Then, and only then, do you realize: It's NOT just a piece of metal.

ESWS: Just A Piece Of Metal

To a surface sailor, it's quite a feat:
Like the mountain climber who reaches the top of a peak.
They will long remember this day
For, in their minds, this will stay.
Whether officer or enlisted, it doesn't matter:
Both had to climb a very steep ladder.
It wasn't easy, but then it wasn't supposed to be.
Like a toll booth, it also has a fee:
Not money, but determination, long hours and team work.
It all starts with that dreaded orange book.
Signatures come at a price,
Questions pressing at you like a vice.
The day of the board is finally here:
You answer the questions loud and clear.
You wait impatiently for the outcome,
One more obstacle, and then you're done.
As you study one more time on what you were taught,
The walk through goes better than you thought.
The CO pins a piece of metal on your chest:
You're a surface warrior: you're one of the best.
It took a long time for this day to come:
Enjoy it! For, on this day, you're not to be outdone.
As this day ends and the excitement settles . . . . .
Can you still say it's just a piece of metal?

This poem really needs no explaining, for I believe it speaks for itself. Christmas back at home sometimes is taken for granted. When you are away you remember the real meaning as it hits you in the face, not able to personally share that feeling with loved ones, due to being far away.

Christmas In The Middle East

Christmas is a special time of year:
Time to celebrate and spread some Yuletide cheer.
Out to sea, you would think a sailor would moan,
For, on this joyous day, they're far from home.
Back at home, people are shopping and making plans,
While their loved ones are in a foreign land.
Looking at the schedule for December,
Making up a list of things to remember,

Are we out to sea, or in port?
If we're in, we know our time will be short.
Picking up gifts in the Middle East,
Getting ready for the Christmas feast,
Buying gold or silver in Bahrain,
Remembering to buy the little one a brand new train.
Making sure packages and letters are ready to go
And maybe a wish for a little snow.
Browsing in Dubai at the local mall,
Standing in long lines to make a call.
Although we are far, far away,
Christmas is still a special day.
To our loved ones, we love with all our might
As we recall these words: "And to all a good night".
As we remember what we are out here for,
Christmas to us means that much more.
To our loved ones, we send our love
And take time to send a prayer for up above.
No matter wherever we are,
Christmas is with us, near and far.

People sometimes take things for granted, especially our families back home. If a sailor is the backbone of a ship, the family is the backbone of the sailor. One hundred eighty days away from the ones we love - - - can take a toll on even the strong at heart. There's not a day goes by that we don't think of family or the ones we love. For some, it is easier than for others. It's our love that gets us through our days and lifts our spirits so that we can fulfill our duties as well as we do. Between the letters, the few phone calls and prayers, each day goes by more quickly than you think. We don't quit thinking, nor forget about the ones we love: it's love that makes us all stronger and better sailors - - - and better persons.

Homesick Blues

I'm on a ship in the middle of the ocean.
Some days I just go through the motions.
Days are long and busy.
At night I go to bed, my head dizzy.
My thoughts are miles and miles away - - -
It's you I think of each day.
Sometimes you don't realize what you've got.
You are my special someone, my dot to dot.
You try to explain to the little one
Daddy will be back, but for now he's gone.
You are the one person in the world
That makes me feel like I'm on a Twirl-A-Whirl.

I know I never wrote you a poem when I was home.
Being out here without you, I feel alone.
Because of the love I have for you,
Out here on the ocean, I'm feeling blue.
Because of you, I make a wish:
To be near the one I dearly miss . . .
Until I'm able to see you once again.
Missing you this much must be a sin,
So remember this, as I close:
You're like a flower, you are my rose.

Six months is a long time to be away from home. You dream of what homecoming is going to be like. Going on deployment can be bittersweet. The day you leave is full of sadness, but does not compare to when the ship returns. On Homecoming Day, emotions are at an all-time high. Some cry and laugh at the same time. You try to prepare yourself, but never really can you even imagine what to expect.

Home At Last

The ship entering the bay in the early morn,
A blast blaring from the ship's horn,
Seagulls gracefully flying about,
People from sailboats giving us a shout.
The smell of the morning air,
The sight of the city is more than we can bear.
The tugs coming toward us is a sight to see:
At that moment, there's no place we'd rather be.
A deep breath is taken as underneath the bridge we pass,
We see a sign that says: HOME AT LAST.
The emotions show as the ship makes it's way to the pier:
The anticipation and excitement on our faces is very clear.
MOORED is the word heard by all.
On the pier it looks like Christmas time at the Mall
As sailors search the pier for a familiar face,
Hearts beating at a faster than normal pace.
As sailors leave, they take a look at the ship's mast.
To themselves they say: "Home at last".

It's amazing what a stuffed bear can do to a little girl, not to mention the effect it had on a father . . . .
This final poem is dedicated to my daughter Kristen Marie Edgar. It was a week before Thanksgiving. We had been in Dubai for a few days and would be underway for the holiday. To be honest, I wasn't looking forward to it. Petty Officer First Class Wilmington came by to give me my mail. Knowing I hadn't received mail in a couple of weeks, she jokingly said: "Looks like somebody loves you." It was a care package with magazines and letters. Sports Illustrated was

great, because we usually only get scores and a brief writeup when we're underway. When I was done, I knew that my fellow shipmates would also enjoy reading them. Receiving letters from my in-laws is always a joy. My wife sent some smoked sausage, which was enjoyed a week later with fellow shipmates while we were watching a movie. I also had two letters, one of which caught my eye; when I opened it, inside was a Winnie The Pooh pin and a brief note from my daughter: "Daddy, TTFN." (Ta Ta For Now!) I remember my last phone conversation with my daughter: she kept talking about Winnie The Pooh, Honey Pot, Tigger and me reading to her. Recalling this conversation brought tears to my eyes. I always tell her "TTFN" on the phone or in my letters. She always tryies to say "TTFN", but gets excited and leaves out the "F". In remembering this, I was compelled to write "The Magic of Winnie The Pooh". (Usually, when I write poems, the rough part is done in thirty minutes with another half hour to smooth it out: for this poem, I was done in twenty minutes and only made two changes.)

In all of my other poems, I was inspired by my shipmates or by events taking place around me. This one, however, was personal and was meant to be for my daughter. When YN1 Wood came by and I asked her to tell me what she thought, she was speechless (and that doesn't happen very often). Before I knew it, other friends asked to read it and they told me it reminded them of their child or of their children. Thus, what started out as a personal poem for my daughter became one I shared with my shipmates . . . Now if THAT'S not magic, I don't know what is!

Needless to say, I was ready for Thanksgiving - - - thanks to my daughter and Winnie The Pooh and friends.

The Magic Of Winnie The Pooh

I got a letter from home the other day:
My wife had a message she wished to relay.
My daughter said: "TTFN",
And with it was a Winnie The Pooh pin.
He's just a stuffy old cuddly bear,
Walking or dancing like he has no care.
My child does not know he's just a storybook tale:
She just hugs onto him when she wants to yell.
Without a hesitation or even a clue,
When she thinks about her Daddy, she picks up her Pooh.
When I am there, she has the comfort of my stare;
When I am gone, she has Mommy and that silly old bear.
We can walk through the store, and of all the toys
It's Winnie The Pooh that gives her the most joy.
She laughs when he is on, and when Tigger starts to bounce,
Especially when he gets ready to pounce.
All she knows is that I'm on a ship, and that I am gone;
She looks for me at the break of dawn;
She clutches onto her Winnie The Pooh bear:
"DADDY, COME HOME", she says with a stare.

R. Allen Stubblefield, Jr.
Lieutenant Commander, U. S. Navy

In October of 1997, while the USS BENFOLD was still out at sea in her first deployment, a new Executive Officer came on board, LCDR R. Allen Stubblefield, Jr. A photo and career profile of LCDR Stubblefield are presented on this page. Welcome aboard !

LCDR Stubblefield was born in Richmond, VA and attended high school in Houston, TX. He graduated from the U. S. Naval Academy in 1984.

After commissioning, LCDR Stubblefield reported to USS REUBEN JAMES (FFG 57). After the commissioning of REUBEN JAMES in March 1986, he served as Auxiliaries Officer and Anti-Submarine Warfare Officer. He reported to the Naval ROTC Unit, University of New Mexico in November 1988, where he served for two years as the Junior and Sophomore advisor and instructor.

LCDR Stubblefield completed Department Head School in July 1991, and reported to USS SIDES (FFG 14) as Combat Systems Officer. He detached SIDES in February 1993 and reported to USS ZEPHYR (PC 8) as Prospective Commanding Officer. After commissioning USS ZEPHYR in Corpus Christi, TX in October 1994, LCDR Stubblefield led ZEPHYR through the initial work-ups, then deployed ZEPHYR to Alaska from July-September, 1995. He was relieved in February 1996 and served in Washington, D.C. at the Bureau of Naval Personnel and on the staff of Director of Surface Warfare until October 1997.

After completing his duties in Washington, LCDR Stubblefield reported to USS BENFOLD as Executive Officer. He served on BENFOLD until May 1999, then detached to proceed to the staff of Commander, Third Fleet in San Diego.

Lieutenant Stubblefield's awards include the Navy Meritorious Service Medal, Navy Commendation Medal (bronze star in lieu of third award) and Navy Achievement Medal. He has received a Masters Degree in Computer Resources Management from Webster University, and Bachelors Degree in Mathematics from the U. S. Naval Academy.

Lieutenant Stubblefield is married to Kimberly Doke of Los Alamitos, CA. They reside in San Diego, CA with their children Patrick and Amy.

The deployment was a very successful one. Several awards were won by the ship and her outstanding crew, among them the prestigious SPOKANE TROPHY AWARD for excellence in Surface Ship Combat Readiness. For a ship to receive this award following its first deployment is a special honor. We present an article summarizing the deployment and the announcement of the Spokane Trophy Award Winner on pages 333 and 334. The trophy plaques are now in the mess hall on board. The three plaques and their inscriptions are shown on page 335.

On March 30, 1998 the ship celebrated her second birthday. It was a day of joy for the officers and crew, having shown to the world during the ship's first deployment that the USS BENFOLD is "The Best Damn Ship in the Navy".

For the remainder of the calendar year 1998, Commander Abrashoff and the crew participated in a number of sea trials and exercises designed to keep everyone ready for any emergency that might occur. These trials are essential, especially considering that crew members are constantly being transferred on board from other assignments and transferred off to other assignments. (Most tours of duty do not exceed 24 months.) The USS BENFOLD also participated in the Annual Fleet Week festivities in San Francisco. (See the photo and article on page 336.)

Constant maintenance of a ship is also required while she is in port. The photo below shows a paint crew working from a scaffolding at the stern of the USS BENFOLD in early 1999.

Various competitions are held involving crew members from a number of ships in the fleet. See the photo and caption on page 337 to see co-author Edgar 'in action', preparing a special delicacy in a healthy cooking competition.

USS Benfold returns home
Lt. Albea, USS Benfold Public Affairs Officer

San Diego--USS Benfold (DDG-65), America's finest destroyer, returned Feb. 19, 1998 from a six-month Middle East Force deployment to the Arabian Gulf. Departing San Diego August 1997, Benfold arrived in the Arabian Gulf in early October and performed several key missions. Benfold joined naval forces already serving under U.S. Central Command, ensuring a Naval presence that provided stability and deterred conflict in the highly volatile region of the Arabian Gulf.

Benfold, with its state of the art weapons system, maintained a capable and potent naval presence in the Arabian Gulf as the crisis in Iraq began to intensify. A tomahawk capable warship, Benfold's primary mission was to respond as necessary to Iraqi non-compliance to the United Nations weapons inspectors. As tensions increased in early October, Benfold was first on the scene, ensuring that a Naval response to any contingency operation was available until the arrival of the Nimitz Battle Group.

Throughout the crisis, Benfold's Tomahawk Team was ready to respond at all times and demonstrated its innovative and highly effective strike organization, cited by Commander Fifth Fleet as one of the best teams in the Arabian Gulf.

"It's a real credit to the Sailors on the strike team that we were able to respond to contingency operations so well. They faced one of the toughest challenges of their careers and were ready should we have gotten the call," said Lt. j.g. Switzer, 26, Cerritos, Calif.

Benfold's tasking also included conducting maritime interception operations. In this capacity, Benfold boarded and inspected merchant vessels sailing to and from Iraq enforcing UN sanctions.

As the U.S. Naval presence increased with the stationing of the Nimitz and George Washington Battle Groups, Benfold operated with both, providing air radar coverage and also air control for carrier fighter and reconnaissance aircraft flying missions over Arabian Gulf waters. Throughout the deployment, Benfold's operations required that the ship sail to the northernmost reaches of the Arabian Gulf to within close proximity of Iranian and Iraqi territorial waters.

"We followed the news as best we could, but we knew all along that we were ready for anything," said Fire Controlman 2nd Class Michael Gurney, 22, of Portland, Oregon. "We had trained long and hard to handle a situation like this."

While deployed, there were several new additions to the Benfold family as 12 wives gave birth while their husbands were serving their country. These fathers will be seeing their new sons and daughters for the first time upon arrival in San Diego. They will be the first off the ship to greet their families.

This is the first deployment for Benfold, which was commissioned in San Diego in March 1996. The fifteenth ship in the class of Arleigh Burke destroyers, the ship is named after Edward C. Benfold, a navy hospital corpsman posthumously awarded the Medal of Honor while serving during the Korean War.

Benfold port visits on this deployment included stops in Singapore, Thailand, Bahrain and Dubai as well as Sydney, Melbourne and Perth in Australia.

USN

COMNAVSURFPAC PRESS RELEASE

98-184

SPOKANE TROPHY WINNER ANNOUNCED

USS BENFOLD (DDG 65) was recently chosen as the winner of the 1997 Spokane Trophy Award for excellence in Surface Ship Combat readiness. This prestigious award was started by President Theodore Roosevelt in 1908 to recognize Naval warfighting proficiency

"During calendar year 1997, the officers and crew of BENFOLD demonstrated unparalleled dedication to combat systems warfighting proficiency and should be proud of this prestigious achievement," said Admiral Archie Clemins, Commander-in-Chief, U.S. Pacific Fleet.

A replica of the Spokane Trophy will be presented to the ship in a ceremony next month.

BENFOLD is a guided-missile destroyer with a crew of about 340 men and women. The ship is homeported in San Diego.

-SURFPAC-

The photo on this page shows the special trophy display case mounted on the wall of the mess hall for all crew members, present and future, to see. The inscriptions on the three trophies are:

Upper Left: USS BENFOLD (DDG-65) 1997 Spokane
                        Trophy Winner. Presented by U.S. Navy
                        League of Spokane.

Upper Right: Naval Trophy: 1997 Spokane Trophy Winner,
                        USS BENFOLD (DDG-65), for outstanding
                        performance in warfare operations and combat
                        systems readiness.

Bottom Center: Commander, Naval Surface Force
                        U.S. Pacific Fleet
                        Battle Efficiency Award
                        1997 Comdesron Battle Efficiency
                        Competition Winner
                        USS BENFOLD (DDG-65)

Fleet Week kicked off Saturday with the Parade of Ships through San Francisco Bay. The USS Benfold, an Aegis guided missile destroyer, steams past the reviewing stand at the municipal pier at Aquatic Park.

Fleet Week kicks off on brilliant day

By Karen de Sa
STAFF WRITER

Skies clear as polished glass, sea flat as an aquamarine tablecloth and sun warm enough for shorts made Saturday a perfect day to worship the wing and the sail.

Before thousands of onlookers, the Navy, Coast Guard and Marine Corps paraded massive sea vessels along the San Francisco waterfront as part of the city's Fleet Week festivities. The event is an annual ritual for many Bay Area residents, as well as an attraction for the tourists with handy cams and binoculars in hand.

While the big boats inched along, most waited eagerly to witness the aeronautic feats of the Blue Angels, a precision flying team made up of Navy and Marine Corps service members in its 52nd year.

James Root is a Blue Angels faithful, proclaiming loudly to anyone listening that he's seen the show 15 times.

"They are the best pilots this country has," the homeless 32-year-old San Francisco man said, leaning over his backpack and bed roll. "We have different pilots that clip lines in Italy and such, but these pilots aren't like that."

Regarding a friend who slept in the sun between two parked cars, Root said: "I'm gonna kick his butt if he doesn't wake up in a couple seconds — he better watch the show."

Despite its militaristic theme, Saturday's event was pure Bay Area. Some old veterans displaying "Why Lie? It's for Beer" signs sat alongside Andean panpipe players and blues-belting saxophonists. Foreign teen visitors in Tommy Hilfiger jackets posed for photos with cloudy, figure eight trails in the skies behind them. A group of Merced County Mennonite girls in long cotton frocks scanned the waterline as foreign and civilian vessels skimmed the waters of the San Francisco Bay.

Then there were those who came to remember. Seventy-year-old Mary Froehlich of Tuscon, Ariz., scanned the Navy vessels and the shores for a sign of bellbottoms or a pea coat, hoping to see in the face of some young sailor a glimpse of her own "old salt," her now-deceased husband.

San Francisco's Fleet Week festivities continue today with an air show from 11 a.m. to 3 p.m. (the Blue Angels will fly from 1 to 2 p.m.) and free tours of the U.S.S. Ogden and the U.S.S. Benfold, both moored at Pier 35.

Various competitions are held involving crew members from a number of ships in the fleet. The photo and caption on this page show co-author Edgar 'in action', preparing a special delicacy in a healthy cooking competition.

HOWARD LIPIN / Union-Tribune

Beyond chipped beef: *Petty Officer Dan Edgar of the destroyer Benfold prepared a Salmon Asparagus Frittata for the Navy healthy cooking contest.*

As of December 1, 1998, there were only three officers on board who had been with the ship since her pre-commissioning days: Command Master Chief Robert J. Scheeler, Jr.; Lieutenant Gerald R. Olin; Lieutenant Kenneth C. Marshall. The CMC left the ship in early December, 1998; Lieutenant Olin in February, 1999; Lieutenant Marshall on March 30, 1999 (the date of the ship's third birthday of her commissioning). All three consented to having their photo taken together in the wardroom of the USS BENFOLD. Two photos are shown on page 339: the first shows, left to right, Lieutenant Olin, Lieutenant Marshall and Commamd Master Chief Scheeler; the second shows Marshall, Scheeler and Olin in front of one of the paintings in the wardroom. We include the career profiles for the two Lieutenants on page 340. (That of Command Master Chief Scheeler was presented earlier in this chapter).

While visiting with the three officers in the wardroom on December 1, 1998, co-author Burgess had the chance to speak with several of the younger crew members who were in the process of preparing lunch for the ship's officers . . . one of the many daily routines that make up life aboard a naval vessel.

Crew members DKSA A. A. Aviles, OSSR John Livingston, Jr. and FC3 R. J. Lee
(Right to Left set the table for the officers' lunch in the wardroom.

Lt. Olin, Lt. Marshall & CMC Scheeler

Lt. Marshall, CMC Scheeler & Lt. Olin

Combat Systems Department   CS Division

ENS Gerald R. Olin

ENS Olin is a native of Phoenix, AZ. He enlisted in the Navy in 1983 as a Fire Controlman. His previous duty stations include USS HAROLD E. HOLT (FF 1074), USS CHOSIN (CG 65), and Aegis Training Support Group, Pearl Harbor. Selected for the Limited Duty Officer program, ENS Olin was commissioned in 1994. He reported aboard as the Systems Test Officer in October 1994.

ENS Olin is married to Gianina M. Olin. They have a daughter, Alexandra Victoria.

Operations Department   OD Division

ENS Kenneth C. Marshall

ENS Marshall is a native of Boston, Massachusetts. He graduated from the University of Rochester in 1994 and received a Bachelor of Arts Degree in Psychology and a minor in Management. After graduation, he tutored for the Upward Bound Program in Atlanta, Georgia before attending the Surface Warfare Officer School in Newport, Rhode Island. In June 1995, he reported aboard as the First Lieutenant.

On Thursday, January 21, 1999, the second Change of Command Ceremony took place at sea during one of the regularly scheduled exercises. Commander D. Michael Abrashoff said farewell to the crew in an emotional speech and turned over command of the ship to Commander Thomas H. Copeman, III.

Commander Abrashoff played a key role in the success of the USS BENFOLD during her first deployment and his 19-month tour of duty as Captain of the DDG-65 will long be remembered. A special poetic salute to the ship's second Captain is presented on this and the following page.

Commander Thomas H. Copeman, III will be leading the USS BENFOLD into the 21st Century and will be her Captain during the six-month deployment, from June to December, 1999. We salute the ship's new leader and wish him well. A photograph and a career profile of Commander Copeman are presented on pages 343 and 344.

On Tuesday, March 30, 1999, co-author Burgess came on board and participated in the ship's third birthday. He presented one of the Audubon Tapestry Afghans to the crew. (See photos on page 345). As part of the celebration, Commander Copeman welcomed FN Brian P. Schrader as the newest BENFOLD warrior. Then he and HTCM Brown, the new Command Master Chief, cut the ceremonial birthday cake. (See the photos on page 346 and 347).

A Salute To Commander D. Michael Abrashoff
2nd Captain of the USS BENFOLD (DDG-65)

I was there on the twentieth day of June
In the calendar year ninety-seven,
On board the USS BENFOLD
At the ceremony that took place at eleven.

Commander D. Michael Abrashoff
Became her new Captain that day:
He would lead the crew of the BENFOLD.
I was honored to meet him that day.

In August, the ship left San Diego,
A six-month deployment ahead.
The crew and its Captain were ready . . . .
And when all had been done and been said,
The BENFOLD was the pride of the Navy - - -
"The Best Ship Afloat" some would say - - -
Garnering the coveted SPOKANE TROPHY
For excellence in readiness underway.

A replica of this solid silver trophy
Is displayed for all crew members to see
With pride, on the wall of the mess hall:
A reflection of hard work while at sea.

I visited the USS BENFOLD
Five times in the next year and a half.
I observed Captain Abrashoff in action:
He worked well with his crew and his staff.

On Thursday, January 21st,
In the calendar year ninety-nine,
Another new leader took over
To continue a tradition quite fine.
When the Change of Command Ceremony
Took place on the deck of the ship,
The air was filled with emotion
As the orders were read from the 'script'.
A feeling of family was present
As Abrashoff turned over command
To Commander Thomas H. Copeman, III:
The crew at attention did stand.
The eyes of the crew members glistened
With tears for a Captain they admired
For excellence, leadership and caring:
In each one career pride he'd inspired.

The students and residents of Audubon
Salute you for all that you've done.
Your tenure on the USS BENFOLD
Helped the ship to be ranked NUMBER 1 !!
She's "THE BEST DAMN SHIP IN THE NAVY",
Well-deserving of the honors received - - -
Thanks to Commander Abrashoff
Who always in his crew has believed.

If ever you come to New Jersey
Be assured that the door's open wide.
Stop by in the Borough of Audubon:
You'll be welcomed with patriotic pride.

Craig E. Burgess

COMMANDER THOMAS H. COPEMAN III

Commander Copeman graduated from Creighton University in May 1981 with a BS in Biology. He was commissioned on April 2, 1982 from Officer Candidate School, Newport, RI. Following Basic SWOS he reported to USS LEFTWICH (DD 984) and served 30 months as Electrical Officer and Main Propulsion Assistant. CDR Copeman then served 24 months as a gas turbine examiner for the CINCPACFLT Propulsion Examining Board. After graduating from SWOS Department Head course he was assigned as commissioning Engineer Officer in USS PHILIPPINE SEA (CG 58) where he served for 44 months. His most recent sea duty was Executive Officer in USS LAKE CHAMPLAIN (CG 57).

CDR Copeman's shore assignments were as a student at United States Army Command and General Staff Course at Fort Leavenworth, Kansas, followed by a tour as an action officer in the Special Technical Operations cell at USSTRATCOM, Offutt AFB, NE. He received a MS in Administration from Central Michigan University while in Leavenworth. Following his XO tour he was assigned to the Chief of Naval Operations staff as a requirements officer in the Theater Air Warfare branch (N865) of the Surface Warfare Division (N86).

CDR Copeman has been awarded the Joint Meritorious Service Medal, Meritorious Service Medal (1 gold star), Navy Commendation Medal (1 gold star), Navy Achievement Medal, as well as various unit citations and campaign awards.

As a special gift for the ship's third birthday party, March 30, 1999,
co-author Burgess presents Commander Copeman a tapestry
afghan which displays historical landmarks in the borough

As crew members watch, Commander Copeman (R) pins the
Command Master Chief insignia on HTCM(SW) Douglas R. Brown.

Following the ship's third birthday celebration, the officers and crew members began making preparations for the second 6-month deployment, which began on June 18, 1999.

As the liaison from Audubon, co-author Burgess was invited to come aboard for a continental breakfast that was prepared for family members and friends. He composed a special poem for Commander Thomas H. Copeman, III, the third Captain of the ship and presented it during his visit. (See poem below and continued on page 349).

He also took some photographs of the events taking place that morning, prior to the ship's departure at 9:15 am. These photos are presented on pages 350 - 354 beginning with one of the ship's new CMC, HTCM(SW) Douglas R. Brown and new Executive Officer, LCDR Todd Leavitt. The final photo is one that clearly reflects the emotion described in co-author Edgar's final poem on the life of a sailor, "The Magic of Winnie the Pooh". Petty Officer Edgar's daughter, Kristen, came on board carrying her Winnie the Pooh doll and . . . as is often said . . . : "A picture is worth a thousand words!"

A Salute To Commander Thomas H. Copemen, III
3rd Captain of the USS BENFOLD (DDG-65)

Commander Copeman came aboard the BENFOLD
In January, nineteen ninety-nine:
He will lead "The Best Ship in the Navy"
And continue that tradition so fine.
He's Captain number 3 of the vessel
And will take her through deployment number 2 . . . .
Then into the 21st Century,
Flying the colors of the red, white and blue.

In his first seventeen years in the Navy
He served both on land and at sea,
Earning Unit Citations and Campaign Awards:
His family is as proud as can be.

His second "family", the Borough of Audubon - - -
All the students and residents there - - -
Is also quite proud of this Captain:
American flags can be seen everywhere !

Commander Copeman keeps in touch with the ship's crew,
As well as with its families and friends.
He's now helping them prepare for deployment - - -
The crew's success on their support depends.
He speaks proudly as the vessel's new Captain,
Praising the crew's excellence and pride.
As her leader, he encourages AND contributes . . .
No secrets from the crew will he hide.

When I first <u>met</u> the ship's new Captain - - -
Just a month after <u>he</u> took command - - -
He impressed me as efficient, yet caring,
As I talked about what had been planned
For the Sailor of the Year's April visit
To Audubon, the crew's 2nd hometown.

He'd already heard of the friendship
With this borough of patriotic renown.
He told me crew members had informed him
Of the gifts and the cards they'd received.
He said that this friendship was special
And something in which he <u>truly</u> believed.

When we met on the ship's third birthday,
Commander Copeman accepted with pride
A Tapestry Afghan from the borough,
With historic landmarks, side by side.

On June 1st the friendship was strengthened
When the ship's new XO came to town
To present a United States Navy Flag
To the students of the proud little town.

Commander Copeman, ONWARD WITH VALOR !
And success for yourself and the crew
Of the "Best Damn Ship in the Navy",
Sailing for the red, white and blue.

When you return from deployment,
Should you get several days "R & R",
You're welcome to come to New Jersey
For a visit - - - by plane and by car - - -
To the proud little borough of Audubon.
We'll greet you with pride, that's for sure,
Then show you what makes us so special - - -
And why our friendship with the Navy will endure.

Craig E. Burgess

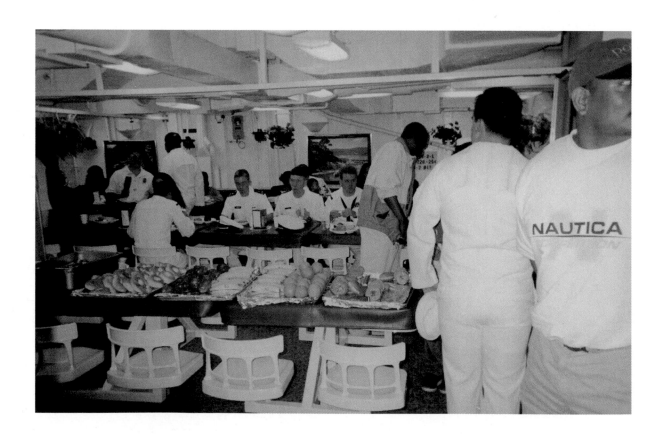

Chapter IV
The Green Wave And The Navy:
The History Of The Friendship

Samuel M. Sampler
U.S. Army

Edward C. Benfold
U.S. Navy

Nelson V. Brittin
U.S. Army

Audubon High School Project Memorial Committee,
announces the dedication of its Memorial to
the Audubon Medal of Honor Recipients.
Monday, July 4, 1994, 4:45 - 6:30 pm.
Audubon High School

 Scott Johnson

Melanie Aubrey

 Anthony Simeone

 Derek Everman

HM3 Benfold's Hometown... Audubon, NJ

Audubon, New Jersey has become the "second home port" for the USS BENFOLD. The ship's sponsor and HM3 Benfold's son still live in the Audubon area. The town has graciously hosted members of the crew for the last two years during their 4th of July festivities. In August, 1995 members of the Engineering Department were in Philadelphia, PA for Land Based Engineering Site training. The town hosted them to a barbecue and softball game. The pride and patriotism of the people of this small town has been a source of inspiration to the entire crew.

EDWARD C. BENFOLD

IN MEMORY OF THE SELFLESS SACRIFICING OF HIS OWN LIFE FOR THE LIVES OF TWO COUNTRYMEN. HE WAS KILLED WHILE DEFENDING THE WOUNDED IN KOREA ON 5 SEPTEMBER 1952

Our journey through history has given you, the readers, some insight into the borough of Audubon, the life story of a local hero and the life of a naval destroyer named in memory of that local hero. We now focus on a very special friendship that has been established between Audubon and the officers and crew of the USS BENFOLD (DDG-65): a friendship that grows stronger with each passing year. As the information on the previous page indicates, "Audubon has become the 'second home port' for the USS BENFOLD". The question is: How did it happen?

The photo shown below, containing the motto of Audubon High School, is a great way to begin to answer the question. It reflects a community in which pride and excellence are not merely words, but a tradition. It also portrays an image of the mascot in Audubon: a mascot symbolizing strength and determination, as well as the surface on which ships in the Navy travel from destination to destination. THE GREEN WAVE is, indeed, a very special mascot ! (See the photo and poem on the next page.)

A Very Special Mascot

The Green Wave

Each High School has a mascot
That helps to showcase pride.
It cheers the student body on
And helps to turn the tide
In favor of the hometown team
In search of one more win !
The mascot is the symbol
That causes heads to spin.

Most mascots are some animal
Or awesome bird of prey
Whose appearance on the field or court
Adds excitement to each day.
Some others are of human beings
Well known both far and wide,
For patriotic efforts,
For strength, or civic pride.

But AUDUBON is quite unique:
Its mascot's really keen !
It isn't man nor animal,
Yet it's strong . . . and very green !!
It even has a golden crest
To help subdue the foe:
Its mascot is a giant wave
That creates an undertow
That sweeps the opposition
Beneath that golden crest.
The Great GREEN WAVE of AUDUBON:
As a mascot, it's the best !!

The growth of the friendship between Audubon and the USS BENFOLD, like the growth of a tall and stately tree, begins with the planting of a seed from which roots take hold and produce a strong trunk. From the trunk come many branches that reach out in all directions from the trunk.

The seed for this special friendship was planted by the Department of the Navy when it made the decision to name one of its new destroyers in memory of Edward C. Benfold. The early growth of the 'roots' received nourishment from a number of sources: Mrs. Joan Henderson Walker, an AHS graduate in the class of 1947, who worked at the Lockheed Martin Combat Systems Engineering Development Site in Moorestown, New Jersey (where the Aegis system for the USS BENFOLD was developed), read about the naming of the new ship in an issue of the Aegis Newsletter and began to 'spread the word' to friends in the borough; Mr. Bob Hoover, another employee at the Moorestown, New Jersey Lockheed Martin site, who made an effort to have the Commissioning of the ship in Philadelphia; Mr. William Westphal, a 1960 AHS graduate and the current Principal of the school, who spoke to students in the Honors International Relations class about the Medal of Honor recipients who had lived and studied in Audubon; members of Murray-Troutt Post #262 of the American Legion in Audubon, who helped keep the memory of the three Medal of Honor recipients alive in annual services on Memorial Day and in special displays at the Post Home.

For the friendship to grow and strengthen, the 'roots' must be watered and fed. In Audubon, the nourishment came from the young citizens in the borough: students who, proud of the patriotic traditions in their community, established the Project Memorial Foundation at AHS and designed - - - and raised all of the money for the construction of - - - a Medal of Honor Memorial. The articles, flyers and photographs on the following 7 pages speak for themselves . . .

PROJECT MEMORIAL FOUNDATION

AUDUBON HIGH SCHOOL
CLASS OF 1994

Scott Johnson
Business & Events Chairperson

Derek Everman
Public Relations Chairperson

Melanie Aubrey
Research & Development Co-Chairperson

Anthony Simeone
Research & Development Co-Chairperson

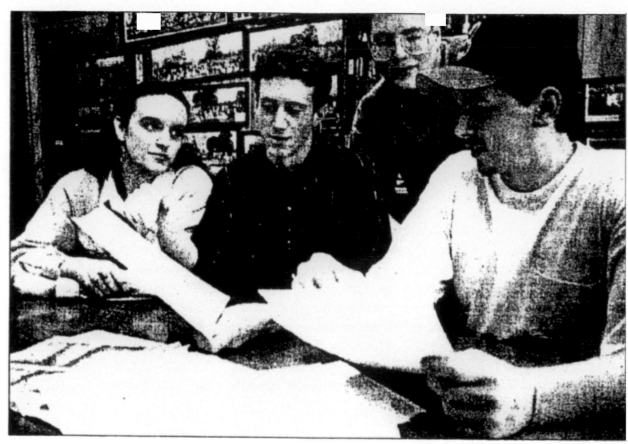

For The Inquirer / MARTY O'GRADY

Four of the Audubon High School seniors planning to raise money for the memorial are (from left) Melanie E. Aubrey, Scott A. Johnson, Anthony C. Simeone, and Derek S. Everman.

Audubon students to honor three heroes

By Christine Lutten
INQUIRER CORRESPONDENT

AUDUBON-- They are fresh-faced teenagers whose only experience with war was sitting in front of the TV watching U.S. Patriot missiles shoot down Iraqi Scuds in Operation Desert Storm.

They've never known what it means to be called to fight.

But five Audubon seniors want to remember three heroic men who had ties to the borough.

On July 4, the teenagers hope to unveil a monument on the high school grounds to honor three Audubon men who were awarded the Medal of Honor.

The monument will be a 5-foot, 6-inch, 8,000-pound wall with each

Three men awarded the Medal of Honor are getting a place in history.

man's face and medal citation etched on it. The teenagers have raised nearly $12,000 to build it.

The borough claims more Medal of Honor recipients than any municipality its size, according to the National Military Order of the Purple Heart.

The students got the idea from Audubon principal Bill Westphal, who spoke to the stidents' Honors International Relations class last fall about ideas for community service projects students could do for a class assignment.

"I was just meandering as I always do, and I started talking to them about our Medal of Honor winners," Westphal said. "A couple of days later five seniors came to my office and said they would like to undertake a project to honor these three people."

Tracking down information required that the students pore over books and call veterans' organizations for data on the personal histories of the men to be honored.

Students to honor 3 heroes

MEMORIAL from S1

Samuel M. Sampler, the borough's first medal recipient, relocated to Audubon after he was awarded the medal for his service in World War I. On Oct. 8, 1918, Sampler, who was born in Texas, threw a grenade at a German position near Etienne, France, killing two Germans. His action forced 28 enemy troops to surrender at a crucial moment and allowed Sampler's troops to move forward. He died in 1979 at the age of 84.

Edward C. Benfold, who attended Audubon High School in the late 1940s, was awarded his medal posthumously for his actions while serving as a Navy hospital corpsman in Korea on Sept. 5, 1952. Benfold was aiding wounded soldiers when two enemy soldiers rushed toward him. Benfold grabbed two grenades and pushed them against the men's chests, killing them and mortally wounding himself.

Nelson V. Brittin, a 1939 graduate of Audubon High School, was awarded his medal posthumously for his action near Yonggong-ni, Korea on March 7, 1951. Sergeant First Class Brittin, who was under relentless enemy fire, pushed forward up a hill, killing 20 enemy soldiers.

The students dove into the project last fall, contacting a contractor and choosing a site. Westphal had envisioned one spot near where the students eat lunch on sunny days. But the students had a grassy area overlooking Edgewood Avenue and Walnut Street in mind.

Oddly, a monument honoring the soldiers from Audubon who fought in World War I sat on that exact site until the 1950s. Westphal, who graduated from the high school in 1960s, remembered seeing it as a child and told the students about it.

"We were surprised," said Scott A. Johnson, 17. "It's sort of ironic that we are putting it there, but obviously

For The Inquirer / MARTY O'GRADY

Carrying a sign about their project to the site are (from left) Scott Johnson, Derek Everman, Anthony Simeone and Melanie Aubrey.

it's a good spot."

Veterans and relatives of the medal recipients have been supportive.

"I have to commend them," said Harry Oswald, 46, of Audubon, a Vietnam veteran who works with the Camden branch of the Military Order of the Purple Heart. Oswald has worked to connect the students with other veterans who might help.

"There aren't many 17-year-olds — there aren't many 25-year-olds — who would want to get involved with veterans," said Oswald, who has lived in Audubon for 18 years.

In 1952 Dorothy Waida was only a few years older than the students in Audubon when her husband, Edward C. Benfold, died in Korea and was awarded the medal. Their only child, Edward Benfold, now 41, said he remembers reading a comic book about medal of honor recipients, including a section about his father.

Waida, now 61, moved to Audubon with her second husband 21 years ago. She said she was surprised to hear that students would have taken on such a project.

"You hear so much about how they don't even want to go into the service. ... It's really something. It's really something," Waida said.

The students have taken steps to raise the money needed.

For example, Johnson walked into a meeting of the Audubon alumni association last Wednesday night and walked out with several hundred dollars more pledged to the project. So far, through mailings to businesses and veterans in Audubon, they have raised about a quarter of what's needed.

The students said they expected one of the biggest fund-raising events to be an athletic contest March 26 pitting police officers from Audubon, Audubon Park and Mount Ephraim against the high school seniors in basketball, volleyball and broom hockey.

For More Information

■ For information on the monument or to make a donation, Audubon High School can be reached at 547-7695.

An artist's drawing shows plans for the five-foot memorial.

361

Memorial Description

All Impala Black Granite - Total Pieces 6

Monument

Dimensions:
- **Height: 5 feet 6 inches**
- **Width: 10 inches**
- **Length (per section): 3 feet**
- **Weight (per section): 2,700 pounds**
  - **Total Weight: 8,100 pounds**

Polished: Front, Back & Top
Rock Pitch: Sides

Base

Dimensions:

- **Height: 10 inches**
- **Width: 18 inches**
- **Length (per section): 48 inches**

Polished: Top
Rock Pitch: Front, Back & Sides

Designs:

Carving:

- **Skin Frost Carving**
- **Triple Border Lies**
- **Stars (Polished)**
- **Olive Spray**

Etching:

- **Three Soldier Profiles**
- **Three Medals of Honor**

Lettering:

- **600 Characters**

Student designers of the Medal of Honor Memorial gather for the groundbreaking ceremony (above) and break ground together (below).

AHS Principal William Westphal participates in the groundbreaking ceremony (above) and then joins the four students from the class of 1994 for a group photo (below)

An artist's depiction of the completed Medal of Honor Memorial Site on the campus of Audubon High School.

Scott Johnson

Business & Events Chairperson

Melanie Aubrey

Research & Development Co-Chairperson

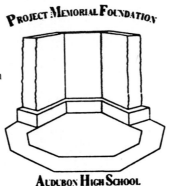

PROJECT MEMORIAL FOUNDATION

AUDUBON HIGH SCHOOL

CLASS OF 1994

Derek Everman

Public Relations Chairperson

Anthony Simeone

Research & Development Co-Chairperson

Project Memorial Fundraisers

1.   The Audubon, Audubon Park, and Mt. Ephraim police will be competing against Audubon High School seniors in athletic contests on Saturday, March 26. Tickets will be $3 for students and $5 for adults. There will be a $1 discount for tickets purchased before March 26. All proceeds from this event will go towards Project Memorial.

2.   Direct mailings have been made to all Audubon and Mt. Ephraim veterans (over 1,000 contacts). This was begun in December and will be completed in February.

3.   Direct mailings will also be sent to Audubon businesses in February. There are over 200 businesses in town and Project Memorial will recognize any corporate donation, of $50 or more, with a plaque.

4.   The POW/MIA Awareness Committee of Gloucester and Camden Counties, along with KC Printing, has donated one hundred T-shirts to be used as a fund raising project. These Project Memorial T-shirts will be sold for $10.

5.   A community initiated social whose benefits will be donated to Project Memorial will be organized by two members of the Audubon Board of Education. This event will not involve the students at the high school. The date for the social will be May 14th.

6.   A town drive will be organized to fund Project Memorial. Community organizations will be asked to help in the distribution of flyers to every house in Audubon. The date for the drive has yet to be determined.

7.   Audubon's Murray-Troutt Post #262 of the American Legion has agreed to and is in the process of organizing a spaghetti dinner. The proceeds will be donated to Project Memorial. The date for the dinner will be April 30th and tickets will be sold at $3 for children and $5 for adults.

8.   A donated Project Memorial sign will be erected on the site of the future memorial. This sign will be used to launch an advertising campaign. Contact will be made with the Retrospect, Courier Post, Philadelphia Inquirer, and the TV news. Such press coverage is anticipated to energize and create more support for Project Memorial.

9.   A "Buy a Brick" fundraiser will be established. Certificates ranging from $5 to $40 will be distributed to those individuals who decide to support Project Memorial through this program.

The efforts of these 4 students were reinforced in April of 1994 when a letter was received from the first Commanding Officer of the USS BENFOLD, Mark E. Ferguson, III, accepting an invitation to attend the dedication ceremony for the Memorial on July 4, 1994. (See the letter from Commander Ferguson below).

April 12, 1994

PROJECT MEMORIAL
Audubon Jr.-Sr. High School
Audubon New Jersey 08106-2299

Dear Mr. Everman,

Thank you for your kind invitation to attend the monument dedication. My family and I look forward to attending the ceremony and meeting the members of your project team.

As you know, the USS BENFOLD (DDG-65) is undergoing construction at INGALLS Shipbuilding in Pascagoula, MS. The ship is the most advanced destroyer-class ship in the world, incorporating the AEGIS technology developed by Martin Marietta at Moorestown, New Jersey. The crew, consisting of both men and women, will begin join the ship later this year. As the ship's first Commanding Officer, I welcome the chance to participate in this special event at Audubon School. You are to be commended for your outstanding efforts and patriotism.

Sincerely,

Mark Ferguson
Commander
United States Navy

The roots were being strengthened and the trunk was growing, with branches beginning to appear. The 4 students were honored at a special ceremony at Fort Dix on April 29th, 1994. (See the letter on this page and the news release, dated April 29th, that was published in the Fort Dix newspaper on following page.)

DEPARTMENT OF THE ARMY
HEADQUARTERS, FORT DIX
FORT DIX, NEW JERSEY
April 19, 1994

Office of the Chief of Staff

Mr. William J. Westphal
Principal
Audubon Jr. - Sr. High School
350 Edgewood Avenue
Audubon, New Jersey 08106-2299

Dear Mr. Westphal:

Colonel Michael L. Warner, Commander of Fort Dix, would like to recognize the accomplishments of your students who participated in the Congressional Medal of Honor Project Memorial. He would like to present a High Performance certificate and medallion to Melanie E. Aubrey, Derek S. Everman, Scott A. Johnson and Anthony C. Simeone at the Evening Colors Ceremony to be held at Fort Dix on April 29, 1994 at 4:00 pm.

In addition to this recognition, Colonel Warner would also like to present a national award from General Jack Merritt to the President of the Student Body at the same ceremony.

If the weather on April 29th is good, the ceremony will be held outdoors, across from the Post Headquarters. If there is inclement weather, the ceremony will be held in the Headquarters Command Gym. I have enclosed a map with directions to both locations.

We hope that you and your students will be able to join us for this ceremony. Please call me if you will be joining us for this occasion. I may be reached at (609) 562-3414 if you have any further questions or if I can be of further assistance.

Sincerely,

Susan M. Meyer
Lieutenant Colonel, US Army
Deputy Chief of Staff

368

thePost

Published for the Fort Dix Community. Circulation 10,000

April 29, 1994

Dix honors seniors from Audubon HS

Carolee Nisbet
Editor

Fort Dix will honor five Audubon High School seniors at Evening Colors today for their campaign to make sure their community remembers its heroes.

The students, inspired by Audubon principal Bill Westphal, hope to unveil their project July 4: A curved, three-section monument bearing the names and citations of each of three men from Audubon who were awarded the Medal of Honor.

The students – Melanie E. Aubrey, Scott A. Johnson, Anthony C. Simeone and Derek S. Everman – will be presented Fort Dix High Performance Awards for Excellence by Post Commander COL Michael L. Warner at the 4 p.m. ceremony.

Evening Colors this week will be the first of the season to be held outdoors, and the first to be held at a new site – the field at the corner of Alabama Avenue and North Scott.

The borough of Audubon has more Medal of Honor recipients

Continued on page 3

Dix honors

Continued from page 1

than any other community its size, according to records of the National Military Order of the Purple Heart.

The monument, for which the students are raising nearly $12,000, is set to be placed in a quiet, grassy area near Edgewood Avenue and Walnut Street, on the grounds of the high school. So far, the students have realized about half of the monument cost from donations.

Honored by the monument will be one soldier from World War I, and two who fought in Korea.

Samuel M. Sampler was a corporal in Company H, 142d Infantry, 36th Division, on October 8, 1918. His unit was mounting an advance near St. Etienne, France, and had suffered severe casualties from machine-gun fire. Sampler spotted the position of the enemy machine guns on an elevation, and, armed with German hand grenades he had picked up, he left the line and rushed forward in the face of heavy fire. He advanced to the position, and lobbed three grenades among the enemy, killing two, silencing the machine guns, and causing the surrender of 28 Germans. As a result of his act, the company was able to resume its advance.

Sampler died in 1979 at the age of 84.

The second honoree was a Navy Hospital Corpsman third Class attached to the 1st Marine Division in Korea on Sept. 5, 1952.

Edward C. Benford attended Audubon High School in the 1940s.

He was honored by his nation for gallantry and intrepidity at the risk of his life while saving the lives of others. Benford's company was hit by heavy fire and assault during hours of darkness by a battalion-size enemy force. During the heavy mortar and artillery barrages, Benford resolutely moved from position to position, treating the wounded. From a ridge on the battlefield, he spotted two Marines in a crater, and headed toward them – only to met by two grenades from an enemy soldier. Benford grabbed a grenade in each hand, leaped from the crater and hurled himself against two oncoming enemy soldiers, pushing the grenades against their chests and killing them both. He was mortally wounded by the explosions.

The third honoree, also a graduate of Audubon High School, was awarded the Medal of Honor posthumously.

SFC Nelson V. Brittin, assigned to Company I, 19th Infantry Regiment, was in combat with his unit near Yonggong-ni, Korea, on March 7, 1951. He volunteered to lead his squad up a hill with meager cover against murderous fire from the enemy, and tossed a grenade at the nearest enemy position. Wounded, he refused medical help and continued to move from position to position, tossing grenades and clearing a path for his soldiers with little regard for his own safety. Advancing on a camouflaged, sandbagged machine gun nest flanked by riflemen, Brittin was caught in a hail of automatic fire which killed him instantly.

369

July 4, 1994 was a very special day in Audubon history. Representatives from the Military Order of the Purple Heart, the U. S. Army, the U. S. Navy and community leaders gathered on the campus of Audubon High School for the official dedication of the Memorial Site. Highlights of the ceremony are presented on the next 7 pages.

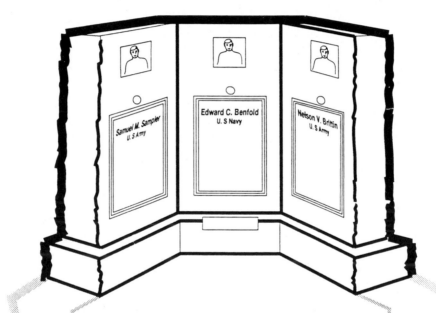

PROJECT MEMORIAL

MONUMENT DEDICATION

July 4th, 1994 – 6:00 pm

A Tribute to Audubon's Congressional Medal of Honor Recipients

FLAG SALUTE / NATIONAL ANTHEM
Alumni Choir
Mr. Richard Smith, Director

INTRODUCTION AND WELCOME
Melanie E. Aubrey, Project Memorial Committee
Audubon High School Class of 1994

INVOCATION
Pastor Steve Shuster, Audubon United Methodist Church
Audubon High School Class of 1974

SPEAKERS
Mayor Alfred W. Murray
Audubon High School Class of 1979

Mr. Albert A. Hujdich, State Commander
Military Order of the Purple Heart

Col. Michael Warner, former Commander of Fort Dix

Commander Mark Ferguson, United States Navy
(future) Commander of USS Benfold

Mr. William J. Westphal, Principal
Audubon High School Class of 1960

Anthony C. Simeone, Project Memorial Committee
Audubon High School Class of 1994

Scott A. Johnson, Project Memorial Committee
Audubon High School Class of 1994

DEDICATION
Derek S. Everman, Project Memorial Committee
Audubon High School Class of 1994

RIFLE SALUTE

TAPS
Melissa Walters
Audubon High School Class of 1996

BENEDICTION
Pastor Steve Shuster, Audubon United Methodist Church
Audubon High School Class of 1974

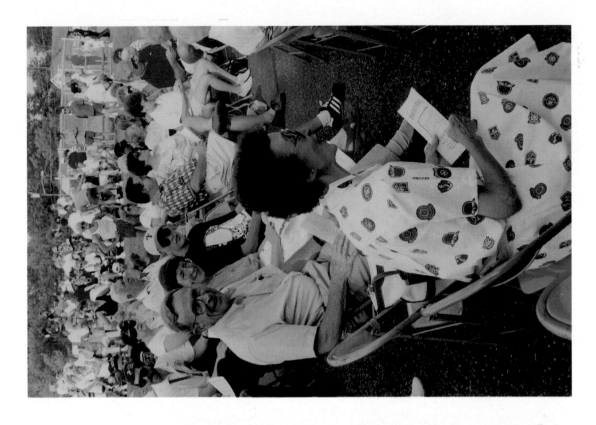

Audubon residents and guests gather on Edgewood Avenue for the official Dedication and unveiling of the Medal of Honor Memorial.

Members of Murray-Troutt American Legion Post #262 pose for a photo with members of the Benfold family (above). Commander Ferguson addresses the citizens and honored guests during the Dedication ceremony (below).

The Memorial is unveiled (above), as members of the military, along with
members of the Audubon Police Department, salute (below).

Following the ceremony, Commander Ferguson joins the 4 members of the Class of 1994 and AHS Principal Westphal at the Memorial site (above). Ferguson and his family then pose for a group shot with members of the Benfold family (below).

The efforts of the AHS Project Memorial Foundation committee members were beginning to reach beyond the boundaries of Audubon. In September, 1994, a feature article on the Project was published in the Philadelphia Inquirer (See page 377); in November, an article appeared in the New Jersey Legionnaire (page 378).

In 1995, the friendship between Audubon and the USS BENFOLD was strengthened by a visit to the borough by some 30 members of the crew, who were in training in Philadelphia, prior to assignment on board. Also, a special page was included in the 90th Anniversary edition of the 4th of July program book in Audubon, focusing on the ever-growing relationship between Audubon and the U. S. Navy (page 379).

Co-author Burgess composed a poem that saluted the ongoing activities of the Project Memorial Foundation, shown in Chapter III. AHS Principal Westphal asked Burgess to present a copy of the poem to Commander Ferguson during the visit of the crew in August. The visit included a ceremony at the Medal of Honor Memorial and a guided tour of the Rotunda at AHS, a reception at the American Legion Post Home, a special service at St. Mary's Episcopal church, a luncheon at the fire hall on Merchant Street and a softball game. Highlights of the visit, along with an article published in early 1996 in the "Bold Defender", the newsletter of the USS BENFOLD, are presented on pages 380 - 386. Less than 2 years after the Dedication of the Memorial site, it was evident that the friendship between the borough and the officers and crew of the ship would be a long-lasting one.

In February of 1996, Burgess received an invitation to attend the Commissioning Ceremony of the USS BENFOLD at the Broadway Pier in San Diego, California. Upon his return from the Commissioning, he contacted both elementary schools in town and another 'branch' of the growing friendship tree sprouted: a pen-pal program between 4th and 5th graders at Haviland Avenue School and Madison Avenue School and members of the crew. Highlights of the first year of this project are presented on pages 387 - 394.

As more and more students began receiving letters from crew members, residents in the borough discussed some other ways in which the growing bonds of friendship could be strengthened. Members of the Women's Club baked cookies and sent them to the crew for the December holidays in 1996. This has become an annual tradition for the local group. When the first LCDR of the USS BENFOLD, Executive Officer Sinclair Harris, left his assignment in early 1997, he prepared a written farewell that was published in the "Bold Defender". His comments included some special thanks to the students and residents in Audubon. (See the letter on page 395).

On June 20, 1997, the Command of the ship was turned over to Commander D. Michael Abrashoff. Prior to his transfer, Commander Ferguson made special arrangements to return to Audubon for a visit with all of the students. We present some highlights of this very 'historic moment' in the friendship on pages 496 - 401

Co-author Burgess was invited to the Change of Command ceremony on board the ship and he took several letters and gifts from the borough for the new Commander, as well as for the outgoing leader. (See the references on pages 402 - 405).

Burgess visited the officers and crew again in mid - July, prior to the start of the first deployment of the ship. He brought more than 17 pounds of salt water taffy and a special greeting card from the borough. (See the card on page 406).

Teens built a monument, found rewards

Raising a memorial was a lesson in life for the students. Now they are receiving honors.

By Amy Zurzola
INQUIRER CORRESPONDENT

AUDUBON — The four Audubon High School seniors had something to prove: To the people who seemed convinced that young people only make trouble, to the naysayers who said it couldn't be done, and most of all, to themselves.

Now, less than a year later, their proof stands like a sentry in five-foot-high black granite, bathed in floodlights under a balmy summer sky.

"We had no idea what we were getting ourselves into," said Anthony Simeone, 18. Simeone and the three other students led Project Memorial, a campaign to erect a monument to Audubon's three Medal of Honor recipients, raising more than $14,000 in donations.

Since then, the group has received commendations and citations from President Clinton, the Military Order of the Purple Heart, civic and veterans groups. In October, they will receive the George Washington Honor Medal from the Freedoms Foundation. The award recognizes individuals and organizations who, through words or deeds, promote an understanding of the nation's heritage, freedom, the private-enterprise system and responsible citizenship.

Katherine Wood-Jacobs, the foundation's vice president for awards, said the national awards jury picked Project Memorial because it was different from the usual youth entries, which are typically essays and speeches.

"We don't get many projects of this type, of youth putting together a memorial," she said.

The three-sided black granite memorial features the faces of the three soldiers — Samuel M. Sampler, Edward C. Benfold and Nelson V. Brittin — who received the nation's highest military honor, given by Congress for risk of life in combat beyond the call of duty.

Sampler led a charge through St. Etienne, France, during World War I. Benfold and Brittin lost their lives in Korea.

The memorial stands in front of the high school, surrounded by flowers, with an American flag fluttering overhead. But 18-year-old Melanie Aubrey, a self-described pacifist, is quick to point out that the project is a celebration of honor, not war.

"The only thing we wanted to stress throughout the project is that this was not a monument to war. We wanted to remember what they did for the country, that they did something very brave and very noble and very special."

For The Inquirer / MICHAEL PLUNKETT

The memorial honors Audubon's recipients of the Medal of Honor. Three of four students who raised the money, (from left) Scott Johnson, Derek Everman and Anthony Simeone, are reflected in it.

Principal Bill Westphal said that since its dedication July 4, the monument has become a popular site. Residents stop by during walks around the neighborhood or pull up in cars to admire the memorial. At night, floodlights shining up at the faces of the three soldiers etched in stone lend an almost ghostly quality.

For the community, the monument represents Audubon's history of military service. It gives the community something to view with pride.

For the students responsible for its creation, it has come to mean much more.

"I got into college because of it," said Scott Johnson, 18, a lanky, blue-eyed boy-next-door who left Aug. 25 to begin classes at Susquehanna University, where he will study business. Through his work in the project, he gained confidence, learning to sell his ideas and himself — qualities he knows he'll need to pursue his goal of owning his own company.

"I was always the one who was willing to be in the background, real quiet and shy," Johnson says. He got over that quickly. He had to. Early in the project, the group solicited funds from a meeting of hundreds of American Legionnaires.

"Basically, we had to get up and beg for contributions. Along the way, you learn to get your point across," he says, laughing.

For strong-willed, gregarious Derek Everman, 18, the politician of the bunch, the rewards were practical experience he'll use in pursuit of his dream· the highest office in the land.

"I'm going to be president," Everman said, with the partly-serious, partly-embarrassed look of a young man out to conquer the world. He will study political science at Rutgers University before, he hopes, entering the U.S. Naval Academy at Annapolis next fall. He took full advantage of the project's "schmooze factor" — kissing babies, hugging people and shaking lots of hands.

Although his scruffy goatee and backward baseball cap may lend Everman the look of a Generation X slacker, he's anything but: a member of the school's newspaper, student government and soccer team, he saw this project as an opportunity not only to honor Audubon's war heroes but to set himself above the rest.

"I'd always been told I had a lot of potential," he said, "but potential doesn't mean anything if you don't do anything with it."

Simeone, dark-haired, intellectual and introspective, said that through the project, he learned about others as well as himself.

"I gained a lot of faith in the human race through this," he said. He will study English at Rutgers, and would like to be an author. And if authors should write about what they know, he figures the exposure to different kinds of people will definitely help him in the long run.

For Aubrey, who will study classical music performance at Temple University, the project was once more in a slew of extracurricular activities that included the school band, newspaper, concert club, cross-country and track teams.

Asserting herself as the only woman in the group wasn't a problem. "I'm a people person," she says, quickly adding: "I'm naturally assertive. I always had my say in everything."

One valuable lesson they all learned — one they'll surely need to survive on campus and off — is group dynamics. For four teens who weren't friends before joining the project, it wasn't always a walk in the park.

"We all bickered. It was a big soap opera," Simeone says with a conspiratorial grin.

"I learned to give in and realize that sometimes people have opinions and that they're valid," Everman said.

But for the controversy and rocky times, none would have left the project. "I couldn't have just walked out; that's not the kind of thing I do," Aubrey said, echoing a theme common to the group.

"Now, when I see the [the monument], I just nod and smile. I'm just relieved that it's in the ground and it's over," Aubrey said.

But, at least for Aubrey, there is one little thing she would have done differently: She wouldn't have ridden through town on the Fourth of July float concocted out of Johnson's huge old station wagon.

"I really didn't want anything to do with patting ourselves on the back. That was a little much."

WORLD'S LARGEST VETERANS' ORGANIZATION

New Jersey
LEGIONNAIRE

Official Publication Of THE AMERICAN LEGION, DEPARTMENT OF NEW JERSEY

VOLUME 9, NO. 2   **TRENTON, N. J.**   **NOVEMBER, 1994**

Students' study project honors medalists

To the Editor:

On July 4th, four Audubon High School students of the graduating class of 1994 unveiled a monument honoring the Borough's three Medal of Honor recipients. While attending a special history class, Scott Johnson, Melanie Aubrey, Derek Everman and Anthony Simeone, inspired by a talk by William Westphal, Principal of their school, adopted "Project Memorial" as their hallmark for the Class of 1994.

In October 1993, their research began, and over the next nine months, the art and design, finances, public relations, and construction under the guidance of William Westphal was completed. A total of $12,000 was raised through friends and community organizations. By February, 1994, their goal was realized and they knew the Memorial would be completed by July 4, 1994. At the ceremony, through the efforts of Congressman Rob Andrews, these students were presented with Citations from President Clinton.

Among the dignitaries attending the ceremony was Commander Mark Ferguson, United States Navy, who will command the destroyer USS Benfold now under construction, and New Jersey State American Legion Commander George W. Diem.

The black marble monument on which the images are inscribed of Samuel Sampler who served in World War I, Edward C. Benfold and Nelson V. Brittin, both of whom served and died in Korea, bridges the generations from those who served to protect to those who live in freedom today, and most importantly, REMEMBER!

"Project Memorial" intends to begin a fund that will provide perpetual care for the monument as well as a scholarship fund to assist those future graduates of Audubon High School who elect to pursue a career in government service.

Thomas F. Costello
Audubon

Shown at the unveiling of a monument honoring Audubon's three Medal of Honor recipients and left to right, Commander Mark Ferguson, United States Navy, future Commander of USS Benfold; Derek Everman, Public Relations; Melanie Aubrey, Research; Scott Johnson, Design & Construction; Anthony Simeone, Art & Research; William J. Westphal, Principal. Audubon High School and Rudy March, Commander of Murray Troutt Post #262, American Legion, Audubon.

WE WELCOME A NEW ADDITION TO OUR AUDUBON FAMILY

Last 4th of July Audubon welcomed Commander Mark Ferguson
and his family to the "Project Memorial" celebration and dedication. Commander Ferguson will return with a few representatives of the crew of the U.S.S.
Benfold. The ship, which has been christened in the name of of Edward
C.Benfold, town son, will be Commissioned early next year.
Audubon, as you know, is the only small town in the United States that has been
home to 3 Congressional Medal of Honor heroes.
The U.S.S. Benfold carries the spirit of our residents, and everyone who lives in
our community is filled with pride that this great ship will forever commemorate
one of our own. There has been a fast bonding between our town and the staff
and crew of the Benfold.There will be a special plaque and portrait presented to
the representative that will be placed in the stateroom of the vessel. This will
serve as a reminder to those who serve upon the Benfold of the blessings, best
wishes and family bond that has been established between them and the town of
Audubon.
We wish them the best and look forward to greeting them on the 4th of July.
They shall be in our midst again in August, at which time we shall have the
opportunity to meet them personally, on a one to one basis. We look forward to
many years of communication and friendship.It is a great time for the family of
Edward Benfold to reflect upon his importance to the small Boro of Audubon
and it's citizens and ultimately to the United States of America.

The 4th of July Committee wishes to thank our resident and friend Bob Hoover,
who took the time, effort and dedication to organize the Benfold celebration. We
again recognize the legacy that "Project Memorial" has created. Thanks Scott
Johnson, Derek Everman, Melanie Aubrey and Anthony Simeone. You too, have
left your mark!

Alfred W. Murray
John T. Hanson
Anthony M. Pugliese.

Introduction from 1995 4th of July Celebration Book

Evidence of the friendship between Audubon and the USS BENFOLD

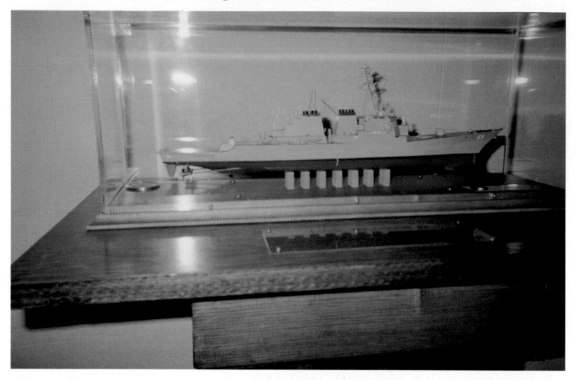

The scale model of the ship presented to the students and on display in the high school Rotunda.

The plaque from the citizens of Audubon on display on the bridge of the ship.

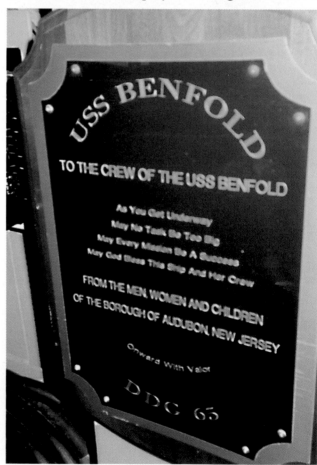

Town, sailors honor Korean War hero from Audubon

By BERNIE WEISENFELD
Courier-Post Staff

AUDUBON — Edward C. Benfold's heroism in battle won him a Medal of Honor and put his name on an Audubon High School monument and a Navy destroyer.

The granite monument, which Benfold shares with two other war heroes from this borough, was the site of a gathering Saturday honoring the Navy veteran, who was killed in 1952 during the Korean War.

The USS Benfold's captain and 30 crew members, Benfold's widow, Dorothy Waida, and officials from the school and Murray-Troutt American Legion Post No. 262 of Audubon gathered on a breezy, sunny day.

Though the Benfold, launched last year, is still being readied for sea duty at a Mississippi shipyard, its engineering crew is training at the Philadelphia Navy Yard. Audubon High School Principal William Westphal learned they were nearby and invited them to visit the monument.

"We want to cement a relationship between the crew of the Benfold and the town," Westphal said.

The ship's crew took part in a Saturday service at St. Mary's Episcopal Church in Haddon Heights, where Benfold attended, then played a softball game against residents. Local poet Craig Burgess, who was the 1963 Audubon High School valedictorian, presented the crew with a poem about students who raised

funds to pay for the monument.

Visiting Audubon, a small town with well-kept bungalows, is "like coming to America," said Sinclair Harris of Washington, D.C., an executive officer of the Benfold. "This is the picture you have."

Ship Commander Mark Ferguson, who attended the monument dedication July 4 last year, said

other crew members will be sent to future ceremonies. Though San Diego will be the Benfold's port, "Audubon is our unofficial hometown," he said. "It makes for a better ship and a better crew" to have young sailors learn of young Benfold's heroism, he said.

The visit gave him "a sense of pride, I guess," said Benfold crew member David Nemcik, 21, of California.

Benfold, who attended Audubon High School in the 1940s, received the nation's highest military honor for action in the Korean War in 1952 that cost him his life, but saved two wounded American soldiers.

A 21-year-old Navy hospital corpsman who arrived in Korea only five days earlier, he spotted two wounded Marines in a frontline shell crater. As he reached them, two hand grenades fell into the crater. Benfold picked up the grenades, leaped from the crater and pushed them into the chests of two enemy soldiers, killing them and himself. The two wounded American soldiers survived.

Benfold's widow and his infant son, Edward J., received his Medal of Honor in 1953. His son now lives in Cherry Hill and still has the medal.

Benfold's widow lives in Audubon and christened the ship last November.

"I stop by once in a while" at the school monument, said Waida, 63, now remarried. "I'm so proud of the kids that started all this."

Edward Benfold's heroic sacri-

> "We want to cement a relationship between the crew of the Benfold and the town."
>
> **William Westphal**
> principal
> Audubon High School

> "Audubon is our unofficial hometown. It makes for a better ship and a better crew" to have young sailors learn of Edward C. Benfold's heroism.
>
> **Mark Ferguson**
> ship commander
> USS Benfold

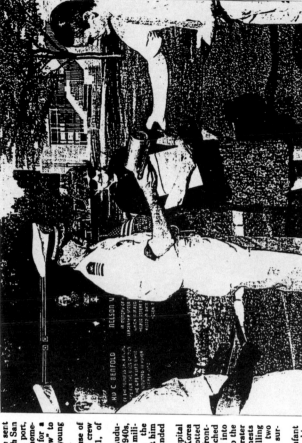

Ceremony: USS Benfold Commander Mark Ferguson accepts a war shell plaque from Audubon's Michael Mertz. Dorothy Waida, the widow of Edward C. Benfold, looks on. Ferguson's Navy destroyer was named after Benfold, a corpsman from Audubon who was killed in the Korean War.

By Al Schell, Courier-Post

fice didn't surprise her, she said. "He would do anything for anyone."

The monument, built last year through the leadership and fundraising efforts of four Audubon High School seniors, also honors

two other Medal of Honor recipients who lived in Audubon: Army Sgt. First Class Nelson W. Brittin, killed in Korea in 1951, received the medal posthumously; Army Cpl. Samuel M. Sampler was honored for bravery in France

in World War I. He died in 1979 at age 84.

"It's a jewel of the town," Westphal said of the monument. "We had 17-year-olds and 75-year-olds digging the hole" for footings.

Ship's crew visits Haddons to learn about namesake

Destroyer is named in honor of former resident Edward Benfold

By Mark Swanson

The Venerable Robert Willing, interim pastor of St Mary's Episcopal Church in Haddon Heights, looked out at the rows of white Navy uniforms in his church one Saturday and smiled.

It is appropriate that so many seamen visit his church, he said, because early Christians often met under overturned boats. The ribs of those overturned boats, he said, must have looked much like St. Mary's own wooden exposed ceiling rafters. Like early Christians, a ship brought them together.

What brought the seamen of the USS Benfold to Haddon Heights was the legacy of one man. That man, Edward Benfold of Audubon, was a St. Mary's member prior to his death in the early 1950s. The ship is the USS Benfold, guided missile destroyer DD(G)-65, named after the man.

Executive Officer Sinclair M. Harris said a commissioning crew such as the Benfold's sometimes have unique opportunities to learn about the person their ship is named after. "It's a

chance to build memories," he noted, ones that will help give their service meaning and depth.

Harris explained that some of the Benfold's crew has been in training at the Philadelphia Naval Shipyard and is stationed nearby. Anticipating this period of training, he said, USS Benfold Commander Mark Ferguson expressed a desire to establish relationships with Benfold's hometown and church. The ship was christened last November at Ingalls Shipbuilding in Pascagoula, Mississippi by Edward Benfold's widow, Mrs. Dorothy Benfold Waida. Also present were Benfold's son, Edward J. Benfold, and granddaughters Nicole and Alexandra. The ship will likely be commissioned at its home port of San Diego in early 1996.

Edward Clyde Benfold was born in 1931, the son of Edward E. and Glenys Benfold of Staten Island. The first few years of his life were spent with relatives in Liverpool, Nova Scotia, and London. He was a skilled horseman and

won numerous horsemanship ribbons.

While in high school, he participated in plays and musical productions. Benfold's father was killed during World War II when the USS Castilla was torpedoed. The son joined the Navy in June 1949. He was trained as a hospitalman and served at several bases before landing at Philadelphia Naval Hospital. He met his wife, the former Dorothy Groff, in 1951 and was married that year. Their son, Edward, was born in May 1952.

Five days after his arrival at the Korean Conflict in September 1952, Benfold was killed while aiding two wounded Marines under heavy artillery fire on the battlefield. In July 1953, Benfold's 14-month-old son was given his father's Medal of Honor at the Philadelphia Naval Base.

St. Mary's Episcopal Church pastor Ven. Robert Willing, Mrs. Dorothy Benfold Waida and USS Benfold Cmdr. Mark Ferguson ask for blessings on Edward Benfold and the ship named after him at the church's Benfold stained glass window.

On a cool sunny Saturday morning in Haddon Heights, Pastor Willing stood before a stained-glass window, dedicated to Benfold in 1953. With Dor-

othy Benfold Waida and Commander Ferguson by his side, Willing asked for a blessing on the departed Benfold and the seamen.

"O hear us when we cry to

thee for those in peril on the sea," said the final hymn, which echoed through the church and through just a few white-uniformed Navy seamen.

Crew members from the USS BENFOLD take a tour of the Rotunda at Audubon
High School (above) and spend some time in the Memorabilia Room of AHS,
viewing highlights of the Medal of Honor Memorial Project (below).

At a ceremony at the Memorial site, members of the Benfold family meet the crew members (above). Later, the crew visits the monuments to World War II, Korean War, and Vietnam War veterans on the grounds of American Legion Post #262 on Chestnut Street (below).

Following the service at the stained-glass window of St. Mary's Episcopal church in Haddon Heights (dedicated in memory of Edward C. Benfold in 1954) crew members sign the guest register (above) while Commander Ferguson talks with Interim Rector, the Venerable Robert Willing (below).

FEATURE

AUDUBON ONCE AGAIN WELCOMES BENFOLD

The City of Audubon, New Jersey welcomed twenty BENFOLD engineers on 19 August 1995. As the engineers were in Philadelphia for ATSG training at the Land Based Engineering Site, it proved a perfect opportunity to visit the hometown of Edward Benfold.

The engineers arrived early Saturday morning at the Audubon Fire House and were met by Mr. and Mrs. Bob Hoover, high school classmates of Benfold, and Mr. Al Murray, the mayor of Audubon. We then began our whirlwind tour of the town of Audubon and the roots of Edward C. Benfold. We visited Audubon High School, site of the Medal of Honor monument erected to Edward Benfold and two other Audubon natives who earned the nation's highest honor. Our next stop was St. Mary's Episcopal Church, where a moving service was given in honor of Edward C. Benfold and the BENFOLD crew, ending on the notes of "Eternal Father," the Navy Hymn. The caravan the trooped over to the Veterans of Foreign Wars building. Tasty refreshments and good conversation were had by all. Then it was back to the Fire House to change clothes, have a few wild rides on the old fire engine, and then off to the

CO, XO AND BENFOLD FAMILY AT THE AUDUBON MEDAL OF HONOR MONUMENT

softball field for a challenge match between the BENFOLD Big Dogs and the Fire House Team. Although the score favored the firemen, the BENFOLD spirit outshone our opponents' bench!

The rest of the day was filled with barbecued hot dogs, burgers, fresh corn and fun and games at the Fire House. Amidst some heated shuffleboard matches and tense pool playing, the BENFOLD had a great day, and we all left with a strong sense of pride for the man our ship represents.

Tuesday, June 04, 1996

Dear Mr. Burgess,

Thank you so very much for very nice letter and the book of poetry. The Commanding Officer was very appreciative of the gesture.

The crew and I welcome the letters from your grade schoolers and will be proud to support the pen-pal program. I ask that the letters initially be addressed to me, so that they can get properly routed. As mentioned in your letter, you will be able to deliever them in person. The ship will arrive in San Diego on 17 July. I ask that you come by Thursday or Friday of that week in the afternoon. I can be reached by calling 1 (619) 556-3869.

Life onboard is really exciting now. We have finished all of commissioning hurdles and are working ourselves up to be a fleet ready asset. The weapons and engineering systems have performed flawlessly. The crew has now settled out and are steadily improving in all areas. In the next few weeks we will shoot lots of surface to air missiles at targets fired at us from the beach. Though we are quite busy, it is the type of activity we came in the navy to do.

I hope this note finds you well. Give my regards to Bob Hoover and the rest of the fine citizens of your lovely town.

Sincerely,

Sinclair M. Harris
Executive Officer
USS BENFOLD (DDG 65)

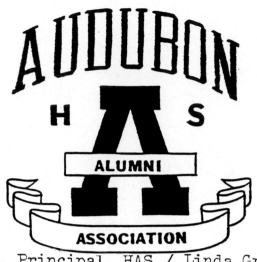

AUDUBON
H A S
ALUMNI
ASSOCIATION

Thursday, June 13, 1996

To   : Roseann Endt, Principal, HAS / Linda Gringeri, Principal, MAS
From : Craig E. Burgess, President, AHS Alumni Association
Re   : PROJECT FRIENDSHIP

I want to thank you for your willingness to participate in the pen-pal project with the crew of the USS BENFOLD. Please extend thanks to the teachers at HAS who took the time to include a letter-writing assignment in their classes. I know that the Captain and crew of the USS BENFOLD will be very excited when they see the 35 letters that have been written by the young citizens in Audubon who attend HAS.
The total number of letters that I shall be taking to San Diego next month is 77!!!

Early in May, I wrote a letter to Commander Ferguson, informing him of our plan to initiate a pen-pal program with the crew of the USS BENFOLD. On Tuesday afternoon, a response to my letter was received, written by the ship's Executive Officer, Sinclair M. Harris. The letter began with the sentence: " The crew and I welcome the letters from your grade schoolers and will be proud to support the pen-pal program."

It would appear that the project is getting off on a good 'foot'. I am scheduled to arrive in San Diego late in the afternoon on Tuesday, July 16th and will be in the San Diego area until Sunday, the 21st.
The letter from Executive Officer Harris informs me that the USS BENFOLD will be returning to port in San Diego on Wednesday, July 17th and I have been invited to come on board on July 18th or 19th to personally deliver the letters.

I shall keep you up to date on what happens during my visit. Officer Harris has informed me that he will see that all of the letters are personally delivered to members of the crew. There is a good possibility that the first communication to your students will be waiting for them at HAS when classes begin in September.

Thank you again for your support of this project.

Craig E. Burgess

Mr. Craig E. Burgess
President, AHS Alumni Association

cc: Mr. John Polomano, School Superintendent
    Mr. William Westphal, Principal,
    Mr. Murray, Mayor of Audubon

388

"A new friendship sets sail" as Audubon High School Alumni Association President
Craig E. Burgess delivers 96 letters from elementary school students to the Executive
Officer of the USS BENFOLD, LCDR Sinclair Harris in July of 1996.

A New Friendship Has Set Sail

An exciting new program has started
In the Audubon, New Jersey schools.
The future seems bright
As some students now write . . .
And may soon learn about naval rules.

The students attend elementary schools
And are writing to friends out at sea.
Each letter they write
Is met with delight
By sailors, as they answer with glee.

These sailors are the crew of the BENFOLD,
A new ship in our great naval fleet.
They have a new home
As the oceans they roam:
It's a town that they know can't be beat !

The BENFOLD is a naval destroyer
That was named for an AHS grad . . .
Commissioned this year
At the large Broadway Pier
In San Diego. The Navy was glad

Because almost 4600
Attended the ship's proudest day:
In red, white and blue
All saluted the crew
In the Navy's traditional way.

The residents who live in Audubon
Are proud of the work that's been done:
The students designed - - -
For the eyes and the mind - - -
A Memorial to please everyone.

It honors three Audubon heroes
Who gave their all, fighting for peace . . .
A tribute sincere
With a message that's clear:
"May our praise for these men never cease !"

Ninety-six letters were written
By students in the 4th and 5th grade,
Then delivered by hand
To those in command - - -
To insure that they weren't delayed.

The students were given a poster
In thanks for the letters they wrote:
Thus, friendship set sail . . .
And the crew will soon mail
A response from their home while afloat.

The crew of the USS BENFOLD
Is proud of it's second hometown,
And the residents there
Are ready to share
With this crew of local renown.

Craig E. Burgess

Students at Audubon's 2 elementary schools proudly display posters they received from the USS BENFOLD in thanks for participating in the pen-pal program with crew members.

The posters were presented in September of 1996 and some students had already received responses to their letters, which they are displaying proudly.

had to empty the sonar dome of water and air. This potentially hazardous evolution was flawlessly executed by STGC Martinez and his team. The operation was repeated at the end of October following some repairs to the Sonar Dome. Other major modifications to be accomplished during this availability include modifications to Combat Systems Maintenance Central and Combat Information Center, SPY-1D radar preservation, EHF communication suite installation, and SIMAS II Upgrade to our Sonar suite. The shipyard period got off to a great start due to the outstanding preparation and documentation of our LPOs: STG1 Salamanca, ET1 Bowen, FC1 Conary, GMG1 Petty, and GMM1 Williams. They and their workcenters were ready to take an active role in the repairs, alterations and improvements to their gear. The ship is well represented at Southwest Marine by LTJG Olin, FC1 Davis and newly arrived FCCS Schance.

Looking ahead, the ship will conduct Sea Trials following the yard period in early December. For Combat Systems this gives us a chance to re-calibrate our weapons and sensor systems, regain our sea legs, and test out some new and modified equipment. These include the latest software in support of Tomahawk operations and a brand new communications system. These state of the art modifications will keep the ship on the leading edge of technology. After that, we will begin preparations for August deployment. These preparations include live weapon firings, scenario training and evaluations during Tailored Ship's Training Availability

Phase 3 (TSTA 3) and Final Evaluation Period (FEP). These graduation exercises will ensure we are ready to join the fleet! Finally, congratulations for the fall go out to our new Chief Petty Officers; GMC Harris and FCC Hacket and our newest Combat Systems Officers of the Watch: STG1 Salamanca.

BENFOLD PEN PALS

Many of our young friends in Audubon, NJ have started corresponding with BENFOLD crewmembers. Children from the fourth and fifth grades in Audubon area elementary schools sent many wonderful letters and pictures to our sailors. The pictures and letters were displayed in the Enlisted Dining Facility for all to see. Each of these letters has been answered by crewmembers who enjoy and look forward to establishing a lasting friendship with the youngsters from Edward Benfold's hometown.

SPORTS DESK 🏆

BENFOLD sports teams have hit the Naval Station with a vengence. Coach (SM1) Murray and the Defenders Softball club, with their 5 -5 record, have become a force to reckon with by all the teams on the waterfront. They presently stand in third place in Medium/Small Ship category and look forward to this year's playoffs. Not to be out done, the Benfold Hoop Masters have run off a string of victories under Coach (GMC) Piper and now a contending for the NAVSTA Crown. Their record is 4 wins and only two losses.

Competition in Captain's Cup is fierce as all departments have posted at least two wins in sports so far. Engineering Department has a slight lead with three victories. In individual accomplishments, SM3 Canale made the cut in tryouts for the Navy Soccer team competeing with World Cup and Olympic level players. And, OS3 Powell and ENFA Wilson have made the cut in tryouts for the San Diego Naval Station Basketball team. Well done to all!

Finally, the following personnel attained scores of outstanding during the annual Physical Readiness Test.

BOLD STATISTICS*

MEALS SERVED	80,000
MILES STEAMED	8000 NM
GALLONS OF FUEL USED	2,000,000 GAL
MISSILES SHOT	10 SM2-MR
BULLETS SHOT	350 5" 54 CAL
WATER PRODUCED	1,900,000 GAL
PAYROLL ALLOCATED	$7,700,000.00

* JAN - NOV 96

Town stages 'a tribute to the human spirit'

COURIER-POST

THURSDAY,
July 25, 1996

Audubon honors one of its hometown heroes

By BRUCE ANDERSON
Courier-Post Staff

AUDUBON — Edward Joseph Benfold was only 4 months old when his father died a hero's death during the Korean War.

"Obviously, I never got to know him myself," said Benfold, 44. "But my mother always told me about his concern and compassion for her and for other people. The people in this area have never forgotten him."

As Benfold spoke, he scanned the rotunda of Audubon High School. More than 40 people had gathered to honor Edward Clyde Benfold at the school he attended before joining the Navy in wartime.

They came to see a scale model of the USS Benfold presented to the school. The actual ship, a Navy destroyer named for the Audubon resident, was designed by Lockheed Martin Corp. in Moorestown and commissioned in March.

But, mostly, they came to talk — about Benfold and about the nature of heroism.

Benfold was awarded the Medal of Honor posthumously in 1953. He had served as a hospital corpsman attached to the First Marine Division in South Korea.

By Carlos Garcia, Courier-Post
Tribute: Edward Joseph Benfold holds his father's medals, including the Medal of Honor Edward Clyde Benfold was awarded in 1953.

During a battle in September 1952, Benfold saw an enemy soldier throw grenades into a crater that held two wounded Marines. Benfold scooped up the grenades, then hurled himself against two enemy soldiers running toward the Marines.

The grenades exploded, killing the enemy soldiers — and Benfold, who was only 20 years old. His heroism saved the two Marines.

Although Audubon's population is only slightly more than 9,100, the borough boasts two other Medal of Honor recipients

Please see BENFOLD, Page 2B

Benfold/Audubon recalls fallen soldier

Continued from Page 1B

— World War I veteran Samuel M. Sampler and Korean War veteran Nelson V. Brittin.

"I think it's a tribute to the character of our people," said 74-year-old Rudy March, commander of Murray-Troutt American Legion Post 262 in Audubon.

Audubon students honor that character in several ways. For instance, they've erected a memorial at the high school in tribute to the Medal of Honor recipients.

And fifth-grade students at Audubon's two elementary schools recently wrote letters to sailors on the USS Benfold,

stationed in San Diego, Calif.

Two representatives from that ship — Master Chief Petty Officer Robert Scheeler, 40, and Petty Officer First Class Bob Riley, 33 — attended Wednesday's ceremony.

"We really enjoy the letters," said Scheeler. "They make us feel appreciated when we're away from our families for a long time."

Audubon High School vice principal Joseph Wall concluded the ceremony with a meditation on heroism.

"This is a tribute to the human spirit," he said. "It transcends age, race . . . all boundaries. No one knows who will be a

hero if the opportunity arises. But we recognize it represents the highest level of human achievement."

At a reception following the ceremony, Anna Mae Hoover drank a soda and shared her memories of Benfold.

"Ed was three years ahead of me at Audubon High School," said Hoover, 61. "Although he was rather quiet and unassuming, he seemed like a normal teen-ager.

"But Ed also became a hero. And that fact should stand as an example to all of us of the incredible good that people are capable of doing."

394

February - April 1997   **Volume 3.1**

BOLD DEFENDER

NEWSLETTER FOR THE FAMILIES AND FRIENDS OF
USS BENFOLD (DDG 65)

PRE-DEPLOYMENT EDITION

FROM THE BRIDGE

Ready to Fight and Win!!! It has been an exciting time in 1997. After completing our short shipyard period in December, the pace has not let up as we complete our training in preparation for deployment. In late January, we headed up to Seal Beach for our weapons onload. After a short inport period, we proceeded to Mazatlan, Mexico under the command of COMDESRON 21 and in company with USS RENTZ (FFG 46) and USS STETHEM (DDG 63). This transit tested our skills in multi-ship operations as well as provided some great liberty during the city's Mardis Gras celebration.

CDR MARK E. FERGUSON III

More recently, BENFOLD was selected to participate in a major exercise with the Commander, Third Fleet, USS Coronado, the First Marine Division, the US Space Command in Colorado, and several other military commands throughout the country. This exercise was significant in that BENFOLD demonstrated new technologies and command and control methods to be implemented by the Navy in the next century.

Specifically, we showcased two new capabilities. First, we demonstrated the potential use of the future arsenal ship in support of a Marine Expeditionary Force operating inland at the Marine Corps base at Twenty Nine Palms. Second, we demonstrated the potential use of this class of ship in defending against theater ballistic missile attack, coordinating with military units throughout the country in the simulated detection and engagement of this type of threat. Our success will help shape the future of Surface Warfare.

We also received notice of a great honor from the Commander, Naval Surface Force Pacific Fleet. The ship was selected to receive four Command Excellence Awards, denoting outstanding performance in the following areas: Logistics Management, Engineering/Survivability, Maritime Warfare, and Command and Control--a clean sweep!!! My congratulations to everyone onboard for their tremendous effort in this, our first full year in commission.

BENFOLD was also fortunate to host the Norwegian CNO for a tour of our ASW systems. In addition, look for us this fall on the History Channel and A&E in the show "DESTROYER". Over the last several days, we were host to a production company filming this series for this fall----watch for us on cable in September!!

Our upcoming schedule is also full of excitement. We have scheduled port visits to Cabo San Lucas, Mexico and to Portland, Oregon for the Rose Festival. More importantly, we will finish our training cycle in April with our Final Evaluated Battle Problem.

For our families, it is time to begin planning for deployment. Mark April 26th on your calendar. The ship will host a pre-deployment fair on that day. It will provide information from Family Service Center, Navy Legal Services, and others so that you will be ready for deployment. This will be an "ALL HANDS" Event and I look forward to seeing you there. If you are unable to make this one, we will have another one in July immediately before our departure.

Lastly, I would like to bid farewell to LCDR Sinclair Harris and his wife Cora as they head off to shore duty in Washington, DC. They have been instrumental in every success enjoyed by the ship and we wish them fair winds and following seas. As sad as saying goodbye may be, the ship has been blessed with another outstanding leader to serve as Executive Officer, LCDR Jeff Harley. On behalf of the crew, I would like to extend a Welcome Aboard to Jeff, his wife Cindy and daughter Emily as they join the BENFOLD Family.

Your BENFOLD Sailors continue to set new standards of excellence in the fleet. As always, their success has as its foundation the love and support of our families at home. Thank you again, for all you continue to do for the ship and our Navy...

SCHEDULE OF ACTIVITIES FOR THE VISIT OF COMMANDER FERGUSON

MONDAY , APRIL 21 , 1997   8:30 am - 2:30 pm

8:30 - 9:00   am   Estimated arrival time at AHS

9:00 - 9:20   am   Discussion of the day's schedule
                        with Mr. Westphal, Principal of AHS

9:30 -10:00   am   Commander Ferguson will meet with the
                        Senior Physics Class at AHS for a
                        presentation and question/answer session.

10:00-11:00   am   Representatives from the 8th grade
                        Citizenship/Geography classes at AHS will
                        meet with Commander Ferguson in the
                        high school Rotunda for a discussion
                        of the USS BENFOLD. Weather permitting,
                        part of the session will take place at
                        the Memorial site on the grounds of the
                        high school. Introductory comments will be
                        made by Principal Westphal and by AHS
                        Alumni Assoc. President Craig E. Burgess.

11:00-11:35   am   - - - - - - - - - - - - - - - - - -

11:45-12:45   Catered Luncheon in the High School Library.
                        Commander Ferguson will greet school and
                        community leaders in an informal setting.

1:00- 1:30   pm   Commander Ferguson will meet with the 6th
                        grade students at MANSION AVENUE ELEMENTARY
                        SCHOOL. The Commander's presentation will
                        include comments about the on-going PEN-PAL
                        program with the crew of the USS BENFOLD.

1:45- 2:15   pm   Commander Ferguson will meet with the 5th
                        grade students at HAVILAND AVENUE ELEMENTARY
                        SCHOOL. The PEN-PAL program with the crew
                        of the USS BENFOLD will be one of the topics
                        covered in this presentation.

The Borough of Audubon is proud to have the opportunity to meet with
Commander Ferguson and learn more about the ongoing activities associated with DDG-65, named in honor of Audubon resident and AHS student
Edward C. Benfold. The Commander's visit will strengthen the ties of
friendship between the Borough and its special naval family, the crew
of the USS BENFOLD.

During his visits to the Audubon schools on April 21, 1997, Commander Ferguson fields questions from students in the elementary schools (above) after giving some examples of the practical application of theories in physics to students at AHS (right).

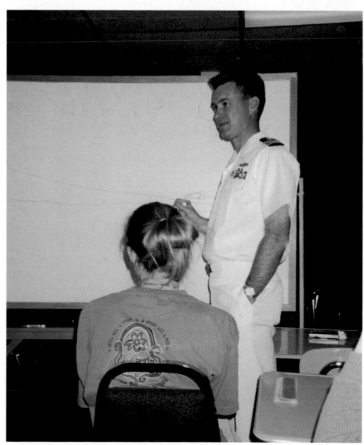

At the reception in the library of AHS, Commander Ferguson receives an Audubon cap (above) and gets acquainted with other student chairpersons from project Memorial (below).

Audubon High School
350 Edgewood Avenue
Audubon, New Jersey
08106-2299
Tel: (609) 547-7695
Tues., April 22, 1997

Commander Mark E. Ferguson III
Captain
USS BENFOLD (DDG 65)
FPO AP 96661-1283

Esteemed Commander Ferguson:

Words can never express how everyone in Audubon feels following your
visit to the borough yesterday. You made a VERY positive impression
on the students in all three schools, both as an officer in the Navy
AND as a person. For that, we are all grateful!

I hope you enjoy the enclosed photo album, containing shots taken
during the visit. As you can see, the photos speak for themselves.

I am in the process of preparing a news release on your visit for
our local papers. As soon as it is published, I shall forward copies
to you and the crew.

I am enclosing a business card so that you may forward to my home
address your new address while at Harvard University. I would like
to be able to keep in touch with you and keep you informed of Audubon/
USS BENFOLD activities during the coming year.

I look forward to meeting your replacement, Commander D. Michael
Abrashoff, when I participate in the Dependents' Day Cruise on
July 2nd.

Respectfully,

Craig E. Burgess

Mr. Craig E. Burgess
President, AHS Alumni Association

PS Enjoy the T-shirt

399

AUDUBON
H **A** S
ALUMNI
ASSOCIATION

Tuesday, April 22, 1997

COMMANDER Sinclair Harris
1007 Pruitt Court S.W.
Vienna, Virginia   22180

Esteemed Commander Harris:

CONGRATULATIONS!!! Commander Ferguson was in Audubon again yesterday and informed us that the 'L' in your title has disappeared. We are all proud of your advancement in rank.

Commander Ferguson spent the entire day in the Audubon schools, talking with students about the USS BENFOLD and about his upcoming year of study at Harvard University.

A catered luncheon was prepared and community and student leaders were invited to get together with the Commander in an informal setting. During conversations with the American Legion Post # 262 members, representatives from the Fire Department (you remember....those 'sluggers' who took on the crew in that famous softball game!), Mrs. Waida, Mr. Ed Benfold and Mr. Bob Hoover, one topic covered was YOU! Everyone wanted to know how you were doing in your new position and all send best wishes for continued success. We still consider you to be part of our 'family' and welcome a visit to Audubon at any time.

Commander Ferguson gave me your new address so that I could write and let you know that the students and the citizens of Audubon are still thinking of you. I also wanted the address because I wanted to thank you again for all you did for me during my visits to San Diego. I participated in the 1st Birthday celebration and have been invited to join the crew on July 2nd for the DEPENDENTS' DAY CRUISE. I am also working on a 'surprise' (don't tell the new Captain and XO!) for the crew prior to the deployment in early August.

In the near future, I shall send you some photos taken at the birthday party and during yesterday's visit by Commander Ferguson. Until then, sincere greetings from everyone in your "2nd Hometown". Please write when you get a chance. I know that the Project Memorial students would enjoy hearing from you.

Respectfully,

Craig E. Burgess

Mr. Craig E. Burgess
President, AHS Alumni Association

400

RETROSPECT

Since 1902

Camden County's Oldest Weekly Newspaper

Serving: Collingswood • Haddon Township • Oaklyn • Woodlynne • Audubon • Haddon Heights • Barrington
Haddonfield • Cherry Hill • Audubon Park • Runnemede • Bellmawr • Mt. Ephraim • Pennsauken • Merchantville

35¢ per copy

Volume 96, No. 38   Collingswood (Camden P.O.), New Jersey, Friday, May 2, 1997

Naval Commander Visits Three Audubon Schools

Monday, April 21, was an exciting day for the students in the Audubon school system.

Commander Mark E. Ferguson III, Captain of the USS Benfold, visited all three schools and spoke with the students about his experiences as a commander in the U.S. Navy. After an informative presentation to Bruce Dyer's physics class, Commander Ferguson spent nearly an hour with representatives from the eighth grade, discussing the role of the USS Benfold in the modern Naval fleet.

The session ended with a visit to the memorial on the high school campus that commemorates the three residents from Audubon who were awarded the Congressional Medal of Honor.

Community leaders then joined student leaders in the high school Library for a catered luncheon and open discussion with the commander.

In the afternoon, Commander Ferguson visited both elementary schools and spoke with the students who have been writing pen-pal letters to members of the crew of the USS Benfold.

Two events are being planned for May by the students in the Project Memorial Foundation at AHS.

Tomorrow, Saturday, May 3, from 4-7 p.m., a Spaghetti dinner to raise funds for ongoing activities will be held at American Legion Post #262 headquarters, Chestnut St. and E. Atlantic Ave. in Audubon.

On Thursday, May 22, services will be held at the memorial to commemorate Memorial Day. For information on both events, call the high school at 547-7695 and ask to speak with principal William Westphal.

QUESTIONING STUDENTS: Sixth grade students learn about the USS Benfold during a question-and-answer session with Commander Mark Ferguson at the Mansion Ave. School, Audubon.

401

Another special tradition in Audubon began on July 4, 1997. The U.S. Navy made arrangements to send the "Sailor of the Year" from the ship to the borough to participate in the events in town. The "Sailor of the year" rode in a special vehicle in the 4th of July Parade, visited with students and residents and got acquainted with the Green Wave, the high school mascot. In 1999, no representative could be sent in July, because the USS BENFOLD would be deployed from June until December. In order that the tradition continue, the U. S. Navy made arrangements to send the "Sailor of the Year" in April. Audubon responded by having a Patriotic Parade in town to welcome our friend. we are proud to present highlights of the three visits below and on the following pages . . . . .

SEPT. – DEC, 1996

BOLD DEFENDER

STG1 Alfred R. Salamanca
Quezon City, Philippines

STG1(SW) ALFRED R. SALAMANCA

Petty Officer Salamanca was born in New Haven, CT and raised in Quezon City, Republic of the Phillipines. He enlisted in the US Navy on 2 February 1978 at Subic Bay.

His previous duty stations include the USS ABRAHAM LINCOLN (SSBN 602), USS JOHN MARSHALL (SSN 611), USS DARTER (SS 576), Puget Sound Naval Shipyard, USS FRANCIS HAMMOND (FF 1067), Fleet ASW Training Center Pacific, USS JOUETT (CG 29), US Naval Hospital Subic Bay, and COMNAVBASE San Francisco.

He is the President of BENFOLD's First Class Petty Officer's Association, which spearheads the command's Adopt-A-School program with Hazel Goes Cook Elementary School. He is also a member of the Alpha Phi Omega Service Fraternity (San Diego Alumni Association Chapter), which performs community service around the San Diego area as volunteers to National City's Christmas in July, KPBS Telephone Fund Drives, Multiple Sclerosis Walk San Diego, Outreach Tijuana of Our Lady of Mount Carmel Church, Boy Scouts, and various FIL-AM projects.

Petty Officer Salamanca's wife Rita hails from Manila, Republic of the Phillipines. They have three sons: Benjamin, Christopher, and Joseph. Their hobbies are fishing and basketball.

July 4, 1997 Sailor of the Year STG1 Alfred R. Salamanca waves his flag from the Judges stand at AHS as the Lions' Club float passes by. The float won first place over-all in the Parade.

Sailor of the Year Salamanca watches as members of the Audubon
Lions' Club pose for a group photo in front of the award winning float. (above)
He then meets with members of the Benfold family. (below)

SOUTH JERSEY

COURIER-POST   Thursday, June 25, 1998   METRO DESK   **486-2408**

GLEN VAN VORST
... USS Benfold Sailor of the Year

EDWARD C. BENFOLD
... Korean War hero

Sailor to continue Audubon tradition

By CAROL COMEGNO
Courier-Post Staff

AUDUBON — The Sailor of the Year aboard the Navy ship USS Benfold will be coming here July 4 to ride in the local parade.

The pending visit of Senior Petty Officer Glen van Vorst continues a tradition that began four years ago when the ship's captain came here to honor Edward C. Benfold, the hometown hero and Medal of Honor winner for whom the ship is named.

Benfold was killed during the Korean War in 1952 while saving the lives of two wounded men. He is one of three Medal of Honor winners from this tiny borough of 10,000 people.

Van Vorst, 34, of Jacksonville, Fla., is a storekeeper among the crew of 300 aboard the destroyer Benfold, which is homeported in San Diego. Every year the Sailor of the Year is sent to visit Audubon.

"I am really excited about the visit to see the town where he (Benfold) lived," the sailor said in a telephone interview from the ship .

The ship's executive officer, Lt. Commander Allen Stubblefield, said van Vorst was select-

┌─ **To keep in touch** ─┐
The Web site address for the Benfold is: **www.navy.benfold.mil.**
└──────────────┘

ed for the award because he had disagreed with some of the prices the ship was paying for supplies and parts and ultimately saved the ship $1 million.

"We have been able to maintain close ties with the town and send someone every year for the Fourth of July. This personalizes a part of the military for them," Stubblefield said.

The ship, commissioned in March 1996, recently returned from a deployment in the Persian Gulf. In 1997, it was rated the best-prepared ship in the Pacific Fleet for combat readiness operations and was awarded the Spokane Trophy for that achievement.

"I just think it's great that the town and the ship do this. You would think after all these years it would be forgotten," said Dorothy Benfold Waida of Audubon, the hero's widow.

Their son, Edward Joseph Benfold, was only 3 months old when his father committed the ultimate act of bravery. He lives in Cherry Hill.

Namesake: The USS Benfold was named after Edward C. Benfold, who died while saving two Marines in the Korean War.

405

COURIER-POST

DAN A. MARTIN
President and Publisher

WILLIAM C. HIDLAY
Executive Editor

ROBERT E. INGLE
Editorial Page Editor

CALVIN J. STOVALL
Managing Editor

8A

TUESDAY
June 30, 1998

OPINION

Remembrance in Audubon

An endearing tradition is evolving in Audubon. It's the presence of a crewman from the USS Benfold in the borough's Fourth of July parade.

The destroyer is named for Edward C. Benfold, an Audubon High School graduate and Medal of Honor winner. He died saving two wounded men in 1952, during the Korean Conflict.

Benfold is one of three men from Audubon to win the Congressional award for bravery in combat. The others are Nelson V. Brittin (also Korea) and Samuel M. Sampler (World War I). No community in America the size of Audubon (9,000) has as many.

The USS Benfold's involvement in Audubon's parade began four years ago with the ship's captain.

Since then, the ship berthed in San Diego has sent its "sailor of the year" annually. This year's attendee will be Senior Petty Officer Glen van Vorst.

"I just think it's great that the town and the ship would do this," Dorothy Waida, Benfold's widow who still lives in the borough, told the *Courier-Post*. "You would think after all these years, it would be forgotten."

Hardly. If anything, the sacrifices made by Benfold, Brittin and Sampler become more treasured as each year passes. That's as it should be, too.

All Around the Towns ... Fourth of July is

Exploding with Festivities

 ## Audubon

Audubon has a Mardi Gras theme for its Fourth of July Parade this year.

The parade will start tomorrow at 8:30 a.m. at Amherst Rd. and Paris Ave. Pre-registered decorated bicycles and floats by organizations, businesses or families will be among the featured attractions.

Athletic events will begin at noon at the high school field and decorated homes will be judged after the parade.

The 7:30 p.m. evening program at the high school stadium will offer live music by the Hayden Brothers and spectacular fireworks by Girone. A dollar donation for the evening's entertainment will be graciously accepted at the gate to help defray expenses.

Rain date is Sunday, July 5.

Special 4th Visitor

SK 1 (SW) Glen van Vorst, the "Sailor of the Year" on board the USS Benfold, will be in Audubon for the Fourth of July and will be riding in tomorrow's parade..Following the parade, Seaman van Vorst will be at Audubon High School to greet everyone and bring greetings from the Naval ship that is named in honor of Edward C. Benfold, AHS student who was killed in the Korean War and awarded the Congressional Medal of Honor.

407

The Green Wave and the Navy:
The Tradition Continues

STOREKEEPER (SK)
SKs operate the ship's storerooms and issue repair parts. Additionally, they prepare requisitions and other orders to maintain supplies at prescribed support levels to satisfy non-stocked departmental requirements. They also manage the ship's inventories, organize warehousing, and prepare items for shipping. SKs also maintain the ship's financial records, acting as the command's budget and accounting officials.

SK1 Glen S. Vanvorst
Jacksonville, FL

There was a special air of excitement in Audubon on July 4th, due to the participation in the annual borough parade of the Sailor of the Year from the U.S.S. Benfold, the naval destroyer (DDG-65) named in memory of Edward C. Benfold, an Audubon student killed in the Korean conflict.

Petty Officer 1st Class SK 1 (SW) Glen van Vorst arrived in town on Friday evening and rode in the parade on Saturday morning, being warmly received by residents. Van Vorst has been a member of the crew of the U.S.S. Benfold since 1994.

As a special gift for borough officials, he brought a photograph of the ship that was taken in Sydney, Australia during the ship's first deployment earlier this year.

Following the parade, van Vorst took a seat on the judges' stand to watch the many floats and musical presentations. He then met with Mrs. Dorothy Waida, Edward C. Benfold's widow and with Benfold's son, Ed, and his family, before taking a tour of Audubon High School.

In the afternoon, there was lunch with the Benfolds, a visit to St. Mary's Episcopal Church in Haddon Heights, where a stained-glass window was dedicated to the memory of Edward C. Benfold in 1953, and visits with members of the Audubon Fire and Police Departments.

Audubon is grateful to the Department of the Navy for making this year's visit a reality. May the tradition continue long into the 21st century.

July 4, 1998, Sailor of the Year Glen S. Vanvorst stands on the Judges' platform in front of AHS (right) along with Audubon Commissioners Donna Sadwin, Brian McPeak and Mayor John Coyle (below).

Sailor of the Year
Vanvorst chats with
Audubon resident
Bob Hoover prior
to the start of the
4th of July Parade
(above) and then
meets with long
time resident John
McDermott to
learn more about
the early days in
the borough. (right)

Vanvorst gets a surprise during dinner at the home of Edward Benfold's son: a 4th of July cake for dessert.

Vanvorst visits the stained-glass window in St. Mary's Episcopal Church that is dedicated to the memory of Edward C. Benfold.

411

 **CRAIG E. BURGESS**
Educator and Poet
327 Washington Terrace
Audubon, New Jersey 08106-2148
(609) 547-2440

Thursday, July 9, 1998

Mr. Bob Hoover
564 Maple Avenue
Audubon, New Jersey   08106

Dear Bob,

I am writing to thank you for your efforts in continuing the tradition of friendship that has been established between the Borough of Audubon and the officers and crew of the U.S.S. BENFOLD.

The visit of Petty Officer First Class SK 1 (SW) Glen van Vorst on July 4th was a great success. Your willingness to assist this year's SAILOR OF THE YEAR during the visit is greatly appeciated and reflects your commitment to this special activity in Audubon.

From your efforts in contacting the ship to learn of the time of arrival in the area of this year's special guest to preparing the truck and the sign for the Parade (and, of course, serving as driver in the parade!) to taking time away from your family on the 4th to be host for Petty Officer van Vorst, your role in this year's visit was a valuable one.

On behalf of all of the residents in the Borough, I wish to extend sincere thanks for all that you have done to insure that the Department of the Navy will see that THE GREEN WAVE AND THE NAVY are, indeed, "PERFECT TOGETHER".

A grateful Audubon resident,

Craig

Mr. Craig E. Burgess
Liaison from Audubon to the U.S.S. BENFOLD

cc: Mr. John Coyle, Mayor
     Mr. William Westphal, Principal, Audubon High School
     Mr. John Frick, Commander, Murray-Troutt Post # 262

412

In 1999, the 4th of July came three months early for the residents in Audubon ! The U. S. Navy sent the "Sailor of the Year" SM1(SW) Michael L. Murray to the borough prior to the ship's deployment. Accompanying Murray on the 7-day visit was MS1 Danny K. Edgar, the co-author of this book.

The information and photos presented on this page were taken from the Commissioning Book for the ship. Both men have received promotions since March, 1996. Petty Officer Murray learned, when he returned to San Diego following the visit, that he had been promoted to rank of Chief Petty Officer.

SM2(SW) Michael L. Murray
Bethlehem, PA

MS2 Danny K. Edgar
Woodridge, IL

SIGNALMAN (SM)
SMs are responsible for all visual signal methods and equipment, including flashing light, semaphore, and signal flags.

MESS MANAGEMENT SPECIALIST (MS)
MSs operate and manage all galley and dining facilities. This includes menu preparation, procurement, receipt, and stowage of all food items for the ship. They also maintain all food service financial returns.

Audubon EXTRA

A Special Publication Commemorating the Alliance between the Borough of Audubon and US Navy Ship USS Benfold   April 1999

Special Patriotic Parade Set

The kickoff event for the visit of Petty Officers Michael L. Murray and Danny Edgar will be a parade, scheduled for 9 a.m., April 17.

The parade route begins at Merchant Street and West Atlantic Avenue and will go west on Merchant to Wyoming Avenue. Turning left onto Wyoming, the parade will pass Mansion Avenue School to Chestnut Street, turn right onto Chestnut and proceed past the Little League complex to the high school and the Medal of Honor Memorial Site.

Following the parade, arrangements are being made for a reception at the Murray-Troutt American Legion Post #262 home on Chestnut Street and East Atlantic Avenue.

Mark your calendar now for this exciting special parade event in our town. Let's welcome members of our "second family" in style!

The Green Wave and the Navy: Perfect Together

This special Audubon newsletter is being sent to all residents to provide an update on the visit to the borough by two members of the crew of the USS Benfold (DDG-65). Due to the fact that the ship will be on its second deployment during the month of July when the sailors normally visit Audubon to participate in Fourth of July festivities, the Navy has agreed to send the Sailor of the Year, Petty Officer SM1 Michael L. Murray, during April. In addition, the Navy will send a second representative, Petty Officer MS1 Danny Edgar, the co-author of the soon-to-be-released book entitled "The Green Wave and the Navy: The History of the USS Benfold." Edgar has written more than 30 poems about life on board a modern naval destroyer. His writings will be part of Chapter III of the book.

The schedule of activities is now being finalized for the visit and, as the official liaison from Audubon to the ship, I am encouraging all residents to come out and meet our two friends at one or more of the events.

Craig E. Burgess

414

Opportunities to Get to Know the Benfold

Sunday, April 18:

As many of you know, Medal of Honor recipient Edward C. Benfold attended St. Mary's Episcopal Church, White Horse Pike and Green Street in Haddon Heights, while a student at Audubon High School. Following his heroic death in Korea, members of the church's Youth Fellowship dedicated a special stained glass window in his memory. This window is special because it contains a stained-glass replica of the Medal of Honor in the lower right corner. Following the 10 a.m. service on the 18th, both petty officers will be the guests of the Parish at a coffee hour session. Petty Officer Michael L. Murray will talk about his being named Sailor of the Year and Petty Officer Danny Edgar will tell us about his writing and about how he became part of the new book currently being written by Audubon resident Craig Burgess about Audubon and the Naval ship.

Wednesday, April 21:

Both Petty Officers will be the special guests at the annual "Senior Spring Social" being sponsored by the Audubon Community Education office. Senior citizens attending this event will have the opportunity to get acquainted with our two visitors and learn more about life on board a modern naval vessel.

This event is co-sponsored by the AHS Student Council and the AHS Intergenerational group. All Audubon senior citizens are invited to attend this annual social. Anyone with questions is encouraged to contact the high school at 547-7695, ext. 185 or 186.

Thurs., April 22:

Both sailors will be visiting all three schools in Audubon today, beginning with sessions at Haviland Avenue School and Mansion Avenue School in the morning. They will then be talking with students at Audubon High School in the afternoon.

This evening, the Audubon Poets have a special reading/signing session scheduled for 7 to 9 p.m., at Encore Books in the Westmont Plaza on Cuthbert Boulevard. Both Petty Officers will be the guests of the writers' group and Petty Officer Edgar will be sharing some of this work on life aboard the USS Benfold with those in attendance. For more information about this event, contact Encore at 854-0505.

Friday, April 23:

The Audubon Poets have their regular sharing session at the Senior Center at Oak Street and Oakland Avenue, from 6 p.m. to 8:30 p.m. Petty Officers Murray and Edgar will be the special guests for the session. The public is cordially invited to come and socialize with our friends from the USS Benfold. This will be the last public appearance for both men during their visit. When they return to San Diego, they will be making final preparations for the next deployment which begins in early May and lasts until late November. The writers' group is planning some special surprises for the sailors and for everyone in attendance, so plan to come out and be part of the "anchors' aweigh" party.

415

❖ LEGION NEWS ❖

| Volume 2, Number 3 | Murray-Troutt Post 262, Audubon, NJ | April 1, 1999 |

AUDUBON PARADE for NAVY CREWMEN

Ave, School to Chestnut St., and down Chestnut St. to the Medal of Honor site. The parade will contain various units including a band, Audubon Fire Dept., and the Post Ambulance Squad.

Following the parade, there will be a reception at the Post Hall. BRING YOUR FAMILY OUT TO GREET THESE MEN OF OUR ARMED FORCES!

Further information at meeting!

The Green Wave Alliance with the USS. Benfold is sponsoring week-long activities with 2 members of the crew from the USS. Benfold, named after our Medal of Honor recipient. Since the Benfold will be deployed over July 4th, arrangements have been completed to have Petty Officer SM1, Michael L. Murray, the ship's SAILOR OF THE YEAR and Petty Officer MS1, Danny Edgar visit Audubon during April 16-23.

*On April 17, starting at 9am, there will be a parade honoring the sailors The Post Honor Guard, led by **Joe Janda**, will lead the parade from W. Atlantic Ave and Merchant St. to Wyoming Ave., pass Mansion*

Since 1902 RETROSPECT

Camden County's Oldest Weekly Newspaper

Serving: Collingswood • Haddon Township • Oaklyn • Woodlynne • Audubon • Haddon Heights • Barrington
Haddonfield • Cherry Hill • Audubon Park • Runnemede • Bellmawr • Mt. Ephraim • Pennsauken • Merchantville

Volume 98, No. 35   Collingswood (Camden P.O.), New Jersey, Friday, April 9, 1999   35¢ per copy

Audubon to Stage Parade for Sailors

The friendship between Audubon and the crew of the USS Benfold continues in 1999 when the "Sailor of the Year," Petty Officer Michael L. Murray, and Petty Officer Danny Edgar, co-author of a soon-to-be-published book on the history of the ship, arrive in town on Saturday, April 17.

The excitement of the visit will be shown that morning as students and residents march in a special patriotic parade through the town.

The parade begins on Merchant St., then goes over to Wyoming Ave. to Chestnut St., then onto Chestnut past the Little League complex to the memorial site on the lawn of the high school.

The parade begins at 9 a.m. and everyone is invited to come out and celebrate the visit from the US Navy.

Both Petty Officers will be in town for a full week and a number of special events have been planned. On Sunday, April 18, St. Mary's parish in Haddon Heights has a coffee hour reception planned, beginning at 11:30 a.m.

On Thursday, April 22, beginning at 7 p.m., both Petty officers will be guests of the Audubon Poets at a reading at Encore Books in the Westmont Plaza. Those in attendance will get a sneak preview of the new book, "The Green Wave and the Navy: The History of the USS Benfold," scheduled for release in December of this year.

Friday, April 16, 1999

Audubon Parade Set Tomorrow

A special patriotic parade will be held in Audubon tomorrow, Saturday, April 17, to welcome two special members of the crew of the USS Benfold.

The parade will begin along the Merchant St. business district at 9 a.m., proceed over Wyoming Ave. to Chestnut St., then past the Little League complex to the Congressional Medal of Honor memorial site on the lawn of Audubon High School.

Participants will include two petty officers from the crew of the Benfold, named to honor the memory of Edward Benfold, one of Audubon's three Congressional Medal of Honor winners. They are the "Sailor of the Year," Michael Murray, and Danny Edgar, co-author of a soon-to-be-published book on the history of the ship.

417

In Our Towns

Audubon embraces ship, crew

By SHARON CHUNG
Courier-Post Staff

AUDUBON

This town of time-honored traditions and patriotic reverence cares for its visitors like family, especially if they're from aboard the USS Benfold.

Navy Petty Officers Danny Edgar and Michael L. Murray, who was recently named the Benfold's "Sailor of the Year," will take center stage during a weeklong tour of the borough beginning Saturday, when a special "Patriotic Parade" will be thrown in their honor.

The pair's visit is part of the ongoing long-distance relationship between the borough's 9,200 residents and the 350-member crew of the Benfold, said Craig E. Burgess, a lifelong Audubon resident and organizer of the event.

The San Diego-based ship is named after Audubon's hometown hero and Medal of Honor recipient Edward C. Benfold, who was killed during the Korean War in 1952 while saving the lives of two wounded Marines.

The annual parade is usually held the Fourth of July. But this year, the Benfold, one of the newest guided-missile destroyers in the Navy's Pacific fleet, is slated for deployment that month. So the borough decided to hold the parade on an ordinary day in April.

"We'll still hold a parade on July 4, but this is a special parade in honor of the

The guided-missile destroyer USS Benfold, based in San Diego, is named after Medal of Honor recipient Edward C. Benfold.

friendship Audubon has with the Benfold," said Burgess, a poet and educator who is working on a book with Edgar on the history and friendship of the borough and the ship.

Burgess said Audubon adopted the Benfold as a "sister ship" in 1994.

Since then, both sides have kept in close contact through annual coast-to-coast visits, letters, holiday cards, gifts and

To attend

■ The parade begins at 9 a.m. at Merchant Street and West Atlantic Avenue and ends at the Medal of Honor memorial site at Audubon High School.

care packages.

See **SHIP**, Page 4B

Ship/Audubon embraces crew of ship named after hometown hero

Continued from Page 3B

"One Christmas the Audubon Women's Club sent 600 homemade cookies to the ship," said Burgess, who has made frequent visits to the Benfold and has acted as liaison with the borough. "The commander said the crew members were so grateful he sent autographed copies of photos of the ship to each and every one of the women."

The parade honored Hospitalman Third Class Edward C. Benfold, USN, one of three can Legion Murray Troutt Post No. 262 in Audubon, said Benfold personnel have been involved with the town since the ship was commissioned in 1996.

"Here we are in a small town like this and we have three Medal of Honor winners," said Frick, referring to two other hometown heroes — Samuel M. Sampler, who charged through hostile gunfire and captured 28 enemy soldiers in France during World War I, and Nelson V. Brittin, killed in the Korean War when he shielded his Army squad from enemy fire.

"From the beginning . . . there has been a really good camaraderie between them and us, and about 15 organizations will be in the parade," Frick said.

In a recent telephone interview from his home in San Diego, Edgar said he and his shipmates are deeply appreciative of the town's friendship.

"The town of Audubon is so patriotic that it reminds me of my home-town," he said. "The crew has developed a strong friendship with the people there. It goes further than that because they actually care.

"Anybody who comes on board (the Benfold) from Audubon gets first-class treatment," he added. "They're like crew members to us. We consider Audubon our second hometown."

Petty officers Danny Edgar (left) and Michael Murray, of the USS Benfold, wave to parade-goers in Audubon Saturday.

AL SCHELL/Courier-Post

Parade in Audubon honors war hero

By JOSEPH BUSLER
Courier-Post Staff

AUDUBON

The morning sun hadn't quite burned through the clouds when the parade started promptly at 9 a.m. Saturday near the Audubon Fire Company.

It started small, led by 13 aging veterans from the Murray-Trout Post 262 of the American Legion, followed by five members of the high-school drum and bugle corps in tri-corner hats, and 11 parents with children.

Medal of Honor winners this borough of 9,200 residents claims as its own, and one of two who died earning it.

The parade grew longer as it snaked along Merchant, Wyoming and Chestnut avenues toward Audubon High School. Scattered groups of residents, most waving 6-inch by 4-inch American flags, stood on corners as the parade passed.

Others stood on their front porches, watching and waving, drawn outside by the din of the drummers and the wail of sirens from police vehicles and four fire trucks. The Durning String Band of Haddon Township added peacock-like beauty as well as gypsy-like music, and Cub Scout Pack 131 . . . well, they were just kids.

Parade organizer and borough poet Craig Burgess, in a red coat and white hat, rode in the back of a pickup truck with Navy Petty Officers Michael Murray and Danny Edgar, members of the 323-member crew of the USS Benfold — the Navy's memorial to its fallen hero.

419

Pomp/Audubon parade honors war hero

Continued from Page 1B

The USS Benfold is an Arleigh Burke-class guided missile destroyer, commissioned in 1996 and based in San Diego. Part of the Pacific Fleet, it bears the Aegis weapon system designed by Lockheed-Martin in Moorestown and is part of the USS Constellation battle group. Its role is to protect the giant aircraft carrier from attack.

Audubon has adopted both the ship named for its hero and the ship's crew. Both are headed for deployment in the Pacific — well away from the troubles in Yugoslavia, for now at least — on June 17.

"We usually have the parade July 4, but we are having it early so the crew members from the Benfold can be here," said Burgess.

Burgess, a lifelong resident, is the architect of the close relationship between the ship and the borough. "I have a time share in San Diego and was there when the ship was commissioned," he said.

Petty Officer Murray, 32, a 14-year Navy veteran and the Benfold's Sailor of the Year, said the relationship with the borough was wonderful.

"The students write us letters and the ladies club sends us Christmas cookies, cards and wreaths," he said. "It's incredible."

A native of Bethlehem, Pa., Murray said he especially enjoyed the string band because "in San Diego, I miss the Mummers Parade." He'll be spending vacation time with his family until May 2, when he will return to the ship.

The parade ended at Audubon High School, where students organized Project Memorial and in 1994 built a granite memorial to the borough's three Medal of Honor winners:

■ Benfold was a Staten Island native whose mother and stepfather — his father was killed in World War II — moved to Audubon when he was a child. A medical field technician with the Marines in Korea, he was killed Sept. 5, 1952. Aiding the wounded in combat, he came upon two Marines in a crater. As he approached, an enemy soldier threw two grenades into the crater while two others charged. Picking up a grenade in each hand, Benfold hurled himself against the onrushing hostile soldiers, killing them and himself when the grenades exploded.

■ Army Sgt. 1st Class Nelson Y. Brittin, who died leading an attack on a hill near Yonggong-ni, Korea, March 7, 1951. Wounded, Brittin refused medical attention and hurled grenades into enemy positions. When his weapon jammed, he leaped into a foxhole and killed its occupants with his rifle butt and bayonet and single-handedly eliminated a machine-gun nest. He accounted for 20 enemy casualties and silenced four automatic weapons before he was killed by a burst of machine gun fire.

In October, the Navy announced it would name one of its 18 new T-AKR troop carriers in honor of this Army hero of two wars.

■ Army Cpl. Samuel M. Sampler, a Decatur, Texas, native who settled in Audubon after World War I. Near St. Etienne, France, on Oct. 8, 1918, he charged German machine gun nests, killing two Germans, silencing the guns and capturing 28 prisoners. He died here in 1979 at the age of 60.

Audubon may have to share two of its heroes with Texas and New York, but local patriots say they know of no other town of its small size in America that can claim three Medal of Honor winners.

"We have three, and two have ships named after them," said Harry Thomas, a World War II veteran and member of the Murray-Troutman American Legion Post.

"Our job now is to get a ship named after Cpl. Sampler."

420

Saturday, April 17, 1999: Co-author Burgess joins Petty Officers Murray and
Edgar on the BENFOLD float for the Patriotic Parade (above). As the vehicle
approaches the high school, members of the Audubon Young at Heart Club
greet them with a banner made especially for the occasion (below).

While visiting the Medal of Honor Memorial on the high school campus, the two Petty Officers get acquainted with Edward C. Benfold's widow, his son and two daughters (above). Later in the day, following dinner at the Benfold residence in Cherry Hill, Murray and Edgar get Flyers' T-shirts (below). Both men are hockey fans.

On Sunday afternoon
both Petty Officers
were special guests of
the Philadelphia Flyers.
Following the second
period of the game,
they were given a ride
on the Zamboni machines
and got a bird's-eye
view of the First Union
Center in Philadelphia.

WOW ! Those Flyers'
T-shirts really
came in handy !!

Murray and Edgar visited
St. Mary's and saw the
stained-glass window
in the church (right).

Later in the week, both
Petty Officers were the
guests of the Mt. Ephraim
Rotary Club and were
given a special gift by
President Bob Cogliser:
a pen. In return, members
of the Rotary Club received
photos of the ship. (below).

Murray and Edgar meet Haviland Avenue Elementary School Principal,
Roann Endt (above) and then field questions from Haviland students (below).

Later in the morning, Murray and Edgar meet the Principal of Mansion Avenue School, Don Borden (above). During the session with students, Edgar presents Borden a photograph of the ship (below). It was a special moment for Borden, who is in his first year as Principal at MAS.

During visits to the high school, Murray and Edgar meet AHS Principal
William Westphal (above) and, during a special Senior Citizens' Spring Social
event - - - sponsored by the students in the Intergenerational Club at
AHS - - - chat with new school superintendent Mrs. Mary Anne Rende (below).

After meeting several of the students who are chair-persons for the Project Memorial Foundation at AHS (above), Murray and Edgar receive Audubon caps in a presentation in the school library. They then placed a decal from the USS BENFOLD at the entrance to the library (below).

After reading several of his poems at a poetry session at a local Encore Books location, co-author Edgar became an honorary member of the Audubon Poets (above). He then joined Petty Officer Murray - - - who was speaking to members of the Audubon Historical Society - - - and got acquainted with several members of the local organization (below).

Friday, April 23, 1999

USS Benfold sends envoys to Audubon

The ship is named after a Korean War hero from the town. Their relationship runs deep.

By Martin Z. Braun
INQUIRER SUBURBAN STAFF

AUDUBON — When Navy Petty Officers Michael L. Murray and Danny Edgar go on shore leave, they usually do not have parades given in their honor or speak to Rotarians and high school students.

But this was no ordinary shore leave.

For the last week, Murray, the USS Benfold's "Sailor of the Year," and Edgar visited Audubon, continuing a five-year relationship between the ship's 350-member crew and the borough of 9,200. Yesterday, the pair, dressed in crisp white uniforms, capped their visit by sharing stories of Navy life with students at Audubon High School.

The USS Benfold, a 505-foot guided missile destroyer based in San Diego, is named after Edward C. Benfold, a Medal of Honor recipient from Audubon who was killed during the Korean War after saving two injured Marines, who were lying in a crater, from enemy grenades. Benfold picked up the grenades, leaped out of the crater and hurled himself against enemy soldiers, killing both them and himself.

The relationship between Audubon and the USS Benfold runs deep, said Craig E. Burgess, an educator and Audubon resident who organized the week's events.

After learning in 1993 that four Audubon High students had helped build a memorial to Benfold, Mark E. Ferguson 3d, the ship's first commander, visited the town on the Fourth of July, 1994. The following year, he returned with 30 crew members. In 1996, Burgess, who had been acting as a liaison between the borough and the ship, was invited to the ship's launch in San Diego.

Since then, the ship's crew and borough residents have exchanged letters, cards and visits. The Audubon Women's Club sends the ship cookies every December, said Burgess. The crew returned the gesture by sending the women autographed photos of the ship. And every Fourth of July, the Benfold sends sailors to march in the borough's parade.

The sailors visited the borough this week because the $1 billion Benfold is scheduled to be deployed to the Persian Gulf in July.

In response to a student's question, Murray said the Navy would not send the Benfold to Kosovo, although the decision could change at any moment.

In his talk to the students, Murray described the ship's 1,500-mile-range Tomahawk missiles and AEGIS radar system, which is built in neighboring Moorestown. AEGIS is so sensitive, Murray said, that seagulls sometimes show up on the radar screen.

The cards and letters sent from Audubon, Murray said, help fight off the loneliness that comes from being at sea for months at a time.

"It's a tough life. It's not an easy life," he said.

430

Murray Troutt Post #262
American Legion
20 Chestnut Street
Audubon, N. J. 08106

June 15, 1997

Commander, D. Michael Abrashoff
USS Benfold DDG 65
Unites States Navy

Commander Abrashoff:

Congratulations of your new command, the USS Benfold DDG 65. The friendship exhibited by Commander Ferguson and the crew, especially their association with "Project Memorial" honoring our Medal of Honor Recipients, is sincerely appreciated by the people of Audubon.

The Audubon American Legion Post #262 was granted a Charter on May 24, 1920 by the National Executive Committee of the American Legion. The total membership numbered 30 at that time.

On January 31, 1931 a replacement Charter was issued to the Post, changing it to Murray-Troutt Post #262. The person requesting this change of the Charter was Harry Mackerell, Post Adjutant, in honor of James L. Murray and William T. Troutt, both of whom died in World War I.

After seventy five years the aim and purpose is still service to the Community, State and Nation, serving in peacetime, as we did during the great conflicts, with dedication and commitment.

The Post has a new home with three monuments dedicated to our veterans of all wars. These monuments are tributes to both the living and to those heroes who fell during these conflicts. (pictures enclosed). We are particularly proud of our three Medal of Honor recipients, an unusual occurrence from a town as small as Audubon with a population of 9,500. This fact speaks volumes in the name of patriotism.

Nelson V. Brittin, U.S. Army, and Edward C. Benfold, U.S. Navy, both died in the Korean conflict. Samuel M. Sampler, though not originally from Audubon, after WWI, chose to live in Audubon and was a member of our Post for 33 years. We are proud that he chose to raise his family within our Community. He received the Medal of Honor for action in France, during WWI. Sam lived to the age of 84.

431

Saint Mary's Episcopal Church
White Horse Pike and Green Street
Haddon Heights, New Jersey 08035
(609) 547-3240
FAX: (609) 310-0565

The Reverend Nathaniel R. Elliott, Jr.
Priest Associate

Friday, June 20, 1997

Commander D. Michael Abrashoff
Captain, USS BENFOLD (DDG 65)
FPO AP 96661-1283

Esteemed Commander Abrashoff:

The entire parish of St. Mary's Episcopal Church in Haddon Heights,
New Jersey, wishes to extend congratulations to you as you begin
your tenure as Commanding Officer of the USS BENFOLD.

Edward C. Benfold, the individual in whose memory DDG 65 was
named, was a parishioner at St. Mary's while a student at Audubon
High School. Following his heroic death in 1952, Edward's friends
and classmates dedicated a special stained glass window at St.
Mary's in his memory.

Enclosed with this communication are several photographs of the
church, a Prayer Book for The Armed Forces and a medallion of the
Episcopal Church Service Cross, along with several newspaper articles
that summarize the activities that took place in Audubon and in
Haddon Heights on August 19, 1995, when members of the crew of the
USS BENFOLD visited the High School and then went to a special service
at St. Mary's.

Our prayers will be with you and the entire crew as you depart for
the Persian Gulf in mid-August.

Best wishes and God's blessing on USS BENFOLD and all who sail in her,

Sincerely,

The Reverend Nathaniel R. Elliott, Jr.
Priest Associate
St. Mary's Episcopal Church
Haddon Heights, New Jersey

432

Borough of Audubon

Board of Commissioners

John J. Coyle, Mayor
Director of Public Affairs & Public Safety

Donna Sadwin, Commissioner
Director of Public Works

Brian McPeak, Commissioner
Director of Revenue & Finance

Commander Mark E. Ferguson, III
USS Benfold

Dear Commander:

On behalf of the residents of the Borough of Audubon, we wish to express our appreciation for all your support, and that of all your officers and members of the USS Benfold, to our community.

Over the past several years, the youth of our community have come to better understand the sacrifices made by our residents that have served in the armed forces, protecting the interests of the United States far from the security of the Borough of Audubon. Most important has been the Project Memorial, honoring Edward C. Benfold and two other residents of this community that are recipients of the Congressional Medal of Honor. Your active participation in this project and your continued inspiration by attending the many events at the Audubon High School are deeply appreciated and have clearly left a positive impression on our youth.

As you leave your command of the USS Benfold, we wish to express our appreciation for your services to this community and wish you continued best wishes. We hope you will visit Audubon as often as your schedule permits.

Sincerely,

Jack Coyle
Mayor

Donna Sadwin
Commissioner

Brian McPeak
Commissioner

DEPARTMENT OF THE NAVY

COMMANDING OFFICER
USS BENFOLD (DDG 65)
FPO AP 96661-1283

OFFICIAL BUSINESS

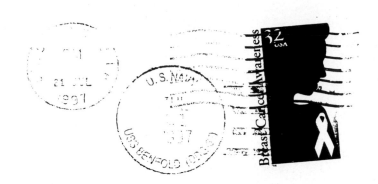

MR CRAIG E BURGESS
PRESIDENT
AUDUBON HIGH SCHOOL ALUMNI ASSOCIATION

COMMANDING OFFICER
USS BENFOLD (DDG 65)
FPO AP 96661-1283

09 July 1997

Mr. Craig E. Burgess
President Audubon High School Alumni Association
350 Edgewood Avenue
Audubon, New Jersey 08106-2299

Dear Mr. Burgess,

Thank you for your kind letter and for your support of USS BENFOLD. I feel honored to be welcomed into BENFOLD's extended family, Audubon High School Alumni Association and the Borough of Audubon.

I know the performance of USS BENFOLD will honor the memory of Edward C. Benfold as well as all the citizens of the Borough of Audubon. Your support solidifies our resolve and our commitment to excellence.

I look forward to continuing the special relationship the officers and crew of USS BENFOLD share with the people of Audubon. Again, thank you for your support.

D. M. ABRASHOFF

434

The visit to Audubon by Commander Ferguson in April of 1997 and the three visits by "Sailors of the Year" from the ship have done a great deal to increase awareness of the special relationship that Audubon has with the officers and crew of the USS BENFOLD. Local organizations schedule sessions to discuss ways to support the student efforts; more and more USS BENFOLD 'covers' and T-shirts are being worn; representatives from all of the armed forces are hearing more about the pride in patriotism that is alive and well in the borough ! This pride has, in turn, resulted in activities that continue to strengthen the bonds of friendship: in September of 1997, community leaders and organizations, as well as all of the officers and crew of the ship received a 1998 calendar with the inscription, "The Borough of Audubon and the Crew of the USS BENFOLD: The Green Wave and the Navy, Perfect Together"; every student and faculty member in all three Audubon schools, as well as the officers and crew of the ship, received a 1999 Pocket Planner and a ball point pen with the same inscription. Both of these gifts were donated by local organizations: The AHS Alumni Association and the Audubon Poets. (See page 437). On June 16, 1999 - - - two days prior to the departure of the USS BENFOLD on its second 6-month deployment - - - co-author Burgess visited the ship and brought an Armed Forces Prayer Book and a Medallion of the Episcopal Church Service Cross for every officer and crew member: a special gift from St. Mary's Episcopal Church in Haddon Heights. (See photo on page 438).

In mid-May, 1999, residents learned that the ship had a new Executive Officer, LCDR Todd Leavitt. LCDR Leavitt is a native of the State of New Jersey and, because of all the information he was receiving about this wonderful friendship with the borough of Audubon, he called and made arrangements to come for a visit on June 1, 1999. He met with the Project Memorial Foundation Committee members and presented them two special gifts from the ship: a 5' shell casing inscribed to the students of AHS and a U. S. Navy Flag. (See the items and photos on pages 439 - 441).

Within the high school, steps were taken to increase student awareness of the lives of the three Medal of Honor recipients. Each November, on Veterans' Day, Principal Westphal and co-author Burgess present a special program to all of the students in 7th grade history classes. The students learn about the items displayed in the Rotunda and in other display cases throughout the building, are given background information on each of the three Medal of Honor recipients, as well as some facts and figures about all of the AHS graduates who have fought for our nation's freedom, and place flowers at the Memorial site. (The letter on page 444, written by two 7th graders to Mr. Westphal in early April of 1999, came as a result of the Veterans' Day presentation in November, 1998. Their ideas received some support from the community and two new benches were installed near the Memorial site prior to the 1999 ceremony.) (Article on pages 442 - 443)

In early 1998, members of the AHS Korean Club initiated a project that resulted in the construction of a walkway leading to the Memorial site. (The walkway was dedicated at the Memorial Day ceremony in May of 1998.) See pages 445 - 446.

The New Jersey Education Association sent a film crew to AHS in May of 1997 to videotape the Memorial Day ceremony. Highlights of the program then aired on Classroom Closeup, NJ, a TV show that features outstanding achievements of students in New Jersey schools. (See page 447.)

We now present highlights of the Memorial Day Ceremonies for 1997, 1998 and 1999. The information and the photos speak for themselves. (Refer to pages 448 - 459).

A Holiday Greeting
To Shine
Throughout Your Year

THE BOROUGH OF AUDUBON
AND THE CREW OF THE
U.S.S. BENFOLD
THE GREEN WAVE AND THE NAVY

THE BOROUGH OF AUDUBON
AND THE CREW OF THE
U.S.S. BENFOLD
THE GREEN WAVE AND THE NAVY
PERFECT TOGETHER
1998

437

Armed Forces prayer books and Episcopal Church Service Crosses are blessed during Services at St. Mary's Church on May 30, 1999 by the Parish Rector, the Reverend Dr. Ronny W. Dower. Both items were gifts from the parish to the officers and crew of the USS BENFOLD.

438

On June 1, 1999, LCDR Todd Leavitt visited Audubon, meeting with community leaders in the AHS Rotunda: (above, l to r) Bob Hoover; Comm. Donna Sadwin; AHS Principal William Westphal; Murray-Troutt Am. Legion Post #262 Commander Bob Phillips. (below, l to r) LCDR Leavitt takes time at the Memorial site for a photo with 1999 Project Memorial Foundation Committee chairs; Joshua Peschko, Gabrielle Horvath, Renato Latini and Sara Kauffman.

AHS students and community leaders proudly display gifts presented to the high school from officers and crew of the ship; a U. S. Navy Flag and a 5 inch shell casing, inscribed to the students at AHS (above) (below) LCDR Leavitt stands with Am. Legion Commander Bob Phillips in front of the WW II Memorial in front of the Post Home on Chestnut Street.

LCDR Leavitt meets with Mrs. Dorothy Waida, widow of Edward C. Benfold and Berta Benfold, wife of Edward's son, during his visit to Audubon (above). He also visited St. Mary's Church in Haddon Heights and saw the stained-glass window dedicated to the memory of Edward C. Benfold (left).

Principal works with students

TINA MARKOE/Courier-Post

Audubon High School Principal Bill Westphal helps students Eric Krout, 18, Erin Bodenschatz, 18, Sarah Royston, 13, and Monica Stillman, 13, as they work on a project to honor Medal of Honor recipients.

By SHARON CHUNG
Courier-Post Staff

AUDUBON

When a student asked Bill Westphal for change of a dollar, the Audubon High School principal reached in his pocket and pulled out three quarters and three dimes, giving the youngster a nickel extra.

Offering an extra coin is just a glimpse of what the school's 900 students stand to gain from Westphal's generous nature as an educator and friend.

But the former math teacher — who taught at the school for 25 years and has spent the last 10 as its top administrator — tends to step away from the spotlight, turning it instead on the accomplishments of his students — all of whom he knows by name.

"We are very close to our kids," Westphal, 57, said recently during his daily lunchtime stroll

Town's Medal of Honor recipients recognized

Organized by the student-led Project Memorial Foundation, the granite memorial, erected outside Audubon High School in 1994, honors the tiny town's three Medal of Honor winners:

■ Navy Hospitalman 3rd Class Edward C. Benfold was a Staten Island native whose mother and stepfather — his father was killed in World War II — moved to Audubon when he was a child. A medical field technician with the Marines in Korea, he was killed Sept. 5, 1952. Aiding the wounded in combat, he came upon two Marines in a crater. As he approached, an enemy soldier threw two grenades into the crater while two others charged. Picking up a grenade in each hand,

Benfold hurled himself against the onrushing hostile soldiers, killing them and himself when the grenades exploded.

■ Army Sgt. 1st Class Nelson Y. Brittin, who died leading an attack on a hill near Yonggong-ni, Korea, March 7, 1951. Wounded, Brittin refused medical attention and hurled grenades into enemy positions. When his weapon jammed, he leaped into a foxhole and killed its occupants with his rifle butt and bayonet and single-handedly eliminated a machine-gun nest. He accounted for 20 enemy casualties and silenced four automatic weapons before he was killed by a burst of machine gun fire. In October, the Navy announced it

would name one of its 18 new T-AKR troop carriers in honor of this Army hero of two wars.

■ Army Cpl. Samuel M. Sampler, a Decatur, Texas, native who settled in Audubon after World War I. Near St. Etienne, France, on Oct. 8, 1918, he charged German machine gun nests, killing two Germans, silencing the guns and capturing 28 prisoners. He died here in 1979 at the age of 84.

Audubon may have to share two of its heroes with Texas and New York, but local patriots say they know of no other town of its small size in America that can claim three Medal of Honor winners.

Compiled by Sharon Chung

around the school.

"You have to be sensitive to them. You can't sell

them short because they can spot a hypocrite better than adults," he said. "The

most important thing to a

See **AUDUBON**, Page 2B

Audubon

Principal works with students on programs

Continued from Page 1B

kid is self-image.

"Good educators measure their successes in the successes of their children," Westphal added. "Recognizing, publicizing and acknowledging people when they do good things is what it's all about. Everyone has something special they can do, and the faculty here reaches out to the kids and we help them develop that self-confidence."

In the few minutes it took Westphal to walk through the hallways and up and down some stairs, his popularity was evident as about a dozen students greeted him.

The school's Project Memorial Foundation, a Westphal-inspired and student-organized program — which began in 1994 with a granite memorial honoring the town's three Medal of Honor recipients   is another example of their camaraderie.

In addition, Westphal gives the students full rein in planning the event, which attracts several hundred spectators annually. Some of the highlights include a procession of state flags, a flag and rifle salute, and a laying of flowers.

"About 200 students participate in Project Memorial. It's a big job and they take pride in it," Westphal said. "It's kind of a surprise what the students come up with every year, but they're in charge."

"They openly schedule meetings with the community," he added. "They learn to interact and deal with each other. They learn how to overcome obstacles and they learn how to delegate responsibility with authority.

"The way all this bonds generations together is a very special feeling," Westphal said. "The process itself is probably more important than the project."

TINA MARKOE/Courier-Post

Audubon High School Principal Bill Westphal talks to seventh-graders Monica Stillman (left) and Sarah Royston. The girls led efforts to get a pair of park benches installed in front of the Medal of Honor Memorial.

At this year's Memorial Day service, two seventh-grade honor students, Monica Stillman and Sarah Royston, who wished to establish a mark for their junior high class, successfully lobbied for a $160 donation from the Audubon Women's Auxiliary of Murray-Troutt American Legion Post 262. The money was used to purchase a pair of park benches, which were installed in front of the Medal of Honor Memorial.

"We wanted to put our class of 2004 out there," Sarah said. "There are a lot of elderly people who like to sit out there, and we thought the benches would be comforting for them. The whole community was responsible for this."

Audubon High School senior Annie Liontas, 17, who actively participated in Project Memorial last month, lauded Westphal for his tireless support.

"He's so energetic and he gets just as excited as the kids do about new ideas. He shapes leaders of the students," said Liontas. "He tells us to lead by example, but that's what he does himself. He's very open-minded.

"A lot of administrators are not willing or open to change, but he is," she added. "He understands where everybody's coming from, whether you're 17 (years old) or 70."

Flanking Liontas were fellow honor students, Eric Krout, 18, and Josh Peschko, 17, who said it's not unusual for their soft-spoken principal to underplay his role as a respected school leader.

"He understands young people and he's very approachable," Krout said. "But he'll brag about the students and not talk about himself."

"He's definitely an unsung hero," Peschko said.

443

April, 1999

Dear Mr. Westphal,

   Hello! My name is Monica Stillman, a 7th grader here in AHS. My friend, Sarah Roisten, and I greatly appreciate the courage of the three soldiers that sacrificed their life for war. So to use our appreciation positivly we would like to get the 7th grade class to contribue to raise enough money to buy a fountain type structure for the memorial. I am the secretary of the 7th grade class and the council and I could put a fund-raiser together. I am also a member of the Student Council and I could talk to them about it. My friend Sarah does know places that sell fountains and it is for a cheap price. If you think our idea is good then please contact me any time during the day.

         Thank you for your time.

                        Sincerely,
                        Monica Stillman
                        And friend: Sarah Roisten

444

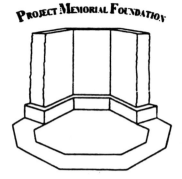

AUDUBON HIGH SCHOOL
350 EDGEWOOD AVENUE
AUDUBON , NJ 08106
PHONE: (609) 547-7695
FAX: (609) 546-8550

KOREAN WAR PROJECT COMMITTEE
Peter Fung
Thomas Hunt
David Proulx

April 9, 1998

Mr. Craig Burgess, President
Audubon High School Alumni Association
329 Washington Terr.
Audubon, NJ 08106

Dear Mr. Burgess:

Thank you. These words don't seem quite adequate to express the appreciation we
feel toward your organization. Had it not been for your organization we would not have
been able to get started on this project. Currently we have ordered our two flag poles
and are awaiting delivery. We have also chosen a contractor and are now in the
process of installing the walkway.

At this time I would like to cordially invite your members to attend the Memorial Day
service for the dedication of this project. The service will be held at 11:00am on Friday,
May 22, 1998, at the site of the memorial. Please let us know if you plan to attend.
Feel free to call me, if you have any questions. Once again, thank you ever so much.

Sincerely,

Peter Fung   Thomas Hunt   David Proulx
Korean War Memorial Project Committee

445

Classroom NJ

New Jersey Education Association's award winning half-hour television show features the outstanding programs in our public schools, and the people who make them work.

STUDENTS HONOR VETERANS AND WAR HEROES IN
MEMORIAL DAY SERVICE AT THEIR SCHOOL

Audubon Jr.–Sr. High Schol

**Featured on
Classroom Close-up, NJ on**

WPHL-TV/WB-17 9:30 am

October 24 & 31

**WWOR-TV/UPN-9 8:00 am
and WPHL-TV/WB-17 6:30 am**

October 25

1997

447

Audubon remembers fallen heroes

By Avi Steinhardt, Courier-Post

The Audubon High School choir sings the national anthem as members of Audubon American Legion Post 262 stand at attention during a Memorial Day observance Friday at the school. The annual event included guest speakers, a wreath-laying ceremony and an award presentation.

FLAG SALUTE

Christine Venable, Project Memorial Committee
Audubon High School Class of 1999

NATIONAL ANTHEM

Audubon High School Choir

WELCOME

Eric Krout, Project Memorial Committee
Audubon High School Class of 1999

INTRODUCTION AND REMARKS

Erin Bodenschatz, Project Memorial Committee
Audubon High School Class of 1999

INVOCATION

Reverend Steven Shuster
Audubon United Methodist Church

SPEAKERS

Lt. Col. Kleppinger, U.S. Army

John Skrabonja, Teacher, Audubon High School

Dick Gallant, National Director of the Military Order of the Purple Heart

LAYING OF WREATH

Jessica Allen, Lilly Fung, Jennifer Tait
Audubon High School Class of 1999

PRESENTATION OF AWARDS

RIFLE SALUTE

TAPS

John Lafferty, Audubon High School Class of 1998
Jennifer Tait, Audubon High School Class of 1999

BENEDICTION

Audubon High School Choir

CLOSING

Annie Liontas, Project Memorial Committee
Audubon High School Class of 1999

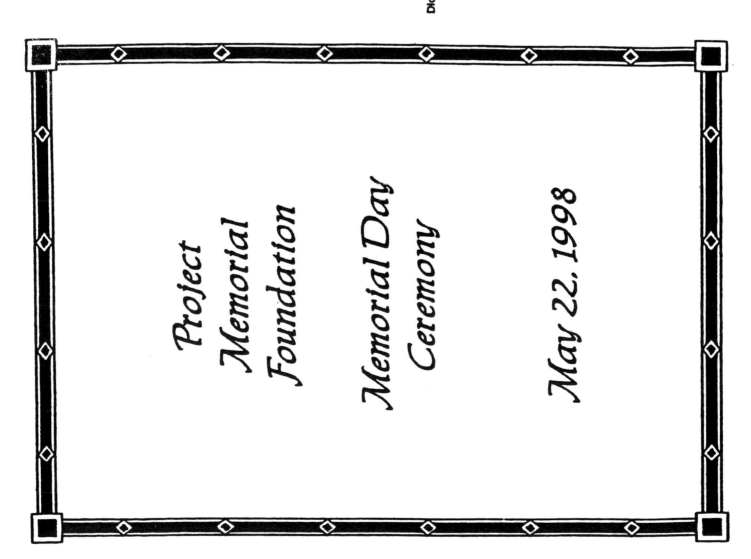

Project
Memorial
Foundation

Memorial Day
Ceremony

May 22, 1998

At the 1999 Memorial Day Ceremony at AHS, members of American Legion Post #262 serve as flag guard (above). Prior to the playing of Taps, members give a Rifle Salute to all veterans (right).

During the ceremony, Lt. Col. Ralph H. Daugherty, Jr. USAF, Ret., presents
Memorial Foundation member Erin Rodenschatz (class of 1999) the Bronze
Patrick Henry Award on behalf of the Military Order of the World Wars (above).
Then students and local residents place flowers at the Memorial site (below)

Following the ceremony, chairpersons Joshua Peschco, Gabrielle Horvath, Renato Latini (holding special Memorial Mug given to the guest speakers), and Sara Kauffman pose for a photo (above). Meanwhile, Bronze Patrick Henry Award recipients Erin Bodenschatz, Annie Liontas and Eric Krout proudly display their citations and medallions for those in attendance (below).

Friday, May 28, 1999

COURIER-POST

South Jersey

Early Memorial Day at Audubon,

By MIKE DANIELS
For the Courier-Post

High school students honor veterans

The Audubon ceremony was staged by 11th-graders serving on the Project Memorial Foundation. The event was kicked off by a performance of the school's

band and a procession of students carrying the flags of the 50 states.

Speakers included two veterans, Richard Gallant and Audubon High graduate Craig Burgess.

In his remarks, Gallant expressed admiration for the students and faculty members who worked on the ceremony.

"Your activity is one of

the finest, if not the finest anywhere in the country," he said.

Burgess read poems written by soldiers during World War II and the Korean War. He also praised the heroism of three Audubon veterans — Samuel M. Sampler, Edward C. Benfold and Nelson V. Brittin — who received the Medal of Honor for heroism in combat.

Sampler, a World War I veteran, was honored for his actions that led to the surrender of 28 enemy soldiers near St. Etienne, France, in October 1918.

Sampler died in 1979.

Benfold and Brittin both died in action during the Korean War in 1952.

Benfold saved the lives of two wounded soldiers; Brittin led his company to victory in a battle.

Thursday's ceremony was held on Edgewood Avenue, next to the granite memorial dedicated to the Medal of Honor winners. The ceremony provided a chance to show off park benches and a new walkway leading to the memorial, that was donated by the Audubon Women's Auxiliary.

JOHN JABLONSKI/For the Courier-Post

Audubon High School students carry flags of 50 states Thursday at a ceremony honoring veterans. From left: Karl Lynn, Ashley Schmidt, Rosemaria Carrado and Brianna Carroll.

As co-authors of this book, we are very proud to be part of this great friendship. We decided to send out a questionnaire to several of the ship's officers, to the Mayor, several educators and some residents in Audubon AND to members of the Benfold family to find out what they thought about what has been happening. These are some of the comments we received:

*

I first became aware of the connection between Audubon and the ship when I was first named to command in November 1993. At that time, I was the first, and only, officer named to the crew. My first action was to research the history of the ship, her namesake, and any other information I could locate. My goal was to identify the unique aspects of the ship's history upon which to build her character and reputation. The crew must have a link with the past to forge the future . . . and hopefully I could capture that past in the ship's crest and motto for a start.

Between that time and the spring, I became aware of Mrs. Waida and her son, Edward through the office of the Secretary of the Navy. I also became acquainted with the amazing efforts of the Borough to construct the memorial to the Medal of Honor winners. My first visit to the town was on 04 July 1994, when I was privileged to speak at the dedication of the memorial. We also watched the parade, attended the picnic at Mayor Murray's home, and met Mrs. Waida and Edward for the first time. On behalf of Lockheed Martin - - - we were able to present a painting of the ship to the school at that time.

What struck me then, and remains with me today - - - are the vivid images of patriotism and the intense pride of the town on the 4th of July. The bunting on the houses, the flags on all the lawns, the little league and children riding their bikes in the parade - - - along with obvious pride in the creation of the monument - - - struck me as I have seldom been before. It was the manifestation of a type of patriotism, loyalty to community, and pride in our past that I have rarely seen, let alone experience outside of the military. To share that day with my family was a searing experience - - - one that I wanted the ship to experience as well. I thought it essential the crew learn about the town that could create such a feeling.

From that came our later visit to bring the crew (about 40) to play softball and ride the fire engine and meet the fire company. Again a high point for me was the privilege of actually driving the fire engine with the crew and firemen onboard (if only around a parking lot). I only stalled it once.

I then committed to having the ship's sailor of the year return to the town on the Fourth of July, whenever possible. I do not know if that continues, but I thought it important the very best of the ship visit and see that pride of your wonderful town.

The other significant memories are of Mrs. Waida and her son, Edward, and their families. Their strength, quiet dignity, and perseverance through years after the death of the ship's namesake comes from a special type of courage, rarely found in this country. They are a family that, in the words of Abraham Lincoln, laid the ultimate sacrifice on the altar of freedom. Holding Edward Benfold's Medal of Honor was another great privilege of my life. What I remember most is their explanation of how Edward's father lost his life in the sinking of the merchant ship SS Castilla during the Second World War, when Edward was just a boy. Then, in the Korean War, Edward also made the ultimate sacrifice and was awarded the Medal of Honor.

The ship's motto, "Onward With Valor", is dedicated to this amazing family. It attempts to capture how their sacrifice for our freedom is carried on by the next generation - - - and forges the link from the past to the future of my ship and crew.

Sincerely,

Mark E. Ferguson III
Captain, USN

*

The tour of the Memorial to Audubon's fallen heroes from the three wars was the most moving event that I personally participated in. I can't conceive of many other towns of Audubon's population giving three of her sons to the defense of our great nation in the same way. It symbolized what we all cherish in the military . . . a people that are patriotic not only in word but in deed, even unto death. The tribute of the people of Audubon was a fitting memorial and one that I will not forget.

The other most memorable activity was communications with Audubon's children. I will speak to this activity below.

The relationship between the people of Audubon and USS BENFOLD is unique. In the five ships that I have been assigned, I have never seen anything like it. I had the privilege to correspond with many of Audubon's elementary school youth during my tour on BENFOLD. We also receive cookies, and other treats from the women of Audubon for Christmas. Lastly, the trip to Audubon (especially the fire engine ride) was a pure delight. These were my personal examples of acts of friendship that the people of Audubon showed us. These acts and the kindness of the people made us all feel like we had the backing of the people in America that really mattered. What the people of Audubon did came not with political purse-strings or baggage, not with the hope of some plush government contract, or some other monetary benefit. It came out of a pure and patriotic heart. It came from ordinary people just like us who cared about the sailors and defenders of their freedom. It came from AMERICANS.

To the people of Audubon, New Jersey; I may never sail on a ship as fine as BENFOLD again. And, I may never get the opportunity to visit your beautiful and wholesome town again. Thus, I want to let you know that I deeply appreciate all the kindness that you consistently showed me and the officers & crew of BENFOLD. Your outstanding hospitality, graciousness and spirit of patriotism were fantastic. Your love for us sustained us over the long hours of watch far from family and friends. As future crews inhabit BENFOLD, the memory of the relationship between a town and her ship may have its ups and downs. But for me, a simple sailor, a veteran . . . the memory of our visit with you, and our kinship, will always bring a smile to my face and warm my heart. GO GREEN WAVE !!

LCDR SINCLAIR HARRIS

461

*

When I took command of the ship in June of 1997, I received a special briefing from my predecessor on the special and enduring friendship USS BENFOLD has with the community of Audubon. The life of Edward Benfold resonates with the crew and, posthumously, he provides inspiration with us all. It is through our relationship with the citizens of Audubon that we honor him.

As our daily lives become more hectic and stressful, we often times forget about our roots and the basic values that gave us a firm anchoring in life. By pausing and reflecting on the heroism of Edward Benfold, we are refreshed or renewed and we re-commit ourselves to a greater purpose. By continuing a relationship with the Benfold family and citizens of Audubon, we are reminded how important our core values are.

The Sailor of the Year is awarded to that First Class Petty Officer who best reflects the life of Edward Benfold: Honor, Courage, Commitment. The Chief Petty Officers make a recommendation to me and I have final approval for their recommendation. The Sailor of the Year Program is a fantastic program and the person selected feels honored by being able to participate in the Fourth of July festivities.

COMMANDER D. MICHAEL ABRASHOFF,
CAPTAIN, USS BENFOLD, 1997 - - -

*

As Command Master Chief, I represent the command and the ship's crew. I coordinate the sailor of the year annual visit to Audubon. I have also represented the ship at various civic functions and dedications in Audubon the past four years, during my tour onboard.

Audubon has become the hometown of BENFOLD. Truly our home away from home. I, and members of the commissioning crew have been welcomed home to Audubon, *and we have enjoyed a tremendous sense of belonging there.*

COMMAND MASTER CHIEF ROBERT SCHEELER

*

As Superintendent of the Audubon Schools, I was presented with the idea of a Memorial honoring our three Medal of Honor recipients. I was pleased to support Mr. Westphal and Ms. Beth Canzanese's International Relations class in their community service. The concept of community service is an important aspect of a quality education. So much of our learning takes place outside the classroom and so much is gained in non-traditional learning. Students gain

462

through service because they learn so much about themselves and learn to value the differences in others.

Audubon is a unique community. The pride exhibited by our students is admirable. The Project Memorial Program has enhanced the value of patriotism and has helped our students realize that some traditional values are important to promote and celebrate.

MR. JOHN POLOMANO
Audubon Superintendent until June, 1998

*

Ed and I were married in June, 1951, and we went to live in California as Ed was stationed at Camp Pendleton. Ed was a wonderful person and fun to be with, he loved to dance , and take walks on the beach and talk about our life together after the war, and about our son who was born in May of 1952. He was so happy.

I was the ship's sponsor, I broke the ceremonial bottle of champagne against the bow of the ship. At the Commissioning, I gave the order for all the officers and crew to man the ship and bring her to life. I cried with joy that he was to be so honored.

MRS. DOROTHY WAIDA

*

My entire family was invited to the Christening by Commander Mark Ferguson.

"Who by the way went above and beyond the call of duty not only in locating my family, but also in opening his family and home to us in making the event personable and comfortable. Truly he represents the best ideals of this country and the Navy in his efforts, which I can never forget"

He requested that my two daughters (Nicole Andrea Benfold & Alexandra Kori Benfold) be Maids of Honor to my mother who was the Ships Sponsor. Their role was to escort my mother and assist her in her duties as ships sponsor. (Mostly they just got to sit on the stage and feel important but that in itself was a great experience for them.)

I was asked to speak at the Christening (therefore I also sat on stage with my daughters) and escorted The Honorable Nora Slatkin Assistant Secretary of the Navy to the stage. I read parts of the letter my mother had received from a Marine who served with my father in Korea shortly after his death. In addition I and my daughters joined my mother as she broke the bottle christening and naming the ship.

At the commissioning I was again part of the dais on the ship. My role was to present the ceremonial looking glass "brass old fashioned telescope typical of old seafaring ships".

I have always had this feeling of pride of what my father had done to help others. I have used this as a guide in my life and a standard to look up to in concern for others beyond ourselves. It reminds me of the many who have sacrificed greatly so we all could live free. It is important to me to do what I can in his memory and that of others who have also sacrificed to inspire the young future of this country.

*

Even after I became Mayor, the subject of how to appropriately honor these three heroes in some sort of permanent way was an occasional point of discussion with members of the Legion. Sometime in late 1993, I was approached by Mr. William Westphal, the principal at Audubon High School. Mr. Westphal informed me that a group of students had learned about Audubon's Congressional Medal of Honor recipients, and wanted to create a permanent memorial to them. In our discussions, Mr. Westphal expressed his desire that this project become a community event, as well as a learning process for the students involved. He believed that this project would give the students excellent experience in learning to deal with the public, and the various levels of government that would be involved with such a project.

When news of Commander Ferguson's impending visit for Audubon's 4th of July festivities and the dedication of the new monument was learned, an informal committee was formed to plan for the Commander's impending visit. The committee was roughly comprised of Mr. Robert Hoover, a retired RCA employee who worked on various naval projects, members of the Murray-Troutt Post Legion, members of the Audubon Volunteer Fire Company No. 1, Mr. Westphal, Principal of the High School, and Mr. John Polomano, Superintendent of Schools, and the student officers of the Project Memorial Committee. We would typically meet at the high school and discuss various ideas.

I would say that Fourth of July was one of my proudest days as Mayor of Audubon. This event underscored the superb reputation Audubon has always enjoyed, and certainly brought out the finest in our community. I will always remember Commander Ferguson telling me how he knew the minute he entered Audubon that he was coming to a special place. The thing that formulated this initial impression, was all the American flags that were placed on the poles on Merchant Street.

A couple of weeks later, I received a phone call on my answering machine from the Master Chief. It appeared that there was a certain degree of envy from his superior officers regarding the fire company memorabilia given to him. I immediately contacted Fire Chief Paul Hartstein, who got the Master Chief out of his jam, by sending a "care" package. A few weeks after that, we received several "BENFOLD" baseball hats from a grateful Master Chief.

This relationship also gives the crew members of the USS BENFOLD a better appreciation of their ship's namesake. Through their visits to Audubon and the Benfold family, as well as regular contact between all involved, Edward Benfold is portrayed to those who serve on board his ship as the real person he was, and not some distant memory relegated to the history books. While the crew is comprised of many different people from diverse backgrounds and hometowns, Audubon gives all on board a common link, or living entity to their ship's history.

From my perspective, this friendship serves our common good in a variety of ways. The USS BENFOLD is a wonderful tribute to the memory of one of our own, and remains a constant reminder of the sacrifices made by Edward Benfold, as well as endured by his family. The fact that Audubon can claim three Congressional Medal of Honor recipients is a source of great pride that includes the past, and the present, as well as future generations. This friendship grew out of a high school project, and has evolved to unite our community in pride. This relationship also gives us an opportunity to show the rest of the world that Audubon possesses the spirit, ideals, and values that best reflect our Nation's heritage.

During my tenure in public office, I truly valued my association with the USS BENFOLD. It not only gave me a great source of pride, but made me truly appreciate the friendships that were established. I will always feel privileged to be a part of the initial group that helped establish this friendship. I sincerely hope that what we helped start will continue to grow and endure for many years to come.

Sincerely,

Alfred Murray

*

The current activities between the students and citizens of Audubon and the officers and crew of the USS BENFOLD have provided an extraordinary experience for both groups. Through this partnership both groups have been able to experience patriotic history in the making. This project has brought the citizens of Audubon together and has provided an outlet for young and old to create a part of Audubon's history.

Mr. Craig E. Burgess has made a point of notifying me of the various steps this project has completed and has been a great liaison not only to me, but also between Audubon and the USS BENFOLD. I appreciate all that he has done to coordinate this tremendous and successful project. As the State Senator representing Audubon, I appreciate the opportunity to participate in activities that both honor and salute the residents of this borough. This project is creating something that generations of Audubon residents will honor and cherish.

SENATOR JOHN ADLER

*

My role has been to participate in the Fourth of July festivities with the selected officer from the USS BENFOLD.

I envision that the dedicated Audubon residents will continue the link with the BENFOLD

465

contributions of significant persons are forgotten. This would not be the case at St. Mary's. A stained glass window honoring the memory of Edward had been installed some years previous. In light of the naming of the USS BENFOLD, it seemed appropriate to draw together the officers and crew of the BENFOLD, to experience the <u>place</u> where Edward received his spiritual formation, that may well have played a part in his acts of heroism.

While I no longer have pastoral responsibility, it would be my hope, that there would be an ongoing relationship between Audubon and the officers and crew of the BENFOLD. I would hope that the Parish would play a significant role in the sale and distribution of the projected book.

There will be a mutual benefit to country and to church by keeping alive this relationship.

In January 1998, in my capacity as Chaplain to the QE₂, we unexpectedly embarked in San Diego, but had insufficient time to seek out the ship . . . an intent I would like to have accomplished.

The service, the meeting of the officers and crew of the BENFOLD is one of the highlights of my ministry at St. Mary's, Haddon Heights, NJ.

<u>FATHER ROBERT WILLING</u>

*

The present activity of awareness should provide a response. We of St. Mary's are pleased to share in honoring Edward C. Benfold. Perhaps a role for the parish might be found in the distribution of the book.

<u>FATHER RONNY W. DOWER</u>

On Sunday, August 15, 1999, during the service for the Feast of St. Mary The Virgin, the Passion / Palm Sunday window at the rear of St. Mary's Episcopal Church was rededicated by the Reverend Dr. Ronny W. Dower. The window was repaired and restored with a donation from parishioner Ernest B. Smith in memory of Edward C. Benfold, who was confirmed at St. Mary's on January 30, 1944 and buried from the church on November 12, 1952.

And so, through the ongoing efforts of the students and residents in Audubon and the tremendous support of the officers and crew of the USS BENFOLD, the bonds of friendship have reached across the country and have become strengthened more and more with each passing year. While the U.S. Navy makes it possible for the ship's "Sailor of the Year" to come to Audubon each year and while special visits have been arranged on two occasions - - - by Commander Ferguson in May of 1997 and by Executive Officer LCDR Todd Leavitt in June of 1999, co-author Burgess has served as the Audubon liaison to the ship, traveling from Audubon to San Diego several times each year and bringing greetings and gifts from the borough.

During his visit to the crew on June 16, 1999, Burgess brought copies of several news articles about the friendship, videotapes of the special visit to Audubon by Petty Officers Murray and Edgar in April, 1999, a photo album showing highlights of the visit of LCDR Leavitt on June 1, 1999 and a large greeting card, showing a bear with paws outstretched. This greeting card is presented below, and says: "Think of this card as a GREAT BIG HUG . . . from the students and residents of your 2nd hometown, Audubon, NJ. ONWARD WITH VALOR!" He was then invited to come on board to join family members and friends on Friday morning, June 18th prior to the ship's departure for the second 6-month deployment.

A fitting way to end this chapter on the friendship between the borough of Audubon and the officers and crew of the USS BENFOLD is to present a poem written by 11 year old resident Robert Sweet for a recent writing competition in town. We present it along with a photo taken on June 18, 1999, as the ship departed from San Diego for her 6-month deployment in the Pacific . .

Friendship

The rainbow is nice, just like the star,
But no one can beat how nice you are.
The rainbow is far, as well as the star,
But you are the closest to our hearts.

No one will change that . . . .
Not even the cutest kitty cat.
We'll miss you when you are away,
But in our hearts, you will stay.

Chapter V
The Future
"Onward With Valor" Into The 21st Century

We complete our journey through history with a preview of the future. What lies ahead for the borough of Audubon, for the officers and crew of the USS BENFOLD and for the friendship that has developed between the borough and the ship? As this book entered its final proofreading stage, in early June of 1999, several events took place that may reflect very well our vision of the 21st Century. See if you agree . . . . . .

AUDUBON

The young citizens in the borough already are showing pride in their community, in their country and in their flag. In the 1999 coloring competition, sponsored by the New Jersey State American Legion Association, three 4th grade students displayed patriotism and artistic talent in preparing their entries. We present these three entries on this page and the next

This image was created by Christopher M. Grubb, a student in Mrs. Young's class at Haviland Avenue School.

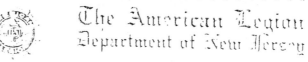

The American Legion
Department of New Jersey

472

This image was created by Eric Bariana, a student in Ms. Storti's class at Mansion Avenue School.

This image was created by Sarah Schroth, a student in Ms. Storti's class at Mansion Avenue School.

 The American Legion
Department of New Jersey

American Legion Post # 262

The borough of Audubon, New Jersey
Is as proud as a borough can be
Of its American Legion Chapter:
It's part of a great family!

The members do more than have meetings
At which they think just of themselves:
They participate in many activities,
Serving as Audubon "elves".

They sponsor a number of dinners
At the home of Post two-sixty-two;
They take part in Memorial services
That honor the red, white and blue;
They donate funds to the borough
To support what brings pride to us all:
Events being sponsored by students
In Winter, Spring, Summer and Fall.

Their role in Project Memorial
Stands out in the hearts and the minds
Of every citizen in Audubon:
Their commitment one not often finds!

The borough of Audubon salutes you,
Legion Post two-sixty-two!
Thank you for serving the borough
And helping make its dreams come true!!

Craig E. Burgess

The Borough Of Audubon
Looking Back With Nostalgia
And Into The Future With Pride

Oh, Little Thrifty Jersey town
Along the Reading Line,
Tho modern and computerized,
The past in you does shine.

One hundred years have come and gone,
Filled with memories so fine - - - - -
The one - room school house, the dairy,
The Bon-Bons come to mind.

The town's first one - room school house,
Dated 1892,
Now is a private residence
Which everyone can view.
It still sits on quaint Cherry Street . . .
Which can be hard to find
On West Atlantic Avenue
Between Washington and Pine.
The street is only one block long
And looks toward the tracks
On which trains still traverse the rails - - -
And take our memories back
To days when each train made two stops
While passing through our town:
At Orston and at Audubon,
Those stations of renown.

The seven farms with Mansion homes
Have long since disappeared
With one exception, grand indeed,
By everyone revered.
The fame of treasured Mansion House
Still lives throughout the town:
George Vail, an artist, lives there now.
His works are well renown.

Those rutted roads of by-gone days
That criss-crossed Audubon - - -
Creating for the borough
The nickname "Mudabon" - - -

Are now fine concrete ribbons
That carry cars and trucks
And even, down by Haddon Lake,
Some flocks of geese and ducks.

The borough landmark, Schnitzler's Hall,
Has now become a store
And many other well-known sites
Are not there anymore:
The National Bank on Merchant Street
Lies vacant and for sale;
The Post Office now just sells stamps,
It no longer sorts our mail;
The town's three movie theatres
Have long since closed their doors,
As have so many businesses - - -
Once vibrant shops and stores.

Where once the little smithy stood
Along the White Horse Pike,
There now are car repair shops,
Gas stations and the like.

WEBER'S COLONIAL DINER
Is a landmark on this Pike:
It's open 24 hours each day,
With a menu patrons like.
In a 1995 newspaper poll
Readers chose this site
"Best Diner in South Jersey":
Many eat there every night!
In May of 1999
You still could have a meal
With everything from soup to dessert
For under $8.00. What a deal!!

During the 20th Century
Many residents fought and died
Fighting for our freedom:
Their efforts aroused much pride.
Students designed a Memorial Site
To honor all veterans of war
AND the town's three Medal of Honor recipients,
From Korea and the 1st World War.

Fond memories of the present day
Include the Greenberg Field,
The very special Memorial Grove,
The USS BENFOLD Shield,
The rebirth seen on Merchant Street,
The Library's new look,
The birth of the FFPLA
And the AUDUBON POET'S book.

As Audubon enters the new millennium,
Her future is looking bright:
So many accomplishments achieved in the past;
So many more now in sight . . . . .
For soon a new ship in the Navy
Will carry Nelson Brittin's name
And a new track will be built at the high school.
The future will bring much acclaim.

May the Lord continue to extend His Grace
On you, special New Jersey town.
Long life and growth in the next century,
Wearing your patriotic crown.

The USS BENFOLD (DDG-65)

The USS BENFOLD (DDG-65), her officers and her crew have achieved much success during the first three plus years since the ship's Commissioning. The Navy has honored her for her performance during the deployment in 1997-1998. The photo below shows LCDR Alan Stubblefield holding a plaque with the replica of the SPOKANE TROPHY, following the presentation of the award on board the ship. Many of the members of the crew have been promoted in rank while serving on this special ship, including, most recently, Petty Officer Michael Murray. Murray was the ship's 1998 Sailor of the Year and came to Audubon for a week in April of 1999. Upon his return to the ship, he learned that he had been promoted to the rank of Chief Petty Officer. Congratulations!

And . . . the future? The poem and photo on the next page speak for themselves . . . .

USS BENFOLD (DDG-65): Onward With Valor

With pride you sail the seven seas,
You wear your namesake well.
What lies ahead in years to come
No one right now can tell.

With each new voyage, you will know
That, as you sail the seas,
Your second family, Audubon,
Sails with you and agrees
That thoughts and prayers will help you through
Each challenge that you face:
Those little gifts - - - and letters too - - -
Will provide a fond embrace.

Fair winds, calm seas and sunshine
Will guide you on your way.
Success to you and your proud crew:
ONWARD WITH VALOR, each night and day!

Craig E. Burgess

"The Green Wave and the Navy" are now, and will continue to be, "perfect together". The students have laid the groundwork for an ongoing friendship over the past six years. The U.S. Navy has strengthened the friendship in many ways and, with the Commissioning of a second ship in memory of a local hero from Audubon, will insure that the friendship stays alive and well.

The article on this page appeared in the AHS newspaper, The PARROT, in late May of 1999 and reflects the pride associated with the visits to the school made by members of the crew.

Sailor of the Year docks at AHS

by Scott Pennock
Parrot Staff Writer

On April 22, the recipient of the Sailor of the Year award visited the AHS library. The presentation was attended by students in the U.S. History II Honors classes and was followed by a luncheon for all who attended.

The Sailor of the Year, Michael Murray, was the first to speak to the crowd of students. He explained that he had been in the U.S. Navy for fourteen years, serving on four ships, one of them being the U.S.S. Benfold.

"The bond between Audubon and the U.S.S. Benfold is very strong," Murray had said.,

The ship was named after Edward C. Benfold, an AHS alumnus and Congressional Medal of Honor recipient. Murray went on to say that he has spent ten years out at sea on the ship.

His position on the ship is that of being in charge of the training program. His official title is Officer of the Deck.

Murray works for the safety of the ship and crew by preparing them for potentially dangerous situations that may occur at sea. Murray later said, "There isn't one day that goes by where I don't learn something new about the ship." Murray's skill, pride and dedication helped him earn the Sailor of the Year award.

Murray is very committed to his job but misses his family life very much. "Missing [my daughter] growing up is the hardest thing," Murray told the audience.

After Murray left the podium to an applauding crowd, Petty Naval Officer Danny Edgar introduced himself. Edgar had been in the Navy for eleven years and has worked on the U.S.S Benfold. When Edgar mentioned the Benfold, he said that it was "the greatest ship in the Navy."

Edgar is currently involved in co-writing a book entitled, *The Green Wave and the Navy*. He has been working hard on the writing process.

While discussing a lifesaving mission he had been a part of, Edgar said that "the greatest thing [he'd] ever done is saved another life."

Edgar later concluded his presentation with a reading of two of his own poems related to the Benfold, Navy and Audubon itself.

Towards the end of the presentation, the Project Memorial Coordinators presented gifts from AHS to Murray and Edgar. They were very appreciative and mentioned that they sent a special surprise gift to AHS.

Sailor of the Year Michael Murray (right) is joined by fellow Benfold crew memberDanny Edgar at a recent AHS student program.

When co-author Edgar returned to the USS BENFOLD following his week-long visit to Audubon in April, 1999, he wrote a thank-you letter to the community and enclosed a poem he had composed. Co-author Burgess encouraged Edgar to include his thoughts in **this** section of the book . . . . . .

"It's breathtaking the experience we had in New Jersey. All towns could take a page from Audubon on Patriotism. Patriotism is what makes this country great. Everyone who is an American should ask himself: 'Why do we love America?'. The answers will vary, but there is no wrong answer. Be proud - - - very proud - - - of the greatest nation in the world ! Brittin, Sampler and Benfold had it; Audubon, New Jersey exemplifies it. The Sailor of the Year (Chief Petty Officer Michael L. Murray) and I wish to thank everyone who made our visit a highlight we will always remember."

Town Fit For Heroes

The sun was out and there was brisk air.
We were slightly cold, but we didn't care.
The little town of 9,000 people was putting on a show:
The people in the streets and parade had a certain glow.

It was patriotism at its best:
We were not outsiders, but honored guests.
What a sight for all to see.
Americans we are proud to be.
We were two sailors from the West Coast,
But the treatment we got, few could boast.

But the best was yet to come:
The people of Audubon were not to be outdone.
We met principals, war veterans, and even the Mayor.
When we finally came to the Memorial, we had to stare.
Three Medal of Honor recipients in one little town.
As we took a deep breath, we took a look around:
We remembered the real reason we were brought here . . . .
And it suddenly becomes clear.

From the heroics of Samuel Sampler in World War I
In the face of diversity, he made his famous run.
Nelson Brittin and Edward Benfold, from the Korean War,
Both died in battle, far from home on a foreign shore.

We came to honor Edward Benfold,
But to us all 3 men were made from the same mold.
Heroes are what we make of them:
They're what hold us together; they are the stem.

Petty Officer 1st Class (SW) Danny K. Edgar

Project Memorial Foundation chairpersons from the AHS Class of 2000 are continuing a tradition of pride and excellence that began with the construction of the Medal of Honor Memorial Site in 1994. This tradition will continue for many years to come.

The four chairpersons - - - Joshua Peschko, Gabrielle Horvath, Renato Latini and Sara Kauffman - - - have learned a great deal from their experience and have felt the joy of working with the community on a program that benefits everyone.

On the next page, we have reproduced another article from the May, 1999 issue of the PARROT. The two staff writers were in attendance at the Memorial Day ceremony and had an opportunity to interview the four Juniors. The article gives some insight into the future, as plans are underway for additional beautification projects at the Memorial site. The photo at the bottom of this page shows the four students and captures the inscription for Nelson V. Brittin, the Audubon hero and Medal of Honor recipient who soon will have a ship in the Navy bearing his name: The USNS BRITTIN.

St. Mary's Episcopal Church continues to show pride in keeping alive the memory of a special parishioner. On page 484 we present parts of a letter that was addressed to the Parish Rector. A donation was being made in memory of Edward C. Benfold and the comments in the letter speak for themselves. The photo shows the newest officer of the USS BENFOLD, LCDR Todd Leavitt, who visited St. Mary's on June 1, 1999 and thanked the Parish for its ongoing commitment to friendship with the crew.

What will the future hold? Page 485 says it all, in two fantastic photographs, each worth at least 2000 words.

482

"A Tradition of Pride and Excellence"

the PARROT

"All the news that's worth repeating"

Since 1927　　　　　May 1999　　　　　Volume 72, Issue 6

Project Memorial honors Air Force

by Rebecca Myers and Scott Pennock
Parrot Staff Writers

Once again, AHS has set aside a day to honor our three Medal of Honor recipients: Samuel Sampler, Nelson V. Brittain, and Edward C. Benfold. The Project Memorial ceremony will take place on Monday, May 27 at 11 a.m. until 12:30. The ceremony is very somber.

Project Memorial was started six years ago by a group of students who wanted to honor our Medal of Honor recipients. They had heard about the three fallen heroes in class and were moved by their stories. They spoke with Mr. Westphal about a possible ceremony to honor the heroes.

Their interest in the heroes sparked the creation of Project Memorial. A marble memorial was built outside of A-building and just recently a walkway was added to the memorial.

The ceremony has become a tradition at AHS. This year the Project Memorial coordinators are Renato Latini ('00), Josh Peschko ('00), Gabrielle Horvath ('00), and Sara Kauffman ('00). They have put together a ceremony that promises to be the best yet. Peschko said, "It's an honor for all of us to be involved with this project."

Pedrick had said, "It's a lot of hard work, but all of it is rewarding." Much care has been put into this year's Project Memorial program.

Guest speakers will include teacher and guidance counselor Mr. John Skrabonja, Superintendent Mrs. Mary Anne Rende, Mr. Dick Gallant, and Poet Frank Burgess. A F-16 fly-over is also tentatively planned and the Bronze Medallion of Patrick Henry will be presented.

The theme for this year's ceremony will be "Air Force Service to America." A great deal of hard work has gone into the planning of this ceremony. The committee has enlisted the help of many students, staff members, and citizens of the community. Students like Pedrick have been asked to organize the flag bearers who will carry the state flags. Shaun Armstrong ('00) and Rebecca Myers ('00) were asked to write the invitations for the guest speakers and other invitees.

Kauffman is happy to be a part of the committee. "I think it's a good program because it gets the students involved in the community," Kauffman said. It's AHS students who helped add the walkway in front of the memorial and who plan to make other additions.

DATE: April 7, 1999

Enclosed is a check for $6,170 to pay for the restoration of the Palm Sunday window. If possible, I would like a plaque placed in the church (perhaps on the rear wall or near the side window dedicated to Benfold) with a suggested inscription as follows:

Rear Wall: "Restoration of Palm Sunday Window given in memory of Edward C. Benfold, U.S.Navy, member of St. Mary's Parish, who gave his life in the line of duty during the Korean War. Recipient of the Congressional Medal of Honor."

Or Side Wall: "this window and restoration of Palm Sunday Window given in memory of Edward C. Benfold, U.S. Navy, member of St. Mary's Parish, who gave his life in the line of duty during the Korean War. Recipient of the Congressional Medal of Honor."

Please feel free to amend the wording as you see fit; however, I want people to see that a parishioner was the recipient of the highest military honor awarded. On a recent visit to the Naval Academy at Annapolis, I was somewhat surprised to see how very, very few from the Navy have been given this supreme honor and recognized that we are one of the few parishes of any faith to have such a distinguished member.

Command Master
Chief Scheeler of
the USS BENFOLD
holds an Audubon
T-shirt (left), while
students, community
leaders and LCDR
Todd Leavitt hold
a United States
Navy flag (below).

The Green Wave
And The Navy

Perfect Together

About The Authors
Petty Officer 1st Class(SW) Danny K. Edgar

Edgar was born in Saigon, Vietnam, while his father was doing a tour of duty there. He was later raised by his grandmother, Hazel Edgar, in Steelville, Missouri. He is a 1987 graduate of Viburnum High School. He reported to Boot Camp in San Diego, California in 1988, graduated there as the honor man of Company 106 and finished Mess Specialist A School while there.

Edgar reported to his first command with the PCU LAKE CHAMPLAIN. He, along with the other 320 crew members, known as Plankowners, started the ship up from scratch and led it to its commissioning into the U. S. Fleet as the USS LAKE CHAMPLAIN. He was recognized as the ship's first "Sailor of the Quarter" - - - the top sailor for a three month period.

Edgar then went on to Navy Recruiting District, Chicago, where he spent 3 years as a recruiter . . . a very demanding and rewarding duty. His next assignment was to NTC Great Lakes, where he worked on the recruit training command, feeding over 14,000 recruits daily.

He reported to the PCU BENFOLD, which is now the USS BENFOLD. He is currently the recordskeeper and wardroom supervisor on board. He is responsible for keeping the food budget for 300 crew members, with a daily allowance which varies from $5.60 - $6.10 a day for one crew member for 3 meals. He also plans menus, prepares food for special events, banquets and luncheons. The USS BENFOLD is currently on her 2nd deployment and will return to San Diego on December 18, 1999.

Petty Officer Edgar's personal awards include two Navy/Marine Achievement Medals, various Campaign and Service Medals and 2 Battle E Ribbons for shipboard excellence. He also received a Letter of Commendation for a lifesaving role he played. (See comments on the poem Danger At Sea). During the 1st deployment of the USS BENFOLD, Edgar received the Enlisted Surface Warrior Specialist (ESWS) Pin.

Edgar is married to the former Laura Young of Woodridge, Illinois. They have one child, Kristen Marie Edgar and currently reside in San Diego, California.

As he looks toward the future, Edgar says: "The Navy in my eleven years has changed slowly, but surely, each year. I can honestly say that the Navy has been very good to me. Just like in any good job, you have to have a good foundation. My wife and child, Marvin and Marie Young and the rest of my family have been that foundation. In the Navy, true leaders like Captain R. K. Martin, LCDR Besteroy and CDR Abrashoff have taught me the importance of taking care of your fellow shipmates. The United States Navy has been and always will be the greatest Navy in the world. Now, and well after I retire, being a sailor or a service member in the greatest nation in the world will always make me stand .tall."

Educator and Poet Craig E. Burgess

Burgess was born in Camden, New Jersey, in 1944 and has lived in the same house in Audubon his entire life. After graduating from Audubon High School as Valedictorian of the Class of 1963, he obtained his degree from Rutgers University in 1967, with a double major - - - in Spanish and German. He served as a Teaching Fellow at the University of Pennsylvania, obtaining his Masters Degree in Education from Penn in 1971 and accepted a position as Spanish teacher in the newly-opened Cherry Hill High School East in September, 1968 - - - a position he held until 1994, when he took early retirement from full-time teaching. Highlights of his career include being named the best teacher of a modern western European language by Johns Hopkins University in 1991, being asked to help write a revision for a college level Spanish text for the Heinle and Heinle company in 1989 (Burgess was the ONLY high school language instructor on the revision committee), and being recommended by students in both 1994 and 1996 for inclusion in Who's Who in America's Teachers.

Burgess was also active outside of the classroom, serving as advisor to the Spanish Club, the Spanish Honor Society, the Adopt-A-Grandparent program and the multi-lingual student literary magazine, PASSPORT. His efforts earned special recognition for the school and the students, who earned 10 international awards for the PASSPORT publication in the five years of its existence. Burgess brought attention to the community efforts of the students in 1993 when he was named the Individual Volunteer of the Year for the state of New Jersey and again in 1995 when he and the activities' director of the Nursing Home where the students visited, Mrs. Amy Maricondi, published a handbook on Intergenerational Caring and Sharing.

After 'retiring', Burgess served for 4 years as President of the Audubon High School Alumni Association and for 4 years as the President of the Camden County Retired Educators' Association and is currently a member of the Audubon LIONS, the facilitator of a local writers' group, THE AUDUBON POETS, and a member of the Board of directors of the WESTMONT THEATRE COMPANY.

Burgess has been elected to the International Board of Governors of the American Biographical Institute and was named an International Man of the Year by the ABI in 1997-1998. In August of 1998, he attended his first Convention of the International Platform Speakers' Association in Washington, DC and took top honors in both the poetry and the speaking ladder competitions.

Having published 4 books of poetry and 2 audio cassette tapes of poetry, set to music at the Trusty Tuneshop Studios in Nebo, Kentucky, Burgess now spends a lot of time in elementary classrooms around the country, introducing poetry to both students and teachers. One of his poems is currently being translated into Hawaiian and three others are hanging proudly on the walls of his Alma Mater, AHS.

During the summer of 1999, Burgess was the recipient of two very special honors. At the 26th International Congress on Arts & Communications, held in Lisbon, Portugal in July, he received the ERNEST KAY INTERNATIONAL FOUNDATION AWARD as the Congress Delegate of the year.

In August, Burgess learned that the International Platform Speakers' Association, founded in 1831 by famed orator Daniel Webster and by Josiah Holbrook, had named him to its Board of Governors.

As he looks toward the future, Burgess says: "No one can ever tell what the future may bring. My success in life comes from my parents, the wonderful teachers I had at AHS and my faith in God. As an educator, I have learned that a positive attitude AND an open mind will open doors to incredible experiences. Meeting Petty Officer Edgar and researching this salute to my homctown have opened new doors to adventures for the new millennium."

Bibliography

Audubon Celebration Committee	Independence Day Booklet	1954
" " "	Borough of Audubon, NJ 50th Anniversary: 1905-1955	1955
" " "	Audubon Celebration Book for the New Jersey Tercentenary 1664-1964: People, Purpose, Progress	1964
" " "	Independence Day Booklet	1972
" " "	The Circus Comes to Audubon 4th of July Booklet	1994
" " "	Memories of Audubon, 90th Anniversary Issue: Fourth of July Booklet	1995
Audubon Chapter, S.P.E.B.S.Q.S.A., Inc.	Barbershop Quartet Festival Booklet	1961
Audubon Defender Fire Company	80th Anniversary Booklet	1975
Audubon Fathers Association	Playbill: "Jazze Get Your Gun"	1958
Audubon High School Yearbook	Le Souvenir	1929
	" "	1930
	" "	1947
	" "	1948

Bibliography

Audubon Celebration Committee	Independence Day Booklet	1954
" " "	Borough of Audubon, NJ 50th Anniversary: 1905-1955	1955
" " "	Audubon Celebration Book for the New Jersey Tercentenary 1664-1964: People, Purpose, Progress	1964
" " "	Independence Day Booklet	1972
" " "	The Circus Comes to Audubon 4th of July Booklet	1994
" " "	Memories of Audubon, 90th Anniversary Issue: Fourth of July Booklet	1995
Audubon Chapter, S.P.E.B.S.Q.S.A., Inc.	Barbershop Quartet Festival Booklet	1961
Audubon Defender Fire Company	80th Anniversary Booklet	1975
Audubon Fathers Association	Playbill: "Jazze Get Your Gun"	1958
Audubon High School Yearbook	Le Souvenir	1929
	" "	1930
	" "	1947
	" "	1948

Bibliography continued

Audubon High School
Yearbook   Le Souvenir   1949

                                "   "   1980

Audubon Pupils Program
for Learning Enrichment
(A.P.P.L.E.)   Audubon: 1905-1995
                                90 Years of Community   1995

Borough of Audubon   Community Information Guide   1991

                               Community Profile   1986

                               Dedication Book for the
                               Audubon Public Library Addition   1978

                               75th Anniversary Book   1980

                               Welcome to Audubon   1939

                               Yearly Calendar   1977/1979

                                                                  1983/1989

Danielson, Edgar N.   The History of Audubon (Ditto
                               manuscript in the New Jersey State
                               Library, 185 W. State Street, PO
                               Box 520, Trenton, NJ 08625-0520
                               Call Number: JERSEYANA - Ask
                               Librarian J974, 987, A89, H673)   1941

Department of the
U. S. Navy   USS BENFOLD Commissioning
                               Day Book   1996

                               USS BENFOLD Cruise Book   1998